STATE, SOCIETY, AND LAW IN ISLAM

STATE, SOCIETY, AND LAW IN ISLAM

Ottoman Law in
Comparative Perspective

Haim Gerber

STATE UNIVERSITY OF NEW YORK PRESS

Published by
State University of New York Press, Albany

For information, address State University of New York
Press, State University Plaza, Albany, N.Y., 12246

Production by E. Moore
Marketing by Bernadette LaManna

Library of Congress Cataloging-in-Publication Data

Gerber, Haim.
    State, society, and law in Islam : Ottoman law in comparative
perspective / Haim Gerber.
        p.   cm.
    Includes bibliographical references (p.   ) and index.
    ISBN 0-7914-1877-4 (alk.). — ISBN 0-7914-1878-2 (pbk. : alk.)
    1. Justice, Administration of—Turkey—History. 2. Islamic law—
Turkey—History. 3. Islam—Turkey—History. 4. Turkey—Politics
and government. 5. Turkey—Social conditions.
KKX1572.G47   1994   93-8076
340.5'9—dc20   CIP

10 9 8 7 6 5 4 3 2 1

CONTENTS

INTRODUCTION

Outwardly, this study explores the legal structure of the core area of the Ottoman Empire between the sixteenth and early nineteenth centuries, and its relationship to the sociopolitical structure of that state. In fact, this legal structure is only the empirical data base, and the study seeks to address some wider questions that should be of interest to students of Islam and the Middle East as well as to students of historical legal anthropology. The study casts serious doubt on several fundamental notions concerning the nature of premodern Islamic society—such as the supposed gap between theory and practice, one major expression of which was the province of law: the *shari`a* was sacred, yet in practice always of marginal importance—a gap that had supposedly disastrous consequences for the moral integrity of the Muslim community.

In the case study presented here, this supposed gap hardly existed; and to the extent that it did exist, it was not perceived as morbid or disturbing. The fundamental question that brought me to this topic was my fascination with the (possible) causal relation between Ottoman political and social formations on the one hand and the structure of politics and society in modern Turkey and the Arab world on the other. As far as Turkey is concerned, the characteristic that I find most intriguing is the democratic form of government maintained by this polity for the last fifty years. Most sociologists and historians who deal with this question explain it away by claiming that Turkish democracy is actually false, an epiphenomenon. In this, most of them are deeply influenced by the theories of Max Weber on patrimonialism and sultanism. And in fact, confronting the ideas of Weber with the documentary world with which I became aquainted in Turkey twenty years ago is precisely the intellectual starting point of the present study.

Disregarding real democratic measures like free elections and voluntary changes of government on several occasions, these scholars argue that because the Ottoman polity was rapacious, corrupt, and highly despotic, and because in history there is no such thing as turning over a new leaf, it follows that the Ottoman mentality must somehow still control modern Turkey. To my mind this logic should be turned on its head: To me, modern Turkish democracy is absolutely real, if very problematic and incomplete; and if indeed there is no new leaf in history—an assumption to which I subscribe wholeheartedly—then it follows that there is something wrong with our old image of the structure of the Ottoman state and society. A partial beginning along these new lines of thought was made by Carter Findley in his study of Ottoman bureaucracy in the nineteenth century, where the first stirrings of "rational" bureaucracy are shown to have taken place.[1] But a doubt still lingers, since the writer posits a barely convincing quantum leap, a new dawn in the nineteenth century; the Ottoman past remains dark and sinister, something that had to be swept aside completely to make room for a brand-new rational bureaucracy. I doubt very much whether such decisive ruptures are possible in real history. I will suggest in this book that a certain line of continuity must be sought with the dark age of Ottoman history: the seventeenth and eighteenth centuries. Therefore, deep down, this study has a point to make; but let me assure the suspicious reader that this connection thesis was formulated only after long acquaintance with substantial portions of the evidence that eventually went into the writing of this book.

That long-range possible connection between the seventeenth- and the twentieth-century is the big question I have had in the back of my mind in recent years. But this study is not a full-fledged answer to this question. Here I intend to examine one aspect of the question, that pertaining to the political culture of the central area of the Ottoman Empire in the seventeenth and eighteenth centuries. My original research question asked, how truly despotic was the Ottoman polity in this period? And I intended to pursue this question via an in-depth analysis of the Ottoman legal system at that time—not only because law court records are our best historical source for the reconstruction of center-periphery relations in this state, but also because it seems that the legal system is one of the major points of contact between state and society in any polity. I came to see in the material at hand two distinct threads. On the one hand I perceived that it had the potential to say something new and important about Islamic law between the end of the classical period and the beginning of the twentieth century (a period sometimes referred to as the middle Islamic period). On the other hand I was aware from an early stage that my topic was skirting the old and established discipline of legal anthropology, and I made up my mind to find out whether this study could profit from insights arrived at in that discipline. In fact, it became apparent to me that legal anthropological models were quite an appropriate framework within which to analyze the material. Hence, this study will start with a discussion of legal anthropology, which will thus become the analytical framework of the book. But I will not lose sight of the other topics with which the book deals—Islamic law in the middle period and its links with the structure of the Ottoman polity. The detailed treatment of these last topics may strain the patience of anthropologists reading this book. Some may even claim that the material does not really come within the orbit of anthropology. And they may be at least partly right. I can only say that this is the price any social historian has to pay if he or she wants to venture into the field of interdisciplinary history. The fact is that while pursuing the potential of such interdisciplinary models, I remain deeply enchanted by the specifically Islamic material on which I am working.

Many avenues have led historians in the past decade or so to seek theoretical guidance in anthropology.[2] Those studying the history of the family are most notable here,[3] no doubt because of the traditional centrality of kinship studies in anthropology; but in recent years historians working on popular culture have also turned increasingly to anthropology.[4] In both cases the reason is anthropologists' long acquaintance with and expertise in these topics. Another obvious reason is that traditional history until recently was interested only in the high culture of kings and aristocrats, while the reverse was true of traditional anthropology. My own case may appear different because historians have worked on legal material probably longer than anthropologists have.

But at a deeper level the problem is the same: traditional historians were interested in the "high" level, that of the formal codes of law, while anthropologists were interested in what took place at the "lowest" possible level, that of human existence. As traditional history's elitist preoccupation is now itself history, it seems natural and inevitable that an increasing number of historians will turn to anthropologists (as well as to sociologists) to borrow tools and research questions. No doubt there are difficulties along this path. The main one, as suggested by Darett Rutman, lies in the quintessential difference between the historian and the anthropologist. Historians tend to focus on a single cultural area, strongly bounded by a language and a body of sources, which they proceed to research in ways often barely reminiscent of any other research. In contrast, anthropologists have their eye on existing studies in their field and must be ready to be judged in the light of such work.[5] This is probably largely true even today, when many anthropologists no longer agree that this comparative approach is the hallmark of their discipline and insist that the true nub of the anthropological perspective is cultural orientation—that is, trying to understand societies through their own cultural terms of reference rather than through the biased eyes of the modern Western researcher.[6]

This unwonted humility is, of course, intimately connected with the newly found passionate interest of today's historians in the lives of the common people at ground level. Historians can profit from the work of anthropologists. But it is to be hoped that the comparative approach will not be a casualty of these important new realizations, for it remains a research tool of the utmost importance. For example, in the present study, which deals with the legal system of a particular culture area, the main research question was this : to what extent was the law applied in practice a state law imposed from above or a law bargained over and negotiated between litigants, the state, and society? On the basis of only one case, my main general finding would have been that it was a little of each. But by adding some other cases for purposes of comparison, I have been able to add a deeper and subtler dimension to the discussion. Most historians (including this writer) have grown up academically within the warm and cozy confines of one cultural tradition, which they are convinced they know better than anyone else. And they feel strongly that only someone who has spent at least fifteen years in its archives is entitled to say anything scientific about this entity. This guild feeling and complex socialization process have their merits; but they also have a heavy price in terms of the range of research questions that can be fruitfully discussed. It is incumbent on historians to eventually come round to accommodating a comparative—or in any case a theoretical—element in their work while maintaining a narrow cultural anchorage. In any case, it is along such lines that the present study attempts to proceed. I should emphasize, however, that I am using comparisons mainly for heuristic purposes—that is, to throw into better relief findings I had drawn from my original sources. And in the final analysis it is my case study (and its place in Islamic law) that is the main focus of interest.

Part of my original inspiration came from some recent anthropological studies on other Islamic societies. These studies have underlined the fact that there must be a logically meaningful relation between law and the society surrounding it. The contributions of Clifford Geertz and Lawrence Rosen, in particular, have helped me clarify and formulate my own ideas. In his study on law, Geertz may have been more interested in showing how basic cultural assumptions are hidden in legal material than in analyzing the law itself, but his insight that law is "local knowledge" in a very deep sense was for me an eye-opener.[7] Lawrence Rosen, in his study on the law system of the town of Sefrou, Morocco,[8] has pointed out that law and society are permeated by the same cultural assumptions. The book has justly been criticized for presenting itself as a model of Islamic law past and present, but its basic idea remains important.[9] One possible implication for the history of Islamic law is that this law may be differently structured in different periods and regions. And in fact, recent studies of Islamic law suggest that the old assumption about its immutability are unfounded or at least exaggerated. Students of Islamic law such as Wael Hallaq and Baber Johansen have shown that minute study of the thought patterns of Islamic jurists between the tenth and nineteenth centuries reveals that perceptible changes did take place.[10] What were the real-world circumstances that influenced these patterns of change? I hope this study will contribute toward answering that question.

Of the major problems and theoretical concerns occupying legal anthropologists, some are relevant to the present study. Perhaps the most pervasive is the tension between the law as seen from above—the imposed law code, expressing possibly the ideology of the state or civilization—versus the law in practice as a process of negotiation, a process whereby the lofty code is compromised and becomes subject to the interplay of sociological forces, or is even brushed aside as irrelevant to make room for free negotiation. At base, the logical issue is probably not dissimilar to the fundamental problematic posed by, among many others, Philip Abrams in his *Historical Sociology* as the tension between structure and process.[11] Here the reference is to the issue most basic in understanding social life—the tension between objective, constraining circumstances and the free will of the individual, and the role of each in accounting for social processes. In legal anthropology the best discussion of the problem is offered by Sally Falk Moore,[12] who makes this claim at the very beginning of her book:

> There is a basic tension between the idea that law epitomizes manmade, intentional action, and constitutes the means by which a conscious and rational attempt to direct society can be undertaken, and most thought in the social science, that there are underlying causes of social behavior which are not fully in the conscious control of the actors, yet which are the core of what the social scientist studies.[13]

Moore adds that in her view the first approach is no more than an ideological stand and that in reality societies usually behave according to the dynamic forces on the ground. One reason is that enacted laws are intentionally worded in a general, all-embracing way, so that there is usually more than one way to interpret a given law. Even more important is the basic feature of law in society, which prevents over-rationalization. One factor here—particularly important for this study—is "the piecemeal historical process by which legal systems are constructed." Another is the multiplicity of regulatory sources in any given society and the different contexts in which legal activities take place.[14] In fact, it is widely opined in legal anthropology that the law is carried out not just in the formal courts. Mediation carried on by the lawyers of would-be litigants should unquestionably be considered part of the legal system.[15]

If Moore is of the opinion that formal law is less important than the actual negotiations that take place on the ground, she is cautious enough to phrase her stand so that negotiation itself is rightly seen as negotiable—meaning that although negotiation is a fundamental part of the law in every society, its extent may vary from one society to another.[16] One student of legal anthropology has pointed out that most contributors to this field have—mistakenly in her view—turned their backs completely on the formal codes, possibly as a result of the influence of the Anglo-American legal tradition, where the law is seen as the business of the lawyer.[17] I would suggest that the variations in negotiability among various legal systems may be a major topic of research; in fact, this is one of the points of focus of the present study. Something along these lines is suggested by Lloyd Fallers. At the end of his study on the Soga, a traditional tribal African kingdom located in present-day Uganda, he offers a comparative model for the analysis of some of the better-known cases extant in legal anthropology. The main idea is that the interplay between the imposed law (the positivist law, that is) and law as process need not be always and everywhere the same. It may vary according to circumstances. As this is one of the main points that the present study tries to develop, I would like to go into some detail here.

Fallers compares four major studies that have become classics in legal anthropology, all of them based on African tribes of varying degrees of political development (meant here in the technical-administrative sense, not in any evolutionary sense), a key factor in the model. These studies are on the Tiv, studied by Bohannan; the Arusha, studied by Gulliver; the Lozi, studied by Gluckman; and the Soga, studied by Fallers himself.[18] Of these four, Gluckman's study on the Lozi of Zambia was not only the first but also the inspiration and model for the rest. It is still the most influential study in legal anthropology, introducing as it does the actual legal case witnessed by the researcher. All four societies were very litigious; but Fallers suggests that they were not legalistic to the same extent, meaning that their tribunals varied in the degree to which they tended to "oversimplify disputes in the interest of submitting them to a regime of rules."[19] This somewhat complicated definition really refers to the same old duality between the positivist law and the law as a process of negotiation on the ground. Where the positivist law is supreme, a specific law must be invoked and acted upon. Where negotiation is the rule, everything is open to negotiation and no law is necessarily applied. In the case of Fallers' model we have two different pairs of societies, the Tiv and Arusha on the one hand, the Lozi and Soga on the other. The juridical process was distinctly less legalistic in the first pair than in the second. Let us take the extreme case of the Arusha as an example: "The indigenous dispute-settling gatherings of the Arusha are morally quite holistic and also relatively political. Norms are brought to bear, but there is little attempt to limit consideration to a single, narrowly drawn cause of action or concept of wrong and there is an important element of frank bargaining." Also, there is a strong effort to induce parties to accept the decision rather than to impose it on them.[20] At the other extreme are the legalistic Soga, with a strong tendency on the part of their courts to deal with only one case at a time and to limit the discussion to the particular concept of wrong at issue. The Lozi are near the Soga, though less legalistic. The case of the Lozi deserves a closer look because of the fruitful insights it provides for the analysis of the Ottoman and Islamic materials presented later in this study. It is a particularly good example of the style of analysis and the research questions asked and discussed in legal anthropology.[21]

The Lozi legal system can be said to be one where legalism and substantiveness coexisted. As Moore has shown, this ambiguity was matched by distinct ambiguity in Gluckman's approach.[22] Unlike the Tiv and the Arusha, the Lozi had institutionalized law courts. Gluckman claims—a well-known controversial argument—that a distinction should be drawn between law carried out by a formal court of law and similar things done by other, legally inferior, forums. He specifically adopts Roscoe Pound's definition of law as "social control through the systematic application of the force of politically organized society."[23] Hence, he sees law as corpus juris—that is, the "reservoir of rules . . . on which the judges draw for their decisions."[24] The law is, therefore, the law code, not the process whereby the code is negotiated in practice. It is only one small step from here to the statement that only what goes on in formal courts is truly law. In Gluckman's words, "It is indeed essential to have some word to distinguish forceful processes of social control in societies which have developed courts as against societies which have not reached this stage of political development."[25]

This stand drew a great deal of criticism, an example of which is Moore's statement that as the British excluded from the Lozi courts such matters as sorcery, Gluckman did not become aware of their existence and especially of their social importance; and thus, he saw them as less than fully legal.[26] Though their law was unwritten, the Lozi had a specific concept of law and a rather exact and specific process of adjudication: their judges applied, or sought to apply, a specific law to each case brought before them. When moral principles conflicted with legal principles, they usually preferred the latter, saying, "It is hard, but it is the law."[27] At times they might mitigate such harshness by trying to influence a litigant to act in a way in which the law did not oblige him/her to behave. But very often their process of adjudication also contained powerful holistic, moralistic, and societal principles. This was strongly connected to the fact that the overwhelming number of cases brought before the Lozi court were between husband and wife, or at least between close relatives. Gluckman defined such relationships as *multiplex*. Because relatives had to go on living together, the court was very careful to avoid harsh decisions that might jeopardize the future relations of the parties. Lozi judges explicitly saw as their main task to mediate between close relatives rather than to apply the law in the strict sense. They also strove to get the parties to agree to the developing solution rather than seeing it as one imposed from the outside. In Gluckman's words, "The court tends to be conciliating; it strives to effect a compromise acceptable to, and accepted by, all the parties. This is the main task of the judges . . . in order to fulfill their task the judges constantly have to broaden the field of their enquiries, and consider the total history of the relations between the litigants, not only the narrow legal issue raised by one of them."[28]

Additionally, the Lozi lacked the institution of expert witnessing because, on the whole an average member in this technologically simple society knew about as much as any other member. For this reason, too, the Lozi lacked the fiction of judicial ignorance: judges were acquainted with litigants and freely used this information in court.[29] The Lozi judges were also bureaucrats in addition to being judges, a fact often invoked by them in court to threaten litigants to behave in ways considered socially desirable. Fallers noted that in many of these cases the Soga were more sharply legalistic than the Lozi; thus the Soga judges did not refrain from adjudicating between relatives. Also, in contrast to the Lozi, their role was more professionally restricted to adjudication—leading them, of course, to apply the law more legalistically.

The question is, what is the meaning of the continuum whose existence Fallers was trying to establish? His argument is that the legal differences are explainable by the differences in political organization among the four entities compared. The Tiv and the Arusha before the colonial period were without any form of state power or formal courts. As opposed to this, the Barotse and the Soga had traditional kingdoms, with a ruler and a hierarchy of chiefs who were also judges. Fallers claims that political and bureaucratic development led to growing autonomy of the judicial institution and to the appearance of formal courts and professional judges, along with more nearly formal codes of laws applied in a more nearly imposed way. This by no means entails the elimination of politics—that is, negotiation and bargaining. It only means that the place of politics became now less paramount and less explicit than in the other two legal systems. The present study seeks to find out whether that model can be employed to further our understanding of Islamic law. No evolutionary sequence, and certainly no universal law, is intended here. The same society can at times be highly centralized and bureaucratic and at other times much less so. I am nevertheless confident that taken loosely and treated with caution, the correlation between law and state structure has an explanatory force to it.

Many of the topics mentioned as central to the agendas of legal anthropology are invoked in a specifically Islamic and Moroccan form in Rosen's monograph on Morocco.[30] The study is useful to this one less as a substantive contribution to Islamic law than as an anthropological model, not least because of its sophisticated neo-Weberian character. The study deals with the legal system of the modern Moroccan town of Sefrou—more specifically with the law carried out by the *kadi* of Sefrou—a system of law that Rosen, obviously by mistake, sees as a more or less direct continuation of the system of *shari`a* law of classical Islam.

The study claims that there is an intimate relation in Morocco between law and culture. The writer unravels this relation by pointing out what he sees as the central feature of Moroccan society:

> The central analogy, the key metaphor, that may prove helpful when thinking about the social life of Morocco—and for that matter, of much of the Middle East—is concerned with notions of contract and negotiation. It is an image of the bazaar market-place writ large in social relations, of negotiated agreements extending from the realm of public forum into those domains—the family, history and cosmology, where they might not most immediately be expected to reside. For at the very center of Moroccan life stands not a set of corporate groups—tribe, family, or village . . . but the single individual who draws upon a set of regularized ways to enter into agreements with others and thereby construct a network of obligations as extensive and as fragile as his or her own negotiating capacities.[31]

The same basic concept, according to Rosen, also informs the Moroccan legal system or, more correctly, the law implemented by the *shari`a* court, as well as the internal logic of the court's mode of working. The basic task of that legal system is not, as in the West, to apply a "logically consistent body of legal doctrine," nor even to adjudicate in the hard-and-fast meaning of the term. Instead, "the aim of the qadi is to put people back in the position of being able to negotiate their own permissible relationships without predetermining just what the outcome of those negotiations ought to be."[32] This basic idea has several implications for the Moroccan legal system's mode of working. One claim is that contrary to Western law, which works by the principle of the "logic of antecedents," the Islamic law of Morocco fits more a system of law animated by a "logic of consequences."[33] What this means is that the kind of logic that informs the Western legal system is based on a rigorous application of a body of law to given cases, without bothering about the possible social consequences of the logical decision. As opposed to this, Islamic law is more concerned with the social consequences of the decision, with weighing whether or not these societal consequences are desirable.

Another major characteristic that Rosen sees in Moroccan Islamic law is the unusually wide discretion enjoyed by the *kadi*. This characteristic has to do with what experts have seen as the lack of logical rigor in Islamic law: there is no general idea of contract to guide the *kadi*, only a number of specific types of contracts. As an outcome, almost unlimited discretion is in the hands of the *kadi*. For if the law lacks rigorous standards, the *kadi* is guided only by his own feelings.

It is evident that Rosen here mainly follows Max Weber, who is the leading Western analyst of Islamic law in these terms. Weber saw the unlimited discretion of the *kadi* as the chief characteristic of Islamic law, which he dubbed generally as "*kadi* justice" and saw as the archetype of non-Western legal systems. Thus, in subscribing to the idea that the *kadi*'s discretion in the Islamic legal system was nearly unlimited, Rosen is clearly following Weber. But it is interesting that he does give Weber an important twist. For Weber, Islamic law was judicially primitive and undeveloped. Rosen is not only innocent of the hidden ethnocentric overtones that unquestionably permeate Weber's thought, but he further argues that even on the scientific-judicial level, Islamic law was no less developed and sophisticated than Western law; it is only a different kind of development. Unlike the West's, the law in Islam is informed by the same kind of logic as that which informs the wider society. The *kadi*'s decisions are therefore in accordance with cultural sensitivities and preferences prevalent in his society, not with the artificial logic of the law, as is the case in Western legal systems. No less than in the West, then, the *kadi*'s decisions are consistent, but they demonstrate cultural, not logical, consistency.[34]

This study tries to do something beyond interpret the Islamic material in legal anthropological terms. It seeks also to make a modest contribution to something that is lacking in most of the studies in this field—to add a historical dimension to the legal analysis.

At this point, it seems appropriate to say something about the ongoing flirtation between anthropology and history as seen from the viewpoint of anthropology.[35] If historians now turn to anthropology in search of theoretical insights and research agendas, anthropologists have on occasion turned to history in search of the one element that has traditionally been deliberately and artificially struck out of anthropological explanatory models— change over time. It is well known that anthropology's treatment of history has always been highly ambivalent at best.[36] Structure-functionalist models postulated that any institution not *currently* functional would have to disappear. The past was thereby logically wiped out, so to speak. And though structure-functionalism is now dead and buried, the cultural anthropology that has taken its place is only a trifle friendlier to historical explanations.[37] Cultural tendencies are so deep-seated that they are extremely change-resistant, almost inherent. But as a minor development the revolt against structure-functionalism has resulted also in the appearance of anthropologists who are working with historical material— mostly missionaries' accounts of their first encounters with archaic societies—and even with archival or similar documents, the traditional hallmark of the historian.[38] Even in legal anthropology a subbranch has appeared that goes to the historical sources in search of appropriate research problems.[39] It seems, though, that for some of these anthropologists this is the furthest toward history they are willing to go, claiming that where modes of thinking are concerned, they are content to go on thinking as anthropologists.[40] If this attitude means, in effect, that historical change is left out of the picture, then it seems that something very vital is missed. A snapshot of Italy in 1870 is only a little more historical than one of Italy in 1990 if we do not get an idea of the historical factors and processes that went into creating it. This interest in change probably represents the hard core of the historical way of thinking (though it is often merely implicit and taken for granted by historians themselves), a hard core that is going to prove as difficult for anthropologists to digest as is theory for historians.

The debate over history has been ongoing in legal anthropology, as in other branches of anthropology. This dimension is very well represented, for example, in Sally Moore's introduction to the field, which I have used as a springboard to survey its major problems. As noted earlier, she uses historical change as a device to demonstrate how and why the law cannot be fully rationalized—that is, analyzed as a system whose connecting parts create a total logical harmony. The main reason for this, in her analysis, is that law is constantly changing.[41] Though the use of large doses of history and substantial theoretical commitment in an anthropology book is welcome,[42] I have some problems with Moore's implicit notion of history and historical change. First, history in this analysis stands for the contingent, unsystematic, and unexplainable in social life in general. Second, history tends to be assigned the role of the artificial change introduced from above by nationalist, even socialist, governments, change that tries to undermine original—hence "true"—cultural tendencies.[43] In Moore's case this is quite understandable. In the society she has studied, changes were always introduced from the outside by colonial governments whose considerations were completely divorced from the local scene. Incidentally, there is something very similar to be observed in the case of another well-known scholar, Bernard Cohn, who has been sensitive to history in legal anthropology. In his study dealing with changes over time effected by the introduction of British law into India, history is again seen as something completely contingent, as having no true relation to the indigenous system, like a ship from another planet.[44] None of these scholars is to blame, of course; but this is not necessarily the inherent place of history in social relations. Change can take place as a result of internal chains of development even in non-Western societies—something not usually allowed them; and change can sometimes (not necessarily always) be systematically explained. The present study tries to demonstrate these two points.

In the case of the Ottoman Empire we have a historic empire that though vastly less centrally controllable than a modern state was nevertheless distinctly more so than most societies that have thus far been the subject of research by legal anthropologists. It was less centralistic than modern states for reasons both of ideology and communication. It was not as yet imbued with the nationalistic fervor to impose one culture on all its distinct communities; and an order sent by the ruler, or sultan, might take several months to reach an outlying province. This, of course, also means that such an order was less effective once it finally reached the province. Nevertheless, it was a state that held under a single command some 280 provinces, stretching in the sixteenth century from central Europe to southern Arabia, that could put into battle vast, well-equipped armies, all based on a unified and rather effective tax collection mechanism.

Culturally we have here a literate society, based mainly on the religious output of classical Islam, with large doses of central Asian and Iranian influence. This cultural world featured formal institutions of learning, formal law codes and institutionalized law courts of one form or another, and an intellectual elite fluent in three languages—Arabic, Persian, and Turkish. I would add that another important feature of the society studied here is its distinctly nonritualistic nature.[45] It is difficult to think of any modes of thinking that could alert us to the possibility that seventeenth-century west Anatolian Turkish culture was similar to, say, Bali in being deeply different from modern Western societies in ways observed by Geertz. I have in mind here Geertz's finding that contrary to Western perceptions, the Balinese had no developmental idea of time. Time for them stood still.[46] It is also worth mentioning Rosen's idea that Arab culture had a nonchronological concept of time; storytelling reveals a cultural conception in which it is not the time sequence that plays the key role but the contexts and relationships surrounding the subject of the narrative.[47] Whether this is really a fundamental feature of Arab culture probably remains to be seen; it is certainly not the case as far as Ottoman cultural perceptions are concerned. Even a fleeting familiarity with Ottoman historical chronicles is enough to bring home the realization that their unit of analysis is the calendar year, with the sultanic reign in second place. Time has an arrowlike progression, quite like its perception in the West. This paucity of ritualism may be in a certain sense a far cry from what we find in most societies studied by anthropologists; on the other hand, Ottoman society had an indigenous legal system free from any influence of the West or of modern capitalism. It was a system devoid of lawyers, so that its internal development was connected to cultural and political factors in the wider society—much like in the societies studied by most anthropologists. In many ways then, Ottoman law makes a good case for study and analysis using the tools of the legal anthropologist.

This study is based primarily on law court registers from Istanbul and Bursa, the main cities in this core area of the Ottoman Empire. There are some notable difficulties with this material. In the first place there is no information on other forms of dispute settlement, though there are some hints on mediation in the documents. A more serious problem with the material is that though I was interested in analyzing cases, what is actually available is considerably less than the verbatim thrashing out of problems such as we have with Gluckman's Barotse. There are only after-the-fact summaries compiled by the court secretary. It is known that these summaries were done under the watchful eye of witnesses, so that falsification is not to be suspected here. But the exact words of the litigants are lacking, and the nature of the relation between this summary and the exact words of the litigants can only be conjectured. I shall try however to show that much can be done even with the summaries.

After reading the material concerning the core area of the Ottoman Empire in the seventeenth and eighteenth centuries, one immediately discovers that though a reader can easily recognize the similarity between this legal system and that of, for example, twentieth-century Morocco, the differences are no less striking. One senses something amiss with the oft-repeated conflation of Moroccan law and Islamic law. Ottoman law was Islamic all right, but in some major ways it was substantially different from Moroccan law.

While the *shari`a* court of Morocco deals only with matters of personal status and some matters relating to property, the *shari`a* law court in the central region of the Ottoman Empire covered almost every conceivable area of life, including penal matters. This point is of considerable importance for the general history of Islamic law. It is usually assumed that large parts of the *shari`a*, mainly the criminal parts, remained merely theoretical, reality going by another law altogether with severe psychological consequences. Thus, one sociologist of modern Islam claims the *shari`a* to be a divine and hence unchanging law. However, the realities did change; and because, furthermore, Islamic Middle East thinking between 1258 and 1900 experienced complete stagnation, a centuries-long gulf came into being between thought and behavior. This purported intellectual stagnation is said to have ended only with the late nineteenth-century reformist religious thinkers, who for the first time sought to reconcile the *shari`a* and new bodies of knowledge.[48] I hope to show that this theory is fundamentally incorrect. It is incorrect first of all because during the Ottoman centuries the *shari`a* was enforced over large portions of the Islamic Middle East, which were then under Ottoman rule. In that sense, stagnation never took place, assuming that such an obsolete notion of history can be considered at all seriously. But I will show, moreover, that Ottoman legal jurists had no intellectual problem accommodating into their notion of *shari`a* such new bodies of information as interest charging or new rules of criminal evidence (see chapter 3). In that sense, too, there was never stagnation; processes like Islamic reform were always at work.

It is not merely the case that the *kadi* dealt with, and enforced, major parts of the legal code of the *shari`a*; he also was in charge of enforcing whatever additional bodies of law that happened to be current in that state, whether state legislated, like the agrarian system, or customary, like the law of guilds. Furthermore, instead of decreasing, as is sometimes suggested, the importance of the *shari`a* court increased as time went by. And with this increase, the role of once highly prestigious Islamic institutions that had in the past competed with the *kadi* decreased proportionately. A good example is the near total decline of the *muhtesib*, at least as a legal officeholder. But I will show that the *kadi* successfully rivaled even the military-administrative officials. Moreover, the *shari`a* court was elevated in the Ottoman political-administrative system to the status of a major bureaucratic cornerstone, while the *kadi* was made responsible for many of the administrative operations of the Ottoman government in the provinces. In fact, it could be said that the *kadi* became the most important administrative functionary in the system. I must emphasize, however, that in the real work of the *kadi* there was no confusion whatever between his judicial and administrative functions.

Though my attempts may appear somewhat far-fetched, I will try to accommodate these changes within the anthropological models. My conclusion from analyzing the work of the *shari`a* court in the seventeenth and eighteenth centuries is that it was characterized by a substantial measure of rule enforcement, rather than free-floating bargaining (chapter 1). I then take a long look at the process whereby this situation came about (chapter 2), and reach the conclusion that what we actually see is a rise in the authority of the shari`a court as well as a growing application of sections of the shari`a not formerly in use (such as its "penal" code). In my view it stands to reason that the early period was based more on arbitrariness and bargaining than was the later one, where rule enforcement was more distinct. Thus, the development makes sense also within the anthropological model, not just within the history of Islamic law.

Passing now to the internal structure of the working of the kadi and his court, this was investigated in light of both the Weberian model of "kadi justice," which refers mainly to judicial arbitrariness born of the unlimited discretion at the disposal of the kadi, and the anthropological models detailed previously in this introduction. Whatever the origins or social functions of unlimited judicial discretion in other places, it was not found to exist at all in the area under study. Surprising as it may seem, a major outcome of this study was the finding that most of the classical code of the shari`a was the law, including penal and commercial law, by which the people actually lived. In this area, then, the kadi had no lack of detailed law to go by and had no reason, or indeed ability, to adjudicate off the top of his head, as has been so often claimed by Western "experts." Most of the kadi's decisions and rulings in the area under study were commonsensical and totally predictable. Moreover, the argument that Islamic law was hermetically sealed to change is partially contradicted by the fact that the kadi court in the area under study symbiotically accommodated additional bodies of law, although such additions may or may not be considered legitimate additions to the shari`a, the "true" legal heritage of Islam, depending on one's personal judgment. It is true that major laws of the classical code were strongly change-resistant; but important changes and substantial additions were possible and in fact took place. The view adopted in this study is that these additions are to be considered additions to the shari`a. This statement is no longer entirely surprising after Wael Hallaq so convincingly showed that the old theory of the "closing of the gates of ijtihad (free legal interpretation)" was never more than half-truth at best.[49] Much of the present study is an affirmation of Hallaq's excellent study.

It could not be observed in the area of study that the kadi adjudicated with any element of sensitivity to local social structure or the social origins of litigants. Nor was it possible to detect any reference to lineages or extended families, among whom the *kadi* had somehow to mediate.

Weber's (and Rosen's) argument that a lack of strict logical structure permeating the entire code of laws necessarily resulted in unprincipled adjudication based on nothing more than intuition was found to be completely off the mark in the area under study. Sound as their argument is logically, there is evidently something wrong with it. Apparently the fact of the matter is that although the *shari`a* does lack general principles that would enable it to be applied with ease to ever-occurring new cases, it is detailed enough to cover most possible cases in the first place. As an outcome, I found a legal system that, with a little reinforcement from state law and customary law, was one that worked rather smoothly and was very far from the image of the *kadi* as a judge sitting under the shade of a tree, dispensing justice of obscure origin.

If, in the anthropological cases examined, resonance existed between the legal system and the society and culture, this book argues that such resonance exited in the Ottoman Empire as well. In other words, my argument is that the most fundamental feature of Ottoman society in its core area was the existence within it of a bureaucratic state, and that this fact apparently had much to do with the bureaucratic structure of the law. The resonance is admittedly only partial, and I want to underscore this point. I have shown that systematic application of the *shari`a* took place in fifteenth-century Morocco without the presence of a bureaucratic state; and the penal code of the *shari`a* is presently applied in polities not particularly noted for their bureaucratic characteristics. But it seems to me that within the Ottoman context, maybe even within the context of the premodern Middle East, the connection does make sense. In no other premodern Islamic polity does the *kadi* court seem so important.

To return now to the Ottoman polity. It was first of all a bureaucratic state in the most general sense—a state based on a bureaucracy, a group of people appointed for the purpose of managing its affairs and drawing salaries to do so. To my mind this is the most fundamental fact explaining the expansion of this polity from a frontier principality to a world empire, as well as its extraordinary longevity. In saying this I have in mind a slight polemic with a contending historiographical theory that sets out to explain the Ottoman Empire in different, and to my mind erroneous, terms.

This contending theory comes up in Ernest Gellner's brilliant overview of the sociopolitical history of Islam, which does an excellent job of explaining much of the political history of that civilization—except for this slip, which is in no way detrimental to the work's basic soundness. Moreover, it is exactly Gellner's mistake in interpreting the Ottoman Empire that helps bring about a better and clearer understanding of that polity.[50] Gellner claims that the best theory explaining most of Islamic history is the paradigm suggested by Ibn Khaldun. According to this theory, the driving force in Middle Eastern history has been the interplay between the restless, forceful, primeval tribal population along the frontier and the cultured, hence weakened, settled population. The tension between these two areas provides the ever-recurrent movement in the cycles of dynasties and states: the strong and aggressive power on the fringe exerts pressure on the weak power at the center. The problem with this Middle Eastern theory is that it does not fit the Ottoman Empire, a relatively stable state over a period of some six centuries. Well aware of this problem, Gellner explained away this case by claiming that Ottoman greatness was based on the technical device of the *devşirme*, the levy of Christian boys in the Balkans and their transformation into an effective slave army. According to this theory, Ottoman greatness was predicated on the use of this slave army.[51] One might ask why no other polity in this period hit upon this magic solution. More fundamentally, Gellner's mistake is easily traceable to Max Weber, who a century ago claimed, on the basis of evidence now considered obsolete, that the boy levy was invented in the 1330s—that is, on the eve of the great Ottoman conquests.[52] Modern evidence indicates that the boy levy did not exist before about 1400,[53] when the Ottomans were well on their way to southern Poland. Add to this the recent realization that even in the fifteenth and sixteenth centuries the Ottoman system was not based solely on slaves[54] and the conclusion is evident: the secret of the Ottoman Empire has to be sought elsewhere.

To my mind the greatness of the Ottomans lies in their ability to penetrate into an area greatly weakened by political tensions and then to exploit and mobilize the area to create a large-scale bureaucratic state. This state was based first and foremost on the existence of a massive and solid peasantry—a social feature shared to a degree by Anatolia itself. The Ottoman Empire did not conform to the basic Middle Eastern model of a polity constantly hovering on the borders of a realm occupied by a tribal or nomadic power. Its history conformed more to the bureaucratic model of the great empires. In this respect Albert Hourani was certainly correct in viewing the Ottoman Empire as the apex of Islamic history rather than its nadir.[55]

But I claim more than this. If the Ottoman Empire was merely a bureaucratic patrimonial state, it is inconceivable that it would have awarded a judicial monopoly to the *shari`a* court and the *kadi*, given the independent legitimacy bases of these two institutions. In an extreme patrimonial polity we would expect a legal system based on an entirely subservient state police, not on religious dignitaries often more interested in learning than in power politics. So there must be something more to account for the legal system of this polity. Hence, not only do I claim that the Ottoman Empire was a bureaucratic empire in the sense of being a large centralized state, but I also use the term *bureaucracy* in a rather technical way. Bureaucracy is, of course, a multifaceted term, but the reference to it here is only the Weberian sense. For Weber, bureaucracy was the opposite of two other types of regime. One is the simple tribal chieftainship, where the government is more or less tantamount to the household of the chief. The other is patrimonialism, by which Weber meant total subservience of the state (both society and administrative staff) to the whims of the ruler. Weber in fact defined patrimonialism formally as a polity in which the law of the land is the word of the ruler. As opposed to these two systems, Weber saw bureaucracy, or rational bureaucracy, as a polity based on objective and known rules and laws, characterizing the relations between rulers, administrators and the civil society.

This study claims that Ottoman society in its core area was much closer to this bureaucratic ideal-type than is commonly believed. It claims, in fact, that Ottoman society and polity stood somewhere between the bureaucratic and the patrimonial models. This argument contains two main elements. One is that the actual position of the ruler was far more modest than is implied by the concept of patrimonialism, to say nothing of sultanism, which is an extreme form of patrimonialism characterized by total lack of organized law beyond the unrestrained whim of the sovereign. Such, too, is the role of state officials vis-à-vis the ordinary citizen. The other claim is that Ottoman bureaucracy was permeated by universalistic principles to a greater extent than is usually allowed for. Much of recent scholarship—possibly as a reaction to the trend in former years—has correctly underscored the role in Ottoman administration of patron-client relations and patronage in general—*intisab* in Ottoman parlance. I have no argument with such studies beyond wishing to emphasize that all this should not blind us to the important role of universalistic principles. No less important was the fact that the Ottoman bureaucracy helped bring about a society that was much less kinship oriented in its core area than in geographically more remote parts of the empire. On the whole, the outcome was that the familial pattern among the Ottoman elite tended to the nuclear when compared with, say, families in Syria, to say nothing of Morocco. How did the Ottoman bureaucracy achieve this feat? The reason for this development, I suggest, is that the elite of the core area was the main source of high-level personnel for the entire empire; and because officeholders in that empire were constantly moving around, large families tended to break down. This tendency grew even stronger as the reservoir of elite became increasingly concentrated in a thin layer of core-region families. I argue that the same geographical pattern is important in another way that is connected to the bureaucracy-patrimonialism dichotomy. It seems that much of the predation that took place in the Ottoman Empire in the period under study was not an outgrowth of central policy but rather a violation and subversion of it, mainly by disobedient provincial governors. There are signs that the grip of the center over the provinces grew weaker as they became more far-flung. This meant that bureaucracy was more nearly a reality in the core area of the empire than in its outer provinces.

An important question that remains to be broached at this point is why the bureaucratic Ottoman state gave rise to the particular form of legal system that it did. Part of the answer is more or less self-evident. It is natural for a bureaucratic state to strive for the creation of a relatively unified court system where all sorts of legal business is dealt with. It is less clear why it had to be the *shari`a* court system, and one should probably beware of explaining this in too rigidly functional terms. One may visualize the Ottomans striving to erect an alternative court system. That they did not do so is probably related to the fact that the *shari`a* court system was available to them at no cost whatsoever and that it suited them culturally—not only because it represented Islamic ethics, but also because the Islamic court was an antidote, both political and cultural, to the military administrator, a figure with whom the Ottoman dynasty had a well-known love-hate relationship.

Before plunging headlong into my topic, it seems appropriate to say a few words about my primary sources, which are mainly of three sorts. First, I have used actual records of Ottoman *kadi*s, coming predominantly from the western Anatolian town of Bursa in the seventeenth century but supplemented by several manuscripts and published books that contain genuine *kadi* records, which were largely from eighteenth-century Istanbul and collected for didactic purposes. The second main source that I have exploited is the *Book of Complaints*, recently published in Vienna.[56] This is a huge collection of documents, though a mere sampling of a series preserved in its entirety in the Ottoman archive in Istanbul. By hindsight it turned out to be an extremely interesting source. Its importance seems to me to far transcend the information it provides in the narrow sense. The 2,800 complaints contained in the book cover a period of nine months in 1675; and it turns out that complaints were filed by people from all walks of life and on every possible subject, so that the material lends itself to statistical analysis. In other words, the breakdown of various phenomena in the register may well reflect real-life breakdown. And if this is true, we are afforded here an insight into Ottoman life that would take years of more conventional archival research to obtain.[57]

My third main source is the *fetva* collections, particularly, though not exclusively, of Ottoman *şeyhülislam*s, who were the heads of the Ottoman religious apparatus. The *fetva* (Arabic *fatwa*) is an Islamic legal institution of very early origin. The term refers to a legal opinion of a professional and highly regarded scholar on a certain point of law. The *fetva* was most often used to back legal arguments in the process of adjudication; but it always was, and it remained, a scholarly opinion, not in any sense a binding ruling in a court of law. In the Ottoman Empire the issuance of *fetva*s became highly institutionalized and came to be headed by a *şeyhülislam*, or Grand Mufti, who after the third quarter of the sixteenth century became the officeholder responsible for all religious and legal nominations in the empire, keeping all the while his second hat of *mufti*, that is, a religious scholar in charge of issuing *fetva*s. Several *fetva* collections of such *mufti*s—from about a hundred known to exist—have been published, and these form one of the sources of research in this study.

In the general rush of Ottoman historians to newly found and newly opened Ottoman archives, this source has been almost completely neglected. As an objective source of information, these collections have been pretty much despised; as a source of ideology, beliefs, and culture in the modern anthropological sense they have not so far been considered at all because this aspect of Ottoman studies has barely been touched upon. Yet they are among the few examples of first-person discourse available from this period. The question may possibly be raised as to whether the collections used here can be considered a big enough sample to represent the entire phenomenon. The answer is that these particular collections were not published at all by chance. The last traditional biographer of the *şeyhülislams*, Mustakim Zade, who wrote in the eighteenth century, singled out several of these specific collections as being those that enjoyed particular popularity among the people.[58] Thus I feel justified in considering these collections as much more than a mere sampling; they seem truly to represent the prevalent mode of popular thinking in the time and place of study.

The importance of these collections for the social historian of law is also evidenced in the fact that *kadi* court records in the area of study are replete with *fetva*s emanating from the pens of these *muftis*. Needless to say, these collections are also vitally important as cultural-ideological documents shedding light on the thought patterns of Ottoman religious dignitaries concerning the relations between state and society.

1. THE STRUCTURE OF THE OTTOMAN LEGAL PROCESS IN THE SEVENTEENTH AND EIGHTEENTH CENTURIES

IN THIS CHAPTER I attempt to analyze the main features of the central Ottoman judicial process in the seventeenth and eighteenth centuries, in light of the comparative and theoretical questions raised in the introduction. I shall first investigate the validity of Weber's famous concept of *kadi* justice and then proceed to look at this legal system more closely from the point of view of legal anthropology.

THE VIABILITY OF THE CONCEPT OF *KADI* JUSTICE

Recent years have witnessed a sort of Max Weber renaissance. However, most of this voluminous output seems to be concerned with ever-recurrent interpretations of Weber's views. Almost entirely lacking are studies that subject Weber's ideas to critical examination in light of data bases left untapped by him or that were unknown in his time.[1] Such fresh examinations may yield new insights on the validity and usefulness of Weber's theories in general, and may deepen our awareness of the problems involved in the relation between theory and history.

In this chapter, I propose to confront Weber's sociology of law with Ottoman Islamic law as it was lived and practiced in the central area of that state between the early seventeenth and the mid-nineteenth centuries, in order to check the viability of Weber's famous concept of *kadi* justice.[2] I cannot emphasize strongly enough that my aim in undertaking this study was not a mission to refute Weber or to establish the supremacy of empirical history (raw facts, narrative, and the like) over theory. On the contrary, this study arose from my interest in exploring the relations between theory and history. It is true that along the way I make some critical comments on Weber's opinions of Islamic law, but I found the theoretical framework Weber suggested to be crucial for a comparative study such as the present one.

The Islamic law of the Ottoman Empire seems to be particularly suited to the task of weighing the adequacy of Weber's concept of *kadi* justice (1) because from no other Muslim country has such an abundance of sources survived, and (2) because Weber had in mind to explain, by analyzing the law, something wider and deeper. He was interested in the law because he held the notion that rational, predictable, and dependable law was a root cause of the rise of capitalism in the West from the sixteenth century on. That this was also the period of the heyday and decline of the Ottoman Empire makes this case study a particularly pertinent one. It should also be borne in mind that the Weber thesis (about law) is best investigated in a pre-twentieth-century context, because the massive reforms carried out in almost all Islamic legal systems in the world left this law totally mutilated in comparison to its former self. In most countries it was reduced to dealing merely with family law (marriage, divorce, and the like). If we want to observe Islamic law at work in real-life situations, we have to go back in time—although such an exercise may reveal a great deal about present Islamic societies as well as past ones.

An initial problem with Weber's concept of *kadi* justice is its assumption that Islamic law everywhere is the same, or that differences are negligible. One place where this assumption is taken to task (though not explicitly) is Geertz's study of legal sociology, based partly on Islamic case studies.

Geertz sets out to demonstrate that law is different not only from one culture to another but even within one culture, broadly conceived, because law is an expression of the internal logic and structure of a culture. In this sense it might be said that law is an outgrowth of both the "great" tradition and the "small" tradition, and that what makes its study interesting is tracing the relations between these traditions in different places and periods. To demonstrate the intellectual profit to be gained from such a comparison, Geertz analyzes in this way three societies, two of which— Morocco and Indonesia—are Muslim although the two societies live by legal systems that have only a little in common.[3]

But to come back to Weber, he approached analysis of the world's legal systems by proposing a fourfold classification based on two basic variables: rationality versus irrationality, and formalism versus substantiveness.[4] A legal system was said to be rational when judicial decisions were reached through a process of intellectual reasoning of some sort. When the process was based on some irrational mode of thinking (ordeals by fire and the like), the system as a whole was said to be irrational. Within the rational category Weber differentiated between formal and substantive rationality. The only known exemplar of formal rational law is the Western legal system. In Weber's crucial sentence characterizing this law, formal rational law is found "where the legally relevant characteristics of the facts are disclosed through the logical analysis of meaning and where, accordingly, definitely fixed legal concepts in the form of highly abstract rules are formulated and applied."[5] The key concept in this somewhat elusive rendering is, of course, the logical analysis of meaning. According to David Trubek, this concept means simply that in Western law special attention was given to the intent of those involved in the judicial process. And he adds: "In contract law, this means looking at the intent of the contracting parties; in criminal law, it means deciding whether the accused had the requisite criminal intent."[6] A second major point in the previously-cited sentence from Weber is the far-reaching predictability (and hence, by implication, also fairness and liberality) inherent in Western law, born of the fact that Western law was based on the application of well-known preexisting rules to specific cases, which were applied in a logical manner and without reference to special circumstances.

The substantive rational legal system on the other hand is characterized by the fact that the judge is not bound by any fixed rules but acts arbitrarily and intuitively. While one can think of many examples of this kind of legal system, Weber himself dubbed it *kadi* justice, probably seeing Islamic law as its clearest manifestation.[7] Weber held that the *kadi*'s decisions were purely emotional, entirely unconnected to any rules besides a vague reference to broadly conceived Islamic ethics. Brian Turner is right in asserting that Weber actually had in mind a wider comparison—between East and West, rather than just a comparison between legal systems in the narrow sense.[8] The fact that *kadi* justice was not based on fixed rules of decision also meant that this legal system did not afford any measure of predictability or reliability as far as human rights were concerned. According to Turner, this situation was typical of a patrimonial political system like the Ottoman Empire, characterized as it was by overwhelming state power versus supine societal institutions.

Law in patrimonial systems is glossed as "substantive lawfinding, an amalgamation of sacred and secular law, and arbitrary intervention by the ruler in legal processes."[9] When Weber probes deeper into the problems afflicting the Islamic legal system, we find that targeted for indictment first and foremost is the famous closing of the gates of individual legal interpretation in the twelfth century, which obstructed the further free development of the law. The outcome of this event was progressively fewer fixed rules to direct *kadi*s, their work thus becoming ever less governed by preexisting rules and more by arbitrariness and subjectivity.[10] This naturally remained the situation in the Ottoman Empire, to which was added the problem already noted: that due to the state's patrimonial nature, its legal system was afflicted by heavy state intervention in legal affairs.[11] We thus get a legal system characterized by two main features: arbitrariness and excessive individualism on the part of the *kadi*; and heavy intervention by the state in the legal process.

In the foregoing paragraphs I have taken the liberty of expanding Weber's theory of Islamic law by incorporating into it Turner's views. I will now go a step further and bring in as well Lawrence Rosen's study of Morocco, which expressly adopts the Weberian conceptual framework.[12] Some differences between Turner and Rosen must, however, be noted. Whereas Turner follows Weber in seeing Islamic law in unquestionably dark colors, as oppressive and antiliberal, anthropologist Rosen underscores in the Weberian analysis a line that is to my mind pretty much hidden from sight: the plainly positive proclivity of the Muslim *kadi* to seek substantial social justice well suited to the needs of the community. Put simply, where Turner sees the danger in near total judicial discretion and lack of rules, Rosen sees the potential social benefit and strength of this legal system. Yet they both follow Weber in seeing Islamic law as characterized by mild rules governing the judicial process.

In principle, the Moroccan *kadi* has to go by the 1958 family law. But he can also go by local custom, by analogy, by precedent, and ultimately by what he sees as the public good. One example that is brought forward to demonstrate how these divergent principles work in real life is the suit launched by a woman who asked the court to divorce her from her jailed husband. No article of the family law formally upheld her case, but the *kadi* nevertheless granted the divorce after extensive consultation with social leaders from the area. Especially important in his decision were the uprightness and suffering of the woman, a lady from a good family, as opposed to the lowly origin of the defendant and his despicable character (he was a convicted thief). Thus, the *kadi* decided against the letter of the law and went by what he viewed as the well-being of the community. It is in this way that the Moroccan legal system was said to be suffused by Moroccan culture and ethical preferences, and it was in this sense that the Moroccan legal system was said to be based on substantive rather than formal rationality.

Also pertinent in exactly this context are Clifford Geertz's views on Islamic law, partially based as they are on Lawrence Rosen's field work in Morocco. Geertz accords special importance to the institution of "normative witnessing." In fact, he views it as the most typical institution of Islamic law.[13] The reference is to those permanent witnesses sitting beside the *kadi*, both in classical Islam and in modern Morocco. These witnesses do not have firsthand information concerning judicial cases brought before the court, but they are nevertheless so upright and so intimately involved in the affairs of the community that they are considered qualified to assess the truth of statements made before them.

From the foregoing discussion, one can extract five main features that can be used as a further basis for empirical study: (1) a lack of predictability and reliability due to the absence of a rigorous system of prior laws and rules; (2) arbitrariness on the part of the *kadi* (also resulting mainly from the absence of rules), at times resulting in a violation of rights, even rights that may be considered sacred by the Islamic society (such as property rights); (3) the prevalence, or at least strong involvement, of ethical considerations over strictly legal ones; (4) a strong proclivity on the part of government officials to intervene in the judicial process; and (5) normative witnessing as a paramount feature of the legal system.

On the basis of a substantial number of original Ottoman legal documents originating from the courts of the Bursa/ Istanbul region, I have investigated the Weber thesis and found it wanting on each of the counts enumerated above. In every respect the Islamic law of this region was drastically different from what

Weber suggested it must have been. Therefore, the argument of this study will show that either Weber was completely on the wrong track, or there were substantial differences in the structure of law within Islamdom, or both.

Regarding the issue of predictability, I have chosen three major areas of law and probed the records to find out whether decisions were arbitrary, erratic, and shapeless or whether a consistent pattern could nevertheless be discovered. These areas were family law, criminal law, and civil and commercial law.

It might have been desirable at this point to analyze the actual court scene that unfolded in front of the *kadi*. Unfortunately, it is impossible to reconstruct much of this from the documents currently at hand. No firsthand descriptions of what was said are available, only summaries of the proceedings. A typical case started with a claim (*da`wa*) of one person against another. The defendant either admitted the accusation (*ikrar*), thereby ending the suit, or denied it (*inkar*) and demanded proof (*bayyina*). When the plaintiff could produce evidence, it consisted in almost all the cases I examined of witnesses (I shall speak later of documentary evidence). If no evidence was presented, the defendant was usually offered the oath, which if he took it, cleared him of the charge. In many cases no such oath was necessary, and lack of incriminating evidence was enough to establish innocence. Two important questions come to mind: why was the court following one procedure rather than another? And was the court applying a certain code? These questions are pertinent because I rarely found a case in the area of study where a specific law code or law book was invoked. But on investigation it turns out that the court was applying the *shari`a* procedure, and was following the available *shari`a* manuals. In fact, one *shari`a* manual in particular came to hold sway (entirely through social consensus, of course) in the Ottoman *madrasa* (religious school) and the Ottoman court, a sixteenth-century *shari`a* compilation of Ibrahim al-Halabi entitled *Multaqa al-Abhur*.[14] While the compilation does not mention specific Ottoman innovations in Islamic law (to be detailed later in this chapter), it does constitute a faithful and convenient rendering of the classical Hanafi version of the *shari`a*. Much of this was living law in the area under study; as recent documentary discoveries in Jerusalem have made clear, Ottoman law was partly following here in the footsteps of pre-Ottoman Near Eastern law.[15]

The family law current in the Bursa/Istanbul region in the seventeenth and eighteenth centuries was basically the *shari`a*—

that is, the Islamic law rather than customary law or any other type of law. This is true not only in the sense that the law employed in the court was the Muslim law of family, but also in the sense that on the whole there was no other law in use in the area. The methodological problem referred to here is rendered apparent by looking at Richard Antoun's study on the working of the shari`a court among the village population in contemporary Jordan. We are shown how the shari`a court often forced on those coming before it family law that was at variance with the family law in use by this society. The reference here is to the contradiction between the widespread Middle Eastern custom, whereby the bride's father collects the bride price, and the shari`a law, whereby that money goes to the bride herself.[16] The prevalence of the custom is widely reflected in the work of the court. For example, women often used the denial of the bride price as a legal pretext to achieve an annulment of the marriage or a divorce.

I sought to investigate this point in the documents from the Istanbul region and found that the situation was quite different. Although women in this region often requested and received legal divorce by a wide variety of pretexts, they never, not even once, used the argument of nonpayment of bride price in this context.

By the same token, we should rule out the possibility that this information was not brought to the court because of its illegality; the kadi court records abound with information that was indecent, immoral, and illegal—which did not prevent it from being freely discussed and recorded. Also noteworthy is the fact that in many documents we come across the phenomenon of marriage agreements' being brought to the court to be recorded without there being any particular complication about them.[17] Neither Islamic law nor any other legal system necessitated that kind of procedure, so it seems it might have been the outcome of an awareness on that society's part of the use to which the court might be put in time of death or divorce (when the deferred part of the bride price would fall due and be collected). This enhances the impression that cases violating shari`a regulations would find expression in the kadi records.

It seems likely, then, that the shari`a governed the family law prevalent in the area of study; yet it seems preferable to proceed by analyzing the case material in the records rather than by summarizing law books. And the major family issue in the records is divorce—more specifically, suits brought by women against their husbands in connection with divorce cases.

One of the most widespread types of cases involving family law that appear in the records is *khul`* divorce— that is, divorce initiated by the wife, whether of her own free will or as a consequence of a prior agreement between her and her husband. Such an initiative on the part of the woman would entail the automatic waiver of her financial privileges. In most of the cases cited in the records, the reason adduced for the request is quarrelsome relations.[18] In some cases women even paid sums out of their own pockets to obtain the divorce.[19] No cases were found where the court tried to dissuade women from pursuing their effort to obtain a divorce. By way of comparison, from Paul Stirling's study of two villages in central Anatolia in the 1950s it transpires that such an act on the part of a wife was out of the question: wives who wished for divorce had to run away to their family of origin.[20]

In other cases wives sued husbands and claimed that the latter had made a conditional divorce (in this form: "If so and so happens, my wife is divorced"), and the condition had been fulfilled. Women often seized such opportunities to demand a divorce.[21] In other cases the husband, probably in the context of a familial quarrel, gave his wife permission to divorce herself if she so wished—or at least the wife thought he had, and hence there were a number of lawsuits brought against husbands.[22]

Another ground for divorce was connected with the *shari`a* regulation called *khiyar al-bulugh*—that is, the option given to a girl married off by her guardian when still under age to annul the marriage upon reaching maturity. Again, this option was quite often resorted to.[23] In all these matters, the *shari`a* seems to be the law that prevailed in actual life, not just in theory.

Another area of law worth analyzing in this context is what is called in modern jargon *penal law*. It is well known that the autochthonous categorization was somewhat different then from what it is today, even in Islamic countries. But that matters little for the purposes of the present study. The documents examined indicate quite clearly that in the legal system under consideration a large measure of consistency, and hence predictability, permeated the working of the court. In this area as well, the *shari`a* seems on the whole to be the most important source of law, although, in cases of murder, there was a substantial convergence between the *shari`a* and the *kanun*.

For murder cases to be heard, both the murderer and the legal inheritors of the murdered person had to be present in court. Murder cases being within the confines of the *shari`a* "law of humans," or *huquq al-ibad*, the inheritors served as the plaintiffs, there not being any other authority to fulfill that function. In principle, killing could be either by mistake or premeditated; in the latter case it was murder. In case of murder the *shari`a* gave the plaintiff the right to decide whether the defendant should be put to death through the principle of *kisas* (retaliation) or be liable instead to *diyet* (blood money).[24] This sum was fixed already in classical Islam at ten thousand *dirham* (equivalent to 3.8 grams of silver), the money value of a healthy man as set by the *shari`a*. If the killing was proven to be unintended, the killer was liable only for blood money, which was an equal sum of money. It is noteworthy that the *kanun* here adopted exactly the classical *shari`a* regulation.

The available documents from the Istanbul/Bursa area show that courts usually behaved according to these rules. Thus in one case a woman was brought to court and charged with doping and then strangling to death another woman, whose husband served as the plaintiff.[25] The husband demanded the death penalty, and it was granted. To a degree, at least, the same kind of legal approach to murder cases transpired in cases relating to regions of the empire that were further afield.[26]

In real life this basic rule concerning murder was manifested in several nuances. One such was when the deceased had no legal heirs. The rule then was that the sultan stood in place of the heirs. In one such case from eighteenth-century Istanbul, the case was actually referred to the sultan, whose verdict was death.[27]

If murder was not duly proven, the plaintiff could force the defendant to take an oath. Doing so would establish his innocence. If he refused—which often happened—the plaintiff's case was thereby established. In one case of murder in which a defendant refused to take the oath, the *kadi*'s decision was that he would remain in jail until he was willing to take such an oath.[28] Again, this was entirely in keeping with the *shari`a*. Demands for *diyet* instead of *kisas* were found, too, but they seem less frequent. When such punishments were imposed, they were based on calculation of the present-day equivalent (in Ottoman money) of the aforementioned sum of ten thousand *dirham*.[29] A rare case in this context is one in which a man was sued for murder by the father of the deceased. After the charge was duly proven, the plaintiff demanded blood money, but the defendant retorted that he was unable to pay that kind of money and suggested that the plaintiff demand execution. The *kadi*'s decision was that in such a situation the defendant is liable for neither *kisas* nor *diyet*.[30]

In a case of unintended killing the killer was liable to pay indemnity equivalent to *diyet*.[31] It would be extremely interesting to have examples with detailed debates over the question of whether a certain case was or was not a case of murder. But such cases were not found, other than one, that for technical reasons was not concluded in the account we have of it.[32] Also, negligent homicide is not often at issue. In a rare case we find an Istanbul coachman who beat his horses and made them run so furiously that they killed a small child.[33] The coachman denied he had behaved unreasonably, although a number of witnesses claimed that he had. This case bears out the claim made by some anthropologists that the concept of the reasonable man may well exist in all cultures;[34] but it is noteworthy that traditional Islamic law did not attribute much practical importance to this difference: negligent or not, unintended killing entailed payment of full *diyet*— that is, an amount equivalent to ten thousand *dirham*.

An important area within the Islamic penal law concerned the question of discovered corpses. The *shari`a*, and following it also the *kanun*, ruled that if no individual responsibility for murder could be established, the owner of the house or the inhabitants of the village or quarter were liable for blood money. A large number of documents in our records indicate that this was indeed the situation in the area under study. In an apparently typical case, a man was found dead in a house in Tophane, Istanbul, and no killer was discovered. It was demanded that the owner of the house swear fifty times that he was not the killer. Only then could he pay the blood money.[35] A similar law was at work in the countryside. In one case the body of a man without heirs was discovered in the area of a village belonging to a religious endowment. The manager of the endowment sued the villagers for murder; and after he was unable to prove this accusation, he picked fifty from among their number and demanded the oath from them.[36] In another case, when the body of a man was found at some distance from the built-up area of a village, the heirs requested blood money from the villagers. However, in view of the distance from the village, the following procedure was employed: a *müezzin* (prayer leader) was summoned and instructed to read the call to prayer while witnesses stood on the edge of the village to establish whether the call could not be heard, the court ruled that the village was not liable for compensation.[37]

Another area of the criminal law had to do with grave bodily injury. A great many documents dealt with this problem, and they all convey a certain consistent and detectable logic. Grave harm done to the hand, the leg, or the eye was considered equal to half the value of a fully grown man and entailed the payment of half blood money.[38] Less vital organs entailed smaller amounts of compensation. But again, a very consistent logic prevailed. Thus, knocking out a tooth—a very common grievance—entailed compensation of 5 percent of full blood money (and half that in the case of a woman).[39] In one rare case, though, half blood money was decided for a knocked-out tooth.[40]

Sometimes the bodily harm done to a person was not clear-cut but even here it is evident that compensation was not decided on arbitrarily. It was decided in an ingenious manner: experts were summoned to assess the damage done to the person. The most common type of experts were slave traders, who were asked to look upon the injured person as if he were a slave and to assess the money value of the damage done to him.[41]

Fornication (zina) was also an important area of Ottoman law. Offenses committed by women did not turn up at all in the documents, but I found quite a few committed by men. The punishment meted out was consistent—the shar`i punishment of one hundred strokes because all the culprits in these cases were unmarried men. It is noteworthy that rape came under the same heading.[42] An unfounded accusation of fornication was also considered a severe offense and was punishable by eighty lashes. A related example from Istanbul is the suit initiated by one Ahmed Ağa b. Abd el-Baki, a zaim (fiefholder), against his neighbor, another fiefholder, who cursed him and called him kafir (non-Muslim), kızíl baş (heretic) and zani (fornicator). Because witnesses attested that he was innocent of all these charges, the defendant was condemned to eighty lashes.[43]

Cases of theft were mainly punishable by shari`a regulations; however, it must be emphasized that the penal law of Süleyman did not really supersede the shari`a but was merely added to it. Basically, it accepted the cutting off of the hand as the standard punishment for theft of a certain gravity, but it added some fines for minor thefts.[44] A number of cases of hand amputation as a punishment for theft were indeed found.[45] In a few rare cases, we do find custom-linked types of punishment, such as lengthy imprisonment.[46]

The third area of law I deemed it advisable to review was civil and commercial law. Prevailing opinion once held that this was the one area in which the classical *shari`a* had always been merely theoretical and was not even intended to be carried out in practice. Possibly this was indeed the case in some places. But as a generalization it is certainly belied by the Ottoman case. Thus, as I have shown in another study, the classical Islamic law of partnerships was in full use in Ottoman society.[47] The exact Islamic terms for various types of partnerships are used, and the documents show that these partnerships took the same form as is outlined in the classical law manuals. Needless to say, such use was entirely voluntary; no legal or political authority in Bursa seemed in the least interested in the types of transactions that took place among merchants or artisans.

A broader look at the Bursa and Istanbul records reveals quite clearly that it was not just partnership law that was in use but the entire civil law part of the *shari`a*. An example is the law of bankruptcy. The *shari`a* manuals lay down that anyone unable to pay his or her debt is to be sent to jail pending payment or sufficient proof that he is sincerely unable to pay. A large number of documents from the Bursa/Istanbul area attest that this was exactly the law in use there. Another typical Islamic law of business lays down that a person is entitled to buy an object without seeing it and has the right of rescission immediately after first seeing it. Again, this law was in full use.

These examples could be multiplied. Except in the area of credit relations, where the society in question was truly inventive (see the next chapter), there is a very close match between the *shari`a* and the civil law in use in the area of study. This indicates that the element of consistency, and therefore of predictability, in the judicial process of the *kadi* was very high indeed.

Let us turn now to the internal logic of the process of adjudication and, more specifically, to the question of judicial discretion vested in the *kadi*. If there is one single feature characterizing "*kadi* justice," it is that of the *kadi*'s unlimited judicial discretion. For Weber, this represented arbitrariness; the *kadi* adjudicates strongly, but no one knows what guidelines he uses. For Rosen, the *kadi* mediates leniently rather than adjudicates sternly, which accords well with the social structure. As far as the area under the present study is concerned, both interpretations are, in fact, wide of the mark. In Ottoman society the *kadi* was seen as a strong judge, but he was certainly not adjudicating off the top of his head.

No less than 75 percent of the material he was dealing with was inscribed in shari`a manuals, and the rest was equally well known to the parties and to the witnesses present in each and every case. All of the people present endorsed the entire process with their signatures.

Weber was wrong in assuming that Islamic law was incapable of development after the tenth century. A substantial amount of change did take place, as I will demonstrate later. But he was partly on the right track in asserting that Islamic law was constrained in its development by the sacredness of the shari`a. That does not mean, however, that this law necessarily lost touch with reality. In the first place, reality was not changing at such a pace that the law could easily become out of touch with it. Moreover, Islamic law contains various built-in mechanisms of adaptation. One example is the concept of tazir, an unspecified type of punishment to be decided on by the kadi according to the severity of the offense. What emerges from the area under study is that the role of the kadi in the process of adjudication seems much closer to the European model than has been suggested by either Weber or Rosen.

According to Geertz, the most important feature of the Islamic legal system was the place in it of normative witnessing. Do the documents at our disposal indicate whether this was also the situation in the area under study? Let me say straight away that the central Ottoman area seems in this respect quite different from, for example, Morocco. The first distinct fact in this regard is the place of documents in the legal process. Though clearly secondary to the role of witnesses, documents were nevertheless very important. Thus, in thousands of estates in seventeenth-century Bursa, countless numbers of people are recorded as owing sums of money to the deceased person. There is no question that this vast credit institution rested solely on witnesses. Inheritors would otherwise have had to summon scores if not hundreds of people in order to collect their debts. This was not only unlikely, but there is also no evidence that inheritors were in the habit of doing this. There is not the slightest doubt that the recorded evidence was rarely contested, simply because the court accepted written evidence as a matter of routine.

Additional documentary evidence supports this conclusion. Thus, in one document we find a lawsuit between two parties, one of whom has in hand a document attesting that the other borrowed money from him.[48] The defendant says he actually did not borrow anything and signed the document without really meaning it (muvazaatan). He lost the case. In another document, a man refused to repay a loan of 1,200 piasters denying he had ever borrowed the sum even though the plaintiff produced a genuine-looking document to that effect.[49] Nevertheless, despite the foregoing examples, there is a plethora of documents showing that disputed documents had to be backed by witnesses and were definitely superseded by them. There are no cases of conflict between documents and witnesses; it is simply the case that witnessing was the most widespread kind of evidence.

However, our main issue here is normative witnessing and not witnessing in general. In seventeenth-century Bursa, normative witnessing was used mainly in the context of combating famous and professional robbers. On the whole, it can be stated that this was true for the entire region: normative witnessing did exist, but it was not nearly as important as it had been in classical Islam or is in Morocco. Thus, in a relevant example from Edirne, we read that government officials in that city captured two men who were brought to court and described as "fomentors of evil in the world." A large number of Muslims then declared: "The said two are robbers, day and night they stroll in the said city with weapons, break into the houses of many respectable people, whom they beat and tie up, and then kidnap their wives and carry off their property. That sort of oppression is their permanent habit."[50] The two were condemned to death, although no specific charge was brought against them in the cited document. The case of the city of Bursa may hint at one possible reason that made the society in question particularly sensitive to such a problem.[51] Highway robbery of all sorts was endemic and widespread, while gangs of robbers roamed the countryside—and even the city—entirely unmolested. No wonder that in such a situation the attitude toward robbers was tougher than toward other criminals.

Though most of the extant cases of normative witnessing are of that type, some other cases are worth mentioning. In one, a large group of people, including some religious personages, summoned an individual to court and claimed he was a müteşayyikh (self-styled şeyh). This probably meant a popular religious preacher without formal education or a post. The specific accusation was that he molested people in the city. No decision was given in the case, and it was referred to the central government.[52] Normative witnessing is likewise found in a case where the people of the Yeni Köy quarter of Istanbul launched a complaint against someone from the quarter who was accused of molesting and cursing the people of the quarter, as well as bringing to his house morally suspicious characters. The people of the quarter demanded a verdict of expulsion of the defendant from the quarter. Before this could be done, however, the man undertook to remove himself without a formal verdict.[53]

Many of the normative witnessing cases in the records are against allegedly immoral women, whom the citizens wish to remove from the quarter[54]—a very widespread occurrence in seventeenth-century Bursa.

An extremely interesting case of semilegal involvement of the community is evinced in matters relating to psychiatric institutionalization. In a relevant case from late eighteenth-century Istanbul, a large body of citizens from a certain quarter came to court and claimed against a certain Çokadar Ibrahim that he was crazy (macnun): he used to assault the people of the quarter with weapons, injuring and frightening them. He had been formerly locked away in the Süleymaniye hospital, but he had got out through some mistake and should be returned there. The kadi agreed but had to apply to the sultan to issue the order.[55]

While all these cases evince a certain similarity between the legal system at hand and the Moroccan system as depicted by Rosen and Geertz, there is nevertheless a big difference between normative witnessing here and there. In the Ottoman case, normative witnessing seems to have been used only in cases of habitual offenders; no instance was found of a regular case being decided by this procedure. It might be said that in the Ottoman case normative witnessing served mainly as a functional substitute for modern police records.

That the Ottoman legal system was not based on the social-communal context of the parties to the trial is attested to by the role of the institution of fetva in that legal system. A fetva is a legal question addressed to a mufti—a religious-legal expert especially qualified to provide legally authoritative answers. Such written answers would be presented in court as part of a trial and would be taken into account by the kadi. The relevance of this issue to our topic is that a fetva is a specially drawn-up document worded in such a way as to eliminate all personal and contextual details. Evidently, this is done to prevent the mufti from being influenced in his decision by acquaintance with one or both parties to the case.

The *kadi* court records of the area under study abound with such *fetvas*, which makes the institution an important part of the legal system in question. It should also be borne in mind that the chief *mufti* of the capital, the *şeyhülislam*, was also the foremost religious officeholder in the empire.[56] It may be partly due to this fact that the *kadi* records in Bursa and Istanbul contain *fetvas* in such abundance and that these *fetvas* were taken so seriously by the *kadis*—so much so, indeed, that the party with the *fetva* always won the case. All this indicates quite clearly that far from the communal context being essential to the decision in controversies, the Ottomans saw the opposite as the ideal—that is, neutralizing that effect as much as possible. More important, they also put this ideal into practice.

Brian Turner has observed that the patrimonial nature of Ottoman law consisted of frequent intervention on the part of state officials in the judicial process. Whatever the status of that argument in other areas of Islam, it seems to be completely unfounded in the area being studied here.[57] No single case recorded contains hints to that effect; if such intervention took place secretly, it is doubtful that Turner or any other researcher could know about it, and it is doubly doubtful that anybody could show that other systems—the modern democratic one, for example—are less vulnerable in this regard.

But beyond this exercise in speculation there is some direct evidence that intervention was lacking even in cases where it might have been expected. There is, for example, no shortage of cases where government officials themselves were involved in court cases with ordinary citizens and lost them. One such case concerns a conflict between the citizens of a village in the Istanbul area and the manager of the religious endowment to which the village belonged as well as a number of other state officials connected with state properties in the area. The villagers, the plaintiffs in the case, claim that a large piece of land that formerly had been a pasture area for their village was occupied by the defendants five years earlier and used for the benefit of the sultan's court. Thirty-five villagers from the surrounding areas attest for the plaintiffs, and they win the case in defiance of high state officials in the service of the sultan.[58] There is no hint in this document of any official intervention in the judicial process.

Two cases of murder are also relevant in the present context. One deals with a claim made by ordinary citizens against a fiefholder, who is eventually convicted and condemned to death.[59]

In the second case some youngsters are accused of murdering Feyzullah Paşa, governor of the province of Sivas. The case seems to proceed along quite the usual lines, although a harsher and less orderly procedure might have been expected here.[60]

The issue of official intervention brings us to the wider issue of the judicial system as a reflection of the society's class structure, a topic not really part of Weber's interest. The truth is that it is extremely difficult to show that the Ottoman legal system was used as a tool in class control (see also the special section following). A comparative look at England during this period might be helpful at this point. England is a well-known example of a society in which law, mainly penal law, of course, was a tool in the hands of the upper class to keep the lower classes in their place. A quick look at the criminal law of this period shows what this class difference meant in reality. The available literature[61] shows that throughout the eighteenth century legislation relating to matters of offenses against property was so intensively enacted that by the end of the period about two hundred offenses entailed the death penalty. Theft of property of even trifling value was punishable by hanging. In actuality, the system was a little less harsh than in theory, for one function of this heavy-handed legislation was to augment the possibility of pardon—thus supplying a most powerful leverage of patronage to be used by the aristocracy in controlling the other 97 percent of the population.

The Ottoman Empire presents us with a completely different kind of model. In the legal system in the area under study, there was only one substantial offense against property, punishable in the main by hand cutting. The *kanun*— that is, the Ottoman addition to the field of law—contains nothing really new here. Neither from the *shari`a* nor from the *kanun* is it possible to obtain an idea about the prevailing class structure in this state. If, by definition, the law of a state bears some relation to the prevailing class structure—which seems incontestable to a certain extent—then our conclusion ought to be that Ottoman society was based on a very minor degree of class crystallization. One would be hard put to point to any social layer that could qualify as a ruling class. What is fully apparent is an unquestioned superiority of the sultan, who in turn strives to maintain a loose balance between the various elite groups and the populace. In any event, state intervention in the process of adjudication seems to be completely missing.

In conclusion, I have tried in this section to weigh the value of Max Weber's theory of law, especially with reference to its implications for Islam and Islamic law. But I have tried to go beyond that point, to treat the topic at what seems a more appropriate level: relating the law to the polity of which it constituted a part. What, then, is the connection in the present case study? The answer can be summarized under the title of predictability. We have seen that contrary to Weber's suggestion *kadi* justice in the area under study was characterized by a great deal of predictability and internal consistency. As Turner has claimed, the supposed unpredictability of Ottoman law was an expression of a patrimonial political system, one in which the government was all-powerful and the citizens totally powerless. The extent to which this legal system was predictable would seem to indicate that the Ottoman political system was, in fact, much less harsh than is usually supposed. Patrimonial it may have been, but as such it was rather temperate.[62] A close look at the Ottoman urban scene reveals a society living in quite a "democratic" atmosphere. I shall have much more to say later on this topic.[63]

THE LEGAL ANTHROPOLOGY OF OTTOMAN LAW

In this section I apply to the Ottoman case some of the research categories isolated in the general literature on legal anthropology. For example, a survey of this literature, including the material on Morocco, reveals that the legal system of most of these societies dealt principally with litigation among close blood relatives and tended to treat cases in a highly holistic way. They related lavishly to the past history of the relations among the individuals, trying to mediate between the parties rather than decide sharply without regard to the future relations of the litigants. In a slightly reduced form, this last feature can also be said to apply to the judicial process even among strangers. The primary task of the legal process in these societies was to reach a compromise of some sort between the parties. Consequently, in most of these cases, though not in all, rules were rarely invoked, and cases were not reduced to a skeletal form so that clear and specific rules could be applied. Most of these legal systems did not use written documents or expert witnesses.

Reviewing the Ottoman case in general, I feel strongly that it was much closer to the legalistic-positivist pole than were those above mentioned societies. Gluckman's finding was that most of the cases in his material were intrafamilial; in the case study undertaken here, the opposite was true. Of the thousands of cases that I have reviewed, only a very small fraction revolved around intrafamiliar relations; and the proportion is further reduced if we exclude the cases involving excouples.

Unfortunately, our case material falls short of verbatim statements in court, either by litigants, witnesses, or judges. What we have are only summaries. This does create some problems of interpretation, though to my mind the legal value of these documents is still considerable. To assess some of the problems involved, let us look at three verbatim translations of cases in the form in which they have come down to us.

Case 1

Presented to your highness by your well-wisher.

Mehmed Ağa b. Abubekir, resident of Üsküdar, who had submitted the present petition, claimed in court against Bustani Ibrahim b. Yusuf, mentioned in the petition: "The said Ibrahim struck my son, Süleyman, of whom I am the sole heir, one afternoon five days before the date of this document, at the lower part of his neck, an event that took place at the plain of Haydar Paşa [a neighborhood in Istanbul]. He hit and wounded him intentionally and without any justification, a wound of which he later died. As heir, I demand that the said Ibrahim be executed in retaliation (*kisas*)." After the claim and the denial, the claim of the said plaintiff was confirmed by the witness of Mehmed Ağa b. Abdallah and Mehmed Efendi b. Khayrallah, residents of Üsküdar, whose qualification to give witness (*adalet*) was checked and found acceptable. Consequently, in the presence of the said plaintiff, the said Bustani Ibrahim b. Yusuf was legally found deserving to be executed in retaliation. From the court of Üsküdar to your excellency.[64]

COMMENTS

1. As the first and last sentences of the document show, the custom or the rule in this period, the eighteenth century, must have been to present summaries of cases to the central government. This was not so in earlier periods, and there is no hint that it meant much in legal practical terms (such as the need of local courts to secure approval of verdicts meted out).

2. We get some idea here of the disadvantages inherent in having only summaries of cases. We could surely have made more of the exact words of the litigants and the witnesses. What were

the biases of the judge? Was he influenced by the external appearance of the litigants? Was he influenced by the difference in the social standing of the litigants? All these crucially important questions cannot be discussed because they were not recorded. Nevertheless, there is much that can be done with these summaries.

3. An important example of something that can be done with these summaries is simply to find out the source of law in the judicial decisions reached. Can it be traced to a certain code of law, or is it something the *kadi* made up in an ad hoc fashion? In this particular case, a quick check shows that the *kadi* was quite literally implementing the *shari`a* law relating to murder. The *kadi* does not seem to be looking for a compromise solution or for any special circumstances that might warrant a reduction in the penalty. Perhaps in actuality there was some talk on this point. But the crucial point is that the decision was molded to fit exact, well-known legal categories that are directly derived from the code of the *shari`a* .

4. We do not know what was said about the intention to kill, a crucial element in such a case. It is evident that the witnesses talked only about the act itself. So the intention is decided according to what we would call circumstantial evidence. The thought process of the *kadi* in this case was evidently directed by common sense—what else might the accused in this case have had in mind other than to kill?

5. We do not know who the witnesses were and what exactly they saw. It is possible that the *kadi* questioned them on this point and decided in a way we might consider suspicious, opening the door to the conclusion that the *kadi* had his biases. This is unquestionably a flaw in this source that I see no way of correcting. The same applies to the question of screening the witnesses for Islamic uprightness; we do not know exactly how this was done and whether it reflected hidden biases.

Case 2

Abdulkadir b. Hac Mustafa, citizen of Bursa, concerning whom there is a notification from the head surgeon of the palace (*Ser-i Cerrahan-i Hassa*) that his leg is paralyzed, a claim found correct when checked by the present court, claimed in court against Hüseyin b. Ahmed Kassaboğlu from Bursa: "On Monday, the sixth of Ramazan 1179, sometime after sunset, the said Hüseyin shot me with a rifle near the mosque of Veled-i Habib quarter, hit and wounded me in my left hip. I have now recovered from the wound, but my left foot remains paralyzed. I demand from the said Hüseyin what is incumbent upon him by law." His claim was affirmed by the witness of so and so, whose qualifications as witnesses were checked and found acceptable. Consequently, the said Hüseyin was ordered to pay to the said plaintiff half the blood money of a male person, 5,000 dirhams of silver.[65]

COMMENTS

1. Several of the points made about the former document apply also to this one. Here again, checking the source of the decision indicates that it was based on the classical *shari'a* manuals, not the whim of the *kadi*.

2. Noteworthy in this document is the important role of an expert witness of the highest possible stature, a doctor in the employ of the sultan himself.

Case 3

Ibrahim Ağa b. Ali, originally a resident of the town of Tviran(?) in European Turkey, claimed in court against Feyzullah Ağa b. Abdallah, formerly an officer and treasurer (*beytülmalci*) of the members of the official class (*askeri*) on a certain island: "Hüseyin, father of Hasan, who died as member of the official class on the said island, and whose estate is being held by the aforementioned Ağa [Feyzullah] on the pretext that he had no heir, and my father, Hasan, were full brothers. His father's name was Osman, and his grandfather's name was Ömer, and his mother's name was Fatma, and their origin is the said town. His inheritance goes to me only; he has no heir besides me. I want the said Ağa to be asked on this and that he be ordered to hand over to me the said inheritance." Upon being asked, the said Ağa admitted he had held on to the said estate for safekeeping, in accordance with the register prepared by the assistant judge (*kassam*), but went on to say: "I have no information that the said estate belongs to the said plaintiff." When the said plaintiff was asked to present evidence supporting his claim, along came to court to give witness Ibrahim Ağa b. Osman and Abdulkarim Ağa b. Sufian, free and truthful Muslims, originally from the said town, living temporarily in Tahtakale in the said city. Being asked to testify, they said: "Indeed, Hüseyin, father of Hasan, who died on the island so and so, and whose inheritance is being held by the said Ağa, and Ali, father of Ibrahim Ağa, the said plaintiff, were brothers. Their father's name was. . . . The inheritance of the deceased goes to the plaintiff only, and we know of no other person who is his heir and has a right to his inheritance. To this we testify." This is how each of them testified, and after their qualifications as acceptable witnesses were checked, their testimony was found acceptable. After a verdict and an order were issued accordingly, what happened was written down as requested.[66]

COMMENTS

In addition to points made concerning the first two documents, an important point that comes out in the present one is the possible influence of the government on the judicial process. Here particularly one might expect to find such an influence because a direct material governmental interest is at stake. Yet no sign of any intervention is observable, either in the discourse of the court or in the final decision.

Concerning the three documents presented here as typical examples of what was read in the sources, several points are worth noting. First, we do not observe in these cases much evidence of a negotiation process between the judge and the parties or between the parties themselves. Maybe in reality negotiation did take place, but it is characteristic that the *kadi* strives to mold the discourse of the court into a clear-cut decision stated in terms of the proclaimed Islamic law, or something close to it. There is no compromise solution; the law is pronounced and decided upon or, rather, taken to be common knowledge, and the decision is simply announced. The past or future relations of the parties do not seem high on the list of the *kadi's* priorities, if they are on the list at all.

If these are the conclusions that can be drawn from the three examples presented here, I would like now to broaden the perspective by applying to the entire body of the documents consulted the categories and research questions I have extracted from Rosen's study of Morocco and the rest of the legal anthropological literature reviewed in the introduction.

Evidence: Witnesses

Witnesses are a crucial factor in the Islamic legal process of weighing the evidence, and Rosen aptly underscores the particularly important role here of people with a reputation in the community for uprightness. Rather than probe the content of utterances, Moroccan and classical Islamic law proceeded by weighing the social standing of the utterer.[67] This procedure assumes, of course, small intimate communities. I doubt whether this ideal survived in pure form in the sprawling city of eighteenth-century Istanbul, or even in seventeenth-century Bursa. I have not come across a case where the acceptability of a witness is called into question due to lack of uprightness, and it cannot be claimed that such unfinished cases may have been struck from the record. We know now, especially from cases of mediation (see below) that unfinished cases did go into the records. That no witness was ever overruled is to me a sign that the classical strictness about uprightness of witnesses was considerably relaxed—apparently because familial and quasi-familial conceptions were weaker here (see chapter 5).

However, there is one notable exception. Ottoman law did have the compurgation oath, or collective oath-helping, an oath popular in medieval Europe, whereby a suspect would bring to court a long list of witnesses to attest to his honest nature.[68] While I reject the suggestion[69] that the *kasama* oath in Islamic law is a kind of compurgation (because in *kasama* each person swears he personally has not committed a murder), such an oath does appear in our documents in cases involving *kadhf* (false accusation of actual adultery or of having an adulterous nature). People in the present area of study often brought to court a large number of witnesses from their quarter and asked them to attest to their innocence of such a charge. This, of course, involved both personal acquaintance with the inhabitants of the quarter and willingness on the part of those inhabitants to take the trouble to appear on behalf of the individual involved. Both these conditions conjure up an image of a society akin to the communal ideal type exemplified in Morocco. But *kadhf* was the only case of communal witnessing in my documents.[70]

A study of the role of witnesses in classical Greece sensitizes us to some of the important issues involved here. Contrary to the legal system of the modern West, in which witnesses are supposed simply to "tell the truth," witnesses in Greece performed an entirely different function. Their task was to praise "their" litigant openly and enthusiastically. In trying to account for this unusual situation, Sally Humphreys resorts to the argument that this social feature is a relic of an earlier period in Athenian history, when the community was small and based on face-to-face relations. In such a situation, the role of witnesses was to bring to the public forum the internal opinion of the community on the character of the litigant.[71]

In the evidence at my disposal concerning witnesses, they are never asked about anything but their knowledge of the case; in no instance that I have come across are they cited as pronouncing on anything else. All the evidence points to the conclusion that in the legal system under study witnesses played a role quite similar to their role in Western law. There were hidden biases, of course, but the official ideology and cultural tendency behind the practice are what is important here.

Evidence: The Role of Documents

Despite the fact that evidence in court consisted mostly of witnesses, there is no doubt that, as in medieval Islam,[72] documents nevertheless played a decisive role in various legal contexts in the area under study. The very existence of the voluminous *kadi* records is surely evidence of an intention to have them serve as a future reference. Another important point here is the fact that at the end of every lawsuit one of the parties—the winning side, of course—received a document specifying the details of the case. This party was usually referred to in the document as "the bearer of this document." It is evident that these documents were used socially and judicially. Their very existence probably prevented thousands of additional lawsuits from taking place. Moreover, the court accepted masses of documents as prima facie evidence. Claims of citizens on the government and vice versa were based solely on documentation—claims of income from *waqf*s, taxation, *fetva*s from the *şeyhülislam*, and so on were all embedded in documents. All this was certainly an element of major importance in the work of the court.

Evidence: Voluntary Admission

Scholars of Islamic law tell us that one reason the Islamic criminal law could not be applied in practice is that the rules of evidence were extremely strict, circumstantial evidence being excluded.[73] To a degree this claim is logically true, yet the criminal law nevertheless *was* applied. One major reason for this is the surprising phenomenon that an incredible number of defendants voluntarily admitted guilt. An example is a case of murder reported from Rumelia (the European part of the empire). Two women sued a gypsy and claimed he had murdered their next of kin. They demanded that he be put to death by retaliation (*kisas*). For some inexplicable reason the defendant admitted guilt out "of his own free will," as the document puts it.[74] In another example, an Istanbul woman sued a boat owner and claimed he had forcefully entered her house and raped her. The defendant admitted guilt not just once but in four different court sessions, as the law requires in this case.[75] Again, there is no hint as to what propelled a defendant to admit guilt when no proof was forthcoming.

One can only guess that more people in this period had a guilty conscience than our modern mode of thinking would lead us to expect—possibly an aspect of the more deeply religious nature of that society. What leads us to this conclusion is a related fact that helps to shed some light. In a large number of cases where neither party possessed evidence, defendants were given the opportunity to swear an oath and win the case, yet they declined to do so, thereby automatically losing the case. Such refusal sometimes led to indictment for murder, entailing the death penalty.[76] In such situations it is obvious that the motivating force was indeed a sense of guilt or a fear of God. Such situations are so common in our documents as to lead us to believe that we are confronting here something that was deep and fundamental at the time. The oath was thus seen as an effective judicial tool to secure evidence, something quite reminiscent of the medieval European ordeal, which is no longer seen today as a blind belief in superstition but as an effective judicial tool in the hands of a society highly vulnerable to the ravages of nature and hence deeply religious.[77] One is reminded here of Roy Mottahede's study on loyalty and leadership in medieval Islam, which contains important considerations on the crucial role of oaths in the political life of that society. For example, "the seriousness of oaths is shown most dramatically by the shock and horror with which the medieval Islamic historians discuss those occasions when men openly perjured themselves."[78] David Powers brings in another important example in his study of fourteenth-century Morocco. A lawsuit over a piece of endowed property dragged on for about thirty years and was finally to be decided by the oath's being offered to one of the parties. So after thirty years of stubborn, and possibly expensive conflict, one party could swear and win the case automatically. Yet he refused, thereby losing the case automatically.[79]

I believe we may have here in a nutshell an answer to those who apply to the *kadi* system their own modern way of thinking—

those who question how this system of law could function at all without any technical means to investigate and obtain evidence. The case of the oath suggests that we may be influenced by our hidden ethnocentric blinders concerning this system of law, and that it is time we tried to view this legal system on its own terms. Fear and religiosity may have been tools as effective in the hands of the Ottoman judiciary as are investigative authority and technology in the hands of a modern judiciary.

Judicial Ignorance

Judicial ignorance is one of the most fundamental features of modern Western law, in theory and at least partially also in practice. It means that the judge knows nothing about the parties or the case beyond what is put before him by the litigants. We have seen that one of the main features of the legal systems in tribal Africa was that this theory did not exist: judges were immediately involved in the case as neighbors and fellow tribesmen. The situation was fundamentally different in the case under study here, this being one of the most distinctive features I can discern in the Ottoman legal system. I know of no indigenous Ottoman theory in the matter, but there is no doubt in my mind that the Ottoman habit of transferring judges from one place to another every year effectively achieved impartial arbitration between parties—a concept tantamount, of course, to judicial ignorance. In no case among the thousands that I examined was there any hint that the judge knew anything about the parties involved. And because as I have said, he was usually a foreigner to the town, this is probably a faithful reflection of what really went on.

A Legalistic Versus Holistic Approach by the Court

On the topic of a legalistic as opposed to a holistic approach by the court, there is a large measure of similarity between Rosen's findings from Morocco and most of the case studies I have reviewed from the legal anthropological literature, most notably the Lozi of Barotseland. The main role of the judge in Morocco was to get the parties together in order to thrash out their differences, resolve their conflicts, and then resume the normal course of their relations, which is based on bargaining and negotiation. Litigants were captured holistically—that is, as human beings with ramified relations that had to be taken into account—rather than legalistically—that is, as opposing sides to a legal problem that had a one-dimensional solution. Looking at the evidence available from the central area of the Ottoman Empire, it seems to me that the situation was quite the opposite. In the first place, intrafamilial cases were not found to be prevalent at all; the overwhelming majority of the cases were between total strangers. Second, there is no sign whatsoever that the court was relating to the parties holistically. This is most emphatically true even in cases involving multiplex relations—that is, intrafamilial cases. The social relations of the parties are never weighed. And if it were claimed that possibly the summaries obliterated this aspect of the actual discussion, then the answer would be that the resolution of the cases should also reflect the deliberations. Yet the *kadi* himself is in no case on record the authority who mediated between the parties.

It is interesting and methodologically important that the records examined do contain cases of mediation. An example appears in a lawsuit in eighteenth-century Istanbul, where the plaintiff claims he sold coffee to the defendant for 1,500 piasters and now demands that sum. The defendant claims there was a flaw in the transaction, which made it void. No side has proof, and the *kadi* assigns the oath to the plaintiff, who could thereby win the case. We are told that at this point, before any further action was taken, mediators intervened and got the parties to agree to a compromise.[80] There is a large number of similar cases in the court records, and they all show quite clearly that the judge performed his job and decided the case one way or the other; outside mediators intervened and got the parties to compromise. In fact, mediation often came before the judge decided the case legally.[81] Again, because we have only summaries of cases, I tend to agree that in practice it is possible that the judge had a certain role in the mediation, but to keep the record straight in terms of Islamic law and ethics, he kept these two spheres separate. It is characteristic that in every such case it is stated that outside mediators intervened, and the terms of the compromise are never recorded in the *sicill*, the *kadi's* protocol. For my purposes the important point is that the case was molded to fit legal categories. The formal law was not set aside as something irrelevant. And this is doubly important if we view the law also as a discourse, as the view of the state about how the society should appear.

Criminal Liability and Compensatory Justice

In an important article dealing with penal liability in Islamic law, Lawrence Rosen set out to show yet again how articles of law subtly reflect social and cultural tendencies.[82] But when we compare his findings with the material available from the central area of the Ottoman Empire, fine though important differences emerge. As is well known, killing is treated in Islamic law as part of compensatory justice, as against hudud, the major crimes, whose enforcement is the obligation of the state. In Rosen's view this situation reflects the Arab tendency to limit the number of serious crimes and leave the rest to the province of negotiation between groups that have to go on living together. The liability for killing is also in a way negotiable. As to murder—that is, premeditated killing— classical Islamic law tends to assign intentionality, hence responsibility, according to the weapon used in the killing. If the tool is one usually used in intentional killing (knife, rifle), intention is considered established. Rosen claims that this, too, reflects inherent cultural tendencies: truth and intention become discernible only in the acts of individuals in relation to others. Hence, it is natural to see in the act also the intention. Whether or not this analysis is true of classical Islam, it seems to me not applicable to the central area of the Ottoman Empire. In a large number of legal opinions dealing with killing, there is considerable attention paid to the internal motivation of the killer. An example is the case of Zeyd, who attacked Amr with a lethal weapon. There was a crowd around, so it is taken for granted that Amr could have rescued himself by shouting for help. Instead, he killed Zeyd with a lethal weapon. The *mufti* is asked whether Amr is liable. His answer is that he is indeed liable for *kisas*, death in retaliation.[83] It is evident here that the reasoning behind the decision—which is never detailed by the *mufti*—is that the case was not one of real self-defense; hence, the killing was not justifiable. If there was no interest here in the internal motivation, the weapon alone would be sufficient to establish the case as murder. Although all these *fetva*s mention the weapon of killing, the term *amad* (intention) is always present.[84] In fact, the weapon is rarely dealt with in isolation from the internal motivation. In several cases there is discussion of an apparently unintentional killing with a firearm, and such cases are never pronounced to be murders. An example is the case of Zeyd, who aimed and shot at Amr, but the bullet was deflected from Amr, killing also Bekir. The *mufti* is asked about

Zeyd's liability and his reply is that Zeyd is liable for murdering Amr and unintentionally killing Bekir.[85] In another case, a person attacked somebody with a knife but missed him and killed another person. Again, the *mufti* says the killer is liable here for unintentional killing only.[86] Of course, killing out of self-defense did not entail any liability whatsoever.[87] Killing in self-defense against sexual attack also went unpunishable—provided that the *kadi* interpreted it as a case of self-defense.[88] But note that the intention of killing was not enough to establish a case of killing as murder. The weapon was important in the sense that killing with certain means could not entail liability for murder. A notable example is the case of a man who approached a woman to attack her with the known intention of killing her, yet before he actually attacked her he uttered a terrible shout that caused the woman's death. Although this man had a well known intention to kill, what he actually did was not considered murder.[89]

All in all, I find the subtleties of the jurists' reasoning in deciding whether cases were murder or killing astonishingly refined and rather surprisingly duplicative of the complicated legal logic of modern criminal courts. It is my view that even in the few cases in which only the weapon is discussed, this is only because neither proof nor a commonsensical solution were available.

On the other hand no extensive negotiation is discernible in the records when it comes to physical injuries. What one does see is a very exact, even scientific, approach to assessing the extent of the injury and the compensation due. Such assessment is always done by people declared to be impartial experts.

Expert Witnessing

Unlike the legal systems of all the societies that I have drawn on for comparative material, the Ottoman legal system made extensive use of expert witnessing. An example is a case in which a shipowner through a navigational error wrecked the roof of the Yeniköy dockyard in Istanbul and was sued for damages by the official in charge. The defendant argued that the wind was so strong that the ship was uncontrollable; hence, he was not liable for damages. Summoned were two witnesses said to possess (*itla*) expertise in matters relating to the sea, who said the wind was not strong enough to justify the defendant. Then along came other witnesses, experts in the building industry, who assessed the extent of the damage caused.[90] In another example someone was sued for having caused blindness in one eye to another person. In this case the chief eye expert (*kahhal başî*) [head of a guild?] was summoned to assess the damage inflicted.[91]

Judicial Reasoning

Rosen suggests one can discern three main modes of judicial reasoning in judicial systems. "One is for a set of rules to be articulated and for judges to couch their decisions, however they may actually be reached, in such a way as to give the appearance that they have been derived by a simple process of deduction from the announced rules."[92] The third mode "Consists of the rules being drawn in such a way as to justify a wide range of individual results from which the judge may choose. . . . Considerable leeway for results may be permitted. . . . Rules serve more as guidelines and reasoning consists in the establishment of an individual result within the ambit of the acceptable."[93]

Rosen claims that the third model is, in effect, the mode of reasoning characterizing the Moroccan *kadi*. And it is entirely clear that the first model describes the mode of Western legal reasoning. In amplifying his claim that the mode of reasoning of the Moroccan *kadi* fits the third model, Rosen repeats some of his arguments about the role of the judge as mediator between parties who for the most part have to go on living together. But he adds an interesting Islamic legal argument: a traditional *kadi* in Morocco who faced a serious judicial problem would weigh it in light of the extant juristic literature and point out the extant solutions. Some of them would be "strong"—that is, preferred by tradition; others would be "weak"—that is, less influential. He would then state his choice, the basis for the choice being usually broadly societal.[94] The situation in the central area of the Ottoman Empire seems quite different. I would claim that this legal system rather neatly fits Rosen's first model. There is no extant case where the *kadi* presented several options and chose among them, certainly not according to any concept of social good. The strong version suggested by the traditional jurists is the only one available; it is, in fact, the statement of the law, and there is never any question but that the *kadi* decides according to the law. At least he molds his decision to fit the law as is known to the litigants—exactly as is Rosen's requirement in the first model. (The situation could be somewhat different as far as *muftis* are concerned; see chapter 3.)

When all the evidence on the legal anthropology of the Ottoman legal system is reviewed, the conclusion seems unavoidable that between law and process, and speaking in terms of the model suggested by Fallers and discussed previously, Ottoman law was closer to the pole of positivist law than most other legal systems I have mentioned, particularly the Islamic law of Morocco. As I shall show in the next chapter, Ottoman law contained a very strong element of negotiation in that the interplay between shari`a, kanun, and custom was not entirely, if at all, controlled by the government. But the shari`a , the main body of law in practice in the seventeenth and eighteenth centuries, was more or less cohesive. It was not a formless mass. And even though it was not the product of the Ottoman government, when it came to practice it certainly was a positivist law, more or less in the sense that the English common law was not the product of any particular body yet was nevertheless law, and as such was applied in practice, though with complex relations with law as process.[95]

Class and Status in the Ottoman Court

Legal anthropologists and legal historians have been urging us to look at the law as, among other things, discourse—a statement by the government (broadly conceived) on how the society in question should be in terms of behavior and of etiquette, including proper relations between groups, classes, and so on.[96] No doubt, this is partly the problem of how the society's political hierarchy is reflected in the work of the court. A study of colonial New England, for example, has shown that the class structure of the society was clearly duplicated in the working of the court: most of the suits were initiated by members of the aristocratic elite and were against members of the lower classes. Moreover, members of the elite won proportionately more cases than did common people and got away with lighter penalties when sued in criminal charges. The conclusion is thus reached that the elite received distinctly preferential treatment.[97]

In this section I propose a roughly similar study of class and status in the Ottoman court in the area under investigation. As raw material I have used the collection of court cases by Dabbağzade Numan.[98] On inspection, the collection was found to contain 140 cases of real litigation—that is, cases that had one plaintiff and one defendant and that were resolved judicially. I have analyzed all these cases in terms of the status of the litigants with-

in Ottoman society, which means that a person would be classified according to one of the following categories: (1) as an *askeri*—
that is, a member of the official class; (2) as an *alim*—that is, a religious functionary of some sort; (3) as a commoner—that is, an
ordinary Muslim; (4) as a woman; and (5) as a non-Muslim. These
are well-known distinctions. What they meant in real-life terms at
any given moment in Ottoman history is not at all clear because
investigation of the class history of Ottoman society has scarcely
begun. Even the categories of classification are at present problematic because the terms denoting the categories have changed over
time. For example, in the classical Ottoman Empire the term *ağa*
meant a military officer of some sort. Yet all the evidence at my
disposal seems to indicate that by the eighteenth century the term
had come to denote, in addition, a regular *reaya*, or commoner.

Leaving aside these thorny methodological problems and
turning to the evidence itself, in no less than 71 of the 140 cases
drawn from the source, both the plaintiff and the defendant were
commoners. In an additional ten cases, both parties belonged to
the same social stratum. In addition, in all twenty-two of the cases
classified as being ones in which women were involved, the
women were of the *reaya* class. I draw the following conclusion
from this finding. If in colonial New Haven the court was mainly
used by the aristocracy to regulate and control the lower classes,
this was definitely not so in the case under study, where the court
was used mainly by the common people themselves simply to
smooth the flow of their daily lives. This conclusion is reinforced
if we check the social origin of those who initiated lawsuits. Mary
Baumgartner's conclusion was emphatic that in New Haven it was
mainly aristocrats who initiated lawsuits. But in the society under
study, in all but a few cases, it was the social underdog who initiated the case—women versus men, non-Muslims versus Muslims,
commoners versus members of the elite. The court is seen mainly
as a tool of the common people to defend a modicum of legal
rights.

Of course, the most important question to be considered here
is the outcome of such lawsuits in terms of social class. Whereas
in colonial New Haven the upper class had a clear advantage, this
is distinctly not so here. Women won seventeen of twenty-two
cases against men; non-Muslims won seven of eight cases against
Muslims; commoners won six of eight cases against *askeris*. Only
in the category of commoners against religious doctors do we find
a tie of ten cases each. Thus the *shari`a* court in the area under

study cannot be said to have been a tool of the upper class. On the contrary, it seems more proper to view it as a means for people of the lower classes to defend themselves against possible encroachments by the elite. It might be countered that possibly social inferiors went to court only when they were somehow confident that they would win. But how could they ever know that? And in any case, even if this were so, it merely enhances the conclusion that it was not in the law court that the hierarchy was enacted and concretized, but somewhere else.

If we are to explain this finding in terms of the concept of law as discourse, I would suggest that what is evinced by this situation is an effort on the part of the sultanate, the true locus of government, to curb the political ambitions of the Ottoman elite, especially the lay and military section within it. What I am suggesting here is not that the military class in Ottoman society was not a true social elite, but that there is currently no proof that it was able to employ the *kadi* court to maintain its position. And I must emphasize once again that the statistical evidence tallies perfectly with my intuitive impression of the *kadi* court of seventeenth-century Bursa. Apparently it is untrue, then, to view the Ottoman ruling elite as a homogeneous body having one common adversary, the *reaya*. Infighting within the elite must have been no less important, and upholding the integrity of the *shari`a* court must have been a powerful means for the central government to curb the *askeris* and keep a measure of political balance within the society at large. The next chapter provides further proof of this contention.

2. THE MAKING OF OTTOMAN LAW: THE RISE OF THE *KADI* AND THE *SHARI`A* COURT

IN THE PREVIOUS chapter I analyzed the internal dynamic of the Ottoman legal system as it existed in the seventeenth and eighteenth centuries. It was a snapshot of one particular chapter in Ottoman history that possesses, in my understanding, a substantial measure of internal coherence, which justifies one's seeing it as a single period. But as this chapter will show, that snapshot is the end product of a long period of historical development, stretching more or less from the fifteenth century, so that it cannot be described and analyzed purely in itself. In terms of the anthropological models that constitute the theoretical framework of this study, this chapter will show that what may seem like a fully self-explanatory snapshot of the legal system can be shown as the end product of a historical development. Some anthropologists may object here that this chapter in particular falls outside of the purview of the anthropology of law because it deals more with law codes than with changes in the process that unfolded in the courtroom. My answer is that as the *shari`a* rose, the structure of the legal process became more clearly formed and rule-based than before.

In terms of Geertzian law-as-local-knowledge, this chapter will also show that it is misleading to assume that Islam every-

58

where was the same; even within the subcultures of Islam, changes over time are to be expected. I will try to pinpoint the origins of change. My argument will take a middle way between the structuralists and their opponents: reality is partly to be explained by a structural fit between the law and the society surrounding it, mainly its political dimension; but it is also a continuation of old cultural patterns.

In describing the change that took place in Ottoman law between the fifteenth and the seventeenth centuries, my point of departure is the relations between law and government in Islam. Ottoman development seems to have run counter to recent theories about law and state in classical Islam, especially those of Johansen and Rosen. Rosen claims that the relations between law and the state in Islam are characterized by minimal intervention on the part of the state:

> In the classical Islamic theory of the state [and by implication, of course, also in modern Morocco], law and government were kept largely separate from one another. The state was seen not as the instrument for the application of law, nor were the courts . . . envisioned as vehicles for economic redistribution or the construction of a particular political order. It was the duty of the political authorities to enforce the claims of God—even by maintaining their own courts for the punishment of specific crimes—but beyond that they were to insure that men could carry forth their own affairs without government interference.[1]

This theory of Islamic law is entirely in line with Rosen's theory that the function of law in Islam is merely to get people back on a negotiating track. It may be useful to elaborate here a little by going back to Rosen's source, a study by Baber Johansen[2] that seeks to explain the difference in Islamic law between *huquq Allah* and *huquq al-ibad*—respectively, the laws of Allah and the laws of man. *Huquq Allah* are those laws of the penal code—just five in number—chosen by the *shari`a* as being particularly important and deserving of government enforcement. They are fornication, false accusation of fornication, theft, drinking of wine, and highway robbery. Most notably missing from this list is murder, which like all the rest of the legal code is considered private law to be pushed through the courts by private initiative.

Johansen suggests that at the base of this approach to law and government is the notion that society is composed of small proprietors, the basic relation among whom is complete equality, the only kind of relation necessary to carry out fair business transactions. It is to this approach that Johansen attributes the prohibition of interest: by creating inequality between the parties, interest violates the principle of just exchange.[3] It is only natural, says Johansen, that "the lawyers try to protect the rights of the individual against all possible infringements by the authorities. They do this by closely defining those actions of the political authority that are legitimized as *huquq Allah,* thereby narrowing down the possibility of state interference in the affairs of private legal persons."[4]

Such may be the situation in Morocco and in some other places in Islam past or present. But this study will claim that the description is not necessarily applicable to every Islamic society, and that it is definitely untrue with regard to the Ottoman Empire. There the state had an important role in the creation of a legal system that may have been somewhat similar to Morocco's in the beginning, but that in time developed in a substantially different direction, mainly toward bureaucratization—as reflected in the growing monopolization by the *kadi* of the judicial process. All this was intimately connected with the development of the Ottoman state from a fourteenth-century frontier principality to a world empire two centuries later.

Several scholars support Johansen's statement that classical Islamic states put only slight emphasis on the penal parts of the *shari`a.* Uriel Heyd, for example, observed that "since the very first centuries of Islam . . . criminal justice remained largely outside the jurisdiction of the cadis."[5] Noel Coulson has compiled an important empirical study bearing on this topic.[6] He shows that from the very beginning the incipient *shari`a* had little influence on the activities of the actual ruler, whoever he might be. The ruler delegated authority to his own officials, such as the *shurta,* or police, and paid little heed to the slowly developing idea of the moral superiority of the *shari`a* and the *kadi.* This situation did not change much under the Abbasides, who moreover established alternatives to the *shari`a* court, the so-called *mazalim* courts, which were presided over by the ruler himself. Coulson also claims that according to the ideology of the religious scholars themselves the *shari`a* was not supposed to have judicial monopoly in the Islamic state. One reason is that from the very beginning the *shari`a* was intended more as a basis for arranging relations between man and God than as a legal political document. Another reason is that the *shari`a* developed unusually strict rules of procedure and evidence, such as refusal to accept oral or circumstantial evidence or to accept as a witness anyone but a man possessing "the highest quality of moral and religious probity."[7] Such traits developed, at least partially, because the religious experts were reluctant from the start to come to grips with real-life problems of the law and preferred to see in the *shari`a* a theoretical field of activity. Beyond variations of time and place, therefore, Coulson concludes that "as a general rule . . . [the *kadis'*] province was that of private law—family law, inheritance, civil transactions and injuries, and *waqf* endowments."[8] Joseph Schacht, distilling a vast number of studies on the theory and practice of classical Islamic law, was of the same view.[9] These views are borne out by more recent studies. One such study dwells on the *mazalim* jurisdiction in Mamluk Egypt.[10] It compares the *kadi* court and the *mazalim* court and finds the latter much superior. Whereas the *mazalim* court had the authority to investigate and enforce its decisions, the *kadi* court had no such capabilities and relied mainly on mutual agreement between the litigants.[11] So Nielsen has no hesitation in saying, "It is hardly necessary to point out that only in limited fields did the provisions of the Shari`a apply. What criminal, fiscal and commercial provisions there existed were largely ignored. Shari`a lawyers had themselves contributed to this state of affairs, for when at an early stage its provisions were being left behind by practical developments they had accepted stratagems . . . which avoided the intent of the law."[12]

The question is, where does the Ottoman Empire fit into this picture. The widely held view is that by inventing the *kanun*, or state law, the Ottomans continued and even exacerbated the trend of keeping the *shari`a* on the sidelines. In addition, by creating an immensely strong sultanate they may have created a sovereign whose very word became an arbitrary and whimsical source of law. Both these views, however, are highly exaggerated. I shall deal here with the first issue, leaving the other to a later chapter.

A look at the criminal law enacted by Süleyman the Magnificent around the middle of the sixteenth century—the final and most important version of the Ottoman penal *kanun*—evinces a very special relation to the *shari`a* and completely belies the common view that the Ottomans were seeking to fill in gaps left by the *shari`a*. Their motivation seems to have been much more complex. The simple fact is that the entire body of what we might call the penal code of the *shari`a* finds its way into the *kanun*. The *kanun* merely goes a little further by adding the option (no more than that) of prescribing fines as punishments. We immediately observe that much of what happened in Ottoman legal history in the seventeenth and eighteenth centuries is an outcome of Ottoman state activity, though it could hardly be said that this is the conscious outcome of a fully intended policy.

But let us return to the *kanun* and see how *kanun* and *shari`a* were welded together. The very first article of Süleyman's code deals with fornication and lays down that a defendant accused of that offense—the accusation having been proven in accordance with the *shari`a*—is to receive various fines (given in detail), but only "provided he does not suffer the death penalty."[13] Moreover, one version of this *kanun* says more specifically, "provided he is not to be stoned to death in accordance with the *shari`a*."[14] A further article in the *kanun* sets the explicit *shari`a* punishment for false accusation of fornication, with the possible addition of a fine.[15] In addition, the *shari`a* law concerning murder is simply reiterated by the *kanun*: the punishment for murder is death in retaliation (*kisas*), unless the next of kin of the murdered person chooses to commute it to the payment of blood money.[16] Furthermore, if a corpse is found in a village or neighborhood and the identity of the perpetrator is unknown, the law laid down by the *kanun* is exactly the same as the *shari`a* law—the people living in the village or neighborhood are liable to paying the blood money, but not before swearing fifty times that they did not commit the murder.[17] The infliction of physical harm short of actual killing is treated exactly as in the *shari`a*, often explicitly saying so.[18] Stealing is likewise treated as basically the *had* violation of the *shari`a*—again, with the possible addition of fines.[19]

There are some additional *shari* laws in the *kanun*, less famous than the major *huquq Allah* mentioned so far. I would like here to mention one example because it plays a certain role in my later argument. It has to do with the banishment of criminals or prostitutes from the town quarter or the village on the testimony of a group of trustworthy witnesses, who claim it is their wish. Both Heyd and Schacht make it clear that this is by origin a *shari`a* law.[20]

It must be emphasized, however, that the *kanun* is more than just a reenactment of the *shari`a* by state fiat. Besides the fact that in many articles there is an option of non-*shari`a* punishments, such as fines, there are some new legal concepts and modes of perception. Yet one does not get the impression that these additions may have been the reason for the enactment of the entire penal *kanun*. An important example is the law concerning "disturbers of the peace," *ehl-i fesad*, a generic term to describe habitual criminals, who are to be dealt with by a special messenger of the sultan, whereas the *kadi* is not to interfere in the matter.[21] Another important non-*shari`a* matter in the *kanun* relates to torture, which is mentioned several times. One such context is when a thief is found with stolen property and there is no direct proof to connect him to the act. The *kanun* allows for torture to be applied in such cases in order to secure confession.[22] Finally, the *kanun* bans charging interest of more than 10 percent,[23] thereby implicitly allowing the lower rate—a flagrant violation of the *shari`a* and a point of major importance for the argument of this study (see chapter 3).

The *kanun* also mentions explicitly and on several occasions the *kadi* and his role in applying this code of law—indicating that the Ottomans certainly intended the *kadi*, and as a rule no other authority, to apply the *kanun*. In at least one instance it is clearly specified that officials (*ehl-i örf*) are not to intervene in the matter.

As a cultural document the *kanun* is, therefore, a complex document to interpret. The fact that it enacts the *hudud* as state law poses in itself an almost insoluble puzzle. It is a confirmation of the *shari`a* but also, in a sense, a violation of it, inasmuch as the *shari`a* is God-given. Especially noteworthy is the fact that the *kanun* makes murder a state law, thereby turning the entire concept of *huquq Allah* on its head. At the same time, however, murder is treated in practice (according to the *kanun*, that is) as private law—in other words, by the twin concepts of retaliation and blood money, to be decided on by the next of kin of the murdered individual.

What exactly did the Ottomans wish to achieve, or at least to convey, in enacting the penal *kanun*? My own feeling is that this is not yet entirely clear. They certainly seem to have wished to see the *kadi* as the sole judge in their dominions. But that, of course, does not exhaust the problem. An explanation that does seem convincing is that the Ottomans had a serious problem of legitimation in terms of Islamic political theory, and the *kanun* may have been their answer. In the words of Cornell Fleischer, talking about the historian Ali in the late sixteenth century, "intellectuals of Ali's generation elevated *kanun* from the level of mere temporal, 'secular' legislation to symbolic status. *Kanun* embodied the dynasty's commitment to justice, on which its legitimacy rested."[24] I would suggest that the *kanun* may also have been a cultural product of the bureaucratization that gathered momentum in the sixteenth century and the attendant feeling that a bureaucratic state needs a proper law of its own, even if it is not much more than the duplication of an extant code. If we remember that the code was never before enforced in practice, this thought makes some sense.

Our problem in interpreting the *kanun* as a cultural document does not stop here; it is much more complicated. In fact, there may have been conflicts and disagreements over the *kanun* inside the Ottoman elite. Such evidence comes, for example, from the *fetva* collection of Şeyhülislam Ebu Suud Efendi (d. 1574), who is so intimately associated with the legislative drive of Süleyman the Magnificent. This association is so close that I have thought it appropriate to deal with his opinions as part of the views of Ottoman policymakers rather than as the views of a mere Ottoman *mufti*. A priori it might be thought that Ebu Suud's *fetva*s would faithfully reflect the Ottoman *kanun*, and I am talking here only about the penal *kanun*. Inexplicably, to my mind, this is not at all the case.[25] The penal *kanun* is not even mentioned as such. More meaningfully, when one checks the kinds of punishments prescribed by Ebu Suud for lawbreakers, no *kanun* punishment is ever prescribed. In fact, Ebu Suud is seen as opposed, even aggressively so, to state officials (*ehl-i örf*), who after all had a certain role in the *kanun*. In one case he is asked whether, when people speak of "rough treatment" given to someone apprehended by the law, the reference is to torture by the officials. He replies in a strongly emotional tone that not only is torture absolutely forbidden but that so is any intervention of state officials in the judicial process before the *kadi* has given his verdict.[26] This is somewhat surprising, inasmuch as both torture and the intervention of state officials are sometimes legitimized in the *kanun*. In another case addressed to Ebu Suud, when a Jew complained to the governor that someone had stolen money from him, the governor tortured this man and eventually caused his death. Asked if the Jew and the governor are liable to any punishment, the *mufti* rules that the governor (*sancak bey*) should be made to pay blood money and the Jew should get *tazir şadid* (severe discretionary punishment) *and* long term imprisonment.[27] There are several interesting points in this *fetva*. First, the act of the *sancak bey* is perceived as illegal and hence as a sort of private act, entailing punishment as an ordinary, unintended killing. This is a strange position for a personage as close to the center of political power as Ebu Suud to adopt. It may, in fact, reflect a new trend introduced by the Ottomans of elevating the position of the shari`a court. But the suggested punishment to be inflicted on the denouncer is also strange: imprisonment is neither a shari`a-linked type of punishment nor a type of punishment ever prescribed by the kanun. So it must have been some kind of customary law punishment.

What possible message was Ebu Suud trying to convey by issuing such a fetva? Are we to read into this a veiled criticism of the kanun? But then what is suggested by the non-shari`a punishment? Nor is this an isolated case. Ebu Suud seems to have prescribed long-term imprisonment in any grave case that fell short of a had violation. Thus, someone who sent his servants to kill a third party received that punishment,[28] as did Muslims who encouraged other Muslims to bring wine into town.[29] When specifically asked if the penalty of long-term imprisonment went with any particular violation, Ebu Suud merely answered that it was for the kadi to decide, refraining from any theoretical explanation.[30] I hazard the explanation that Ebu Suud's opinions here reflect an undercurrent of intra-ulema opposition to the kanun, which as a lay creation represented the contribution—and the political position—of the askeris, lay members of the Ottoman official class.

The question is, how much of this legal system was applied in practice and by whom? Heyd claims he has found proof that in the fifteenth and sixteenth centuries the Ottomans made sincere efforts to enforce the kanun in real life, his main evidence being that a copy of the kanun was sent by the central government to every law court with a specific order to implement its content.[31] Further, he shows that in the fifteenth century and the first half of the sixteenth, police officials were actually demanding in court the imposition of fines and other kanun-like punishments.[32] So the kanun must have been implemented to some degree at least. Nevertheless, I claim here that this probably took place only to a limited extent. Heyd himself shows that the kadis in this early period rarely, in fact, passed judgments and contented themselves with recording the bare facts of the cases brought before them. Therefore, it is clear that even in its heyday the kanun was only partially implemented. Exactly why this was the case is not at all easy to say. In any event, because we know that the prevailing law was not the shari`a either, chances are that criminal cases were handled by governors and police officers in ways lacking any procedural consistency or coherence, as in earlier Islamic centuries.

As to the *kanun* after the sixteenth century, Heyd's famous discovery of the decline of the *kanun* seems to me to stand in need of qualification. He claims that "from the second part of the sixteenth century, . . . the criminal code was more and more disregarded."[33] He points out that the Midilli *kanun* from 1709–1710 abolished non-*shari'a* taxes and expressly spoke of the need to revert to the taxes prevailing in early Islam. Further, he cites a late seventeenth-century imperial order to the effect that from then on it would be strictly forbidden to juxtapose the terms *shari'a* and *kanun*, as always used to be done in state documents. Such juxtaposition was now said to be "highly perilous and most sinful."[34] As an ideology the *kanun* no doubt was in crisis at the time. But I think we should look into this process more closely, for there was more to it than decline. Moreover, parts of the *kanun* may be shown as surviving in one form or another even in the eighteenth century. This was certainly the case with the land law, but even the case of the penal *kanun* was complex. In any case, new research on the *kadi* records of seventeenth-century Bursa, as well as some other places, dictates some caution about the so-called decline of the *kanun*.

A general look at the actual legal system current in the Istanbul/Bursa region in the seventeenth and eighteenth centuries presents a more or less rigorous, unified, and coherent system of law. On all these counts one can observe a process of development from the fifteenth to the seventeenth centuries. Let us look first at the role of the *kadi* as the theoretical, and possibly actual, centerpiece of Islamic law. We have seen that in earlier Islamic states this role was more theoretical than real. There is also a widespread notion that in the so-called period of decline of the Ottoman Empire (the period after the sixteenth century), we move into a situation where there is no real law, only arbitrary application of officials' wishes—or whims. Among other things we are supposed to be witnessing an ever-growing encroachment by military governors on the authority of *kadi*s. It is also claimed that the seventeenth century marked a period of disastrous decline in the moral integrity of the *kadi*s, along with other *ulema*.

But all this bears little relation to what the actual sources tell us. Here I want to speak first about the role of the *kadi* in the judicial process. If one reviews the role of the *kadi* in the Ottoman judicial process from the fifteenth century on, a surprising outcome emerges. Heyd says unequivocally that in the earlier period the *kadi* was little involved in what was actually happening: "In most criminal cases recorded in the court registers of the fifteenth and sixteenth centuries . . . no penalty is mentioned at all. Often it is not even mentioned whether or not the cadi found the defendant guilty. The only function the cadi seems to have fulfilled here was to establish the facts."[35] This conclusion is fully corroborated by a large collection of Bursa court documents recently published by Halil Inalcik.[36] The collection contains no penal cases at all, and the author assured me that the collection is a fair replication of the breakdown of actual court cases in fifteenth-century Bursa. A sixteenth-century Ankara *kadi* register that was published in toto confirms the story: there are many criminal cases, but without exception the record contains only a registration of the bare facts of the case.[37] The same is true of sixteenth-century Sophia; although criminal cases are indirectly mentioned in the collection,[38] there is no instance of someone's actual trial for murder. What we do have, for example, are cases of the nomination of individuals to take care of the properties of murdered people's estates and outstanding debts as well as declarations by the relatives of murder victims that they know who the murderer is and that it was not someone from the village or neighborhood (thereby exonerating this group from blood-money liability).[39]

Something quite similar emerges from a study of the law of the Macuka region near Trabzon in the sixteenth century.[40] The author found about twenty criminal cases that were brought before the *kadi*. In one such case the plaintiff alleged the defendant had attacked him with a piece of rock. Though two witnesses verified his version, the matter ends there, no verdict being given.[41] In another case the parents of a murdered person take the killer to court, where he claims that he committed the act in self-defense, the case ending at this point.[42] This pattern is repeated again and again—the *kadi* hears the case but does not decide one way or the other. Only one case in this collection is concluded, in a compromise between the parties in a murder case.[43] It can be concluded from the Trabzon collection that the *ehl-i örf* (state officials) took charge where the *kadi* left off; if this is not self-evident, it is strongly hinted at in some of the documents. In one case it is stated that the session (*meclis*) was convened in the presence of the representative of the governor. In another case it is mentioned that the governor had formerly held a session where a murder case was brought up by the brother of the deceased; a long list of witnesses claim that the killer had a rich criminal past, and it would seem the defendant was found guilty.[44] In no case in the records surviving from this period is it possible to find any hint of the application of one of the most typical *kanun* innovations—torture.

Seventeenth-century Bursa evinces a substantially different situation, indicating that a major change took place in the interim. In about 20 percent of the criminal cases that I consulted in the court records of that town, there was no verdict and no punishment was meted out. In some the verdict is so self-evident as to make it likely that it was given but not recorded. In the overwhelming number of criminal cases, the *kadi* of Bursa delivered the verdict and the penalty, and it would be hard to dispute the conclusion that the role of the *kadi* in this legal system increased rather than decreased. The same seems true of other *kadis* in the core region of the empire. Some of the cases not ruled on by the *kadi* of Bursa were instances of highway robbery in which the criminals were apprehended red-handed; as a result, there was little point in the *kadi*'s dwelling on the case at length.[45] This leads to the conclusion that the *kadi* must have decided most ordinary cases. In fact, the *kadi* was involved even in cases in which we would not normally expect him to be involved. An example is a case in 1658 in which the governor of the area brought to court ten people described as criminals (*şakiler*) and claimed he had apprehended them in an agricultural farm outside of the town preparing to carry out acts of robbery and banditry. The defendants admitted to these charges as well as to some murders committed in the past. They were handed over to the governor for the purpose of carrying out the verdict, which, however, is not expressly mentioned—perhaps because it was so self-evident.[46] Such a case was so clearly within the jurisdiction of the military governor that it is surprising it was brought to the attention of the *kadi* at all.

Bursa *kadis* of the seventeenth century did not refrain from dealing head on with even the most delicate cases—those involving the death penalty. Thus, the Bursa *kadi* acquitted the owner of a coffeehouse charged with killing a client after the defendant produced witnesses to the effect that the death was accidental and that he was in no way involved.[47] Two other Bursa *kadis* in the seventeenth century, when the next of kin opted for retaliation, passed the death penalty on murderers whose guilt had been duly proven.[48] In several other cases Bursa *kadis* ordered the death penalty to be inflicted on highway robbers and perpetrators of other very serious crimes.[49] In no case did I come across a situation in which a *kadi* reasoned that the case was either too complicated for him or outside of his authority.

It seems to me that at least logically and theoretically, a judicial system working on the basis of an increased role for the *kadi* can be expected to work more equitably than one based on Ottoman civil and military officials, as seems to have been the case in the early period. In the Ottoman context the reason is quite obvious: the civil and military officials who might have applied the law in place of the *kadi* were much less educated, in the law or in any other branch of knowledge, and they would have been much less restrained than the *kadi* by religious considerations and Islamic ethics.

Let us consider briefly some potential or real competitors with the *kadi* for judicial monopoly. In the first place, the *mazalim* system disappeared, and there is no equivalent under the Ottomans. So did the classical Islamic *shurta*, or police. The first contender was almost naturally the *muhtesib*—that enforcer of public morals in the marketplace—who is said to have fulfilled a wide range of criminal functions in medieval Islam. With the disappearance of the *mazalim* and *shurta*, the *muhtesib* remained the *kadi*'s only *legal* contender for carrying out adjudication. It is noteworthy that Heyd found the *muhtesib* in the fifteenth and sixteenth centuries bringing criminals to court on several charges.[50] This finding is interesting because it can be stated quite categorically that in seventeenth-century Bursa the *muhtesib* was never found in that capacity. In all the documents in which the *muhtesib* appears, he is the collector of a tax called *ihtisab*—that is, the tax pertaining to the role of the *muhtesib*. But no actual task assignment is ever mentioned in connection with the *muhtesib*.[51] In some other documents in which the *muhtesib* appears, we observe this officeholder's being charged by a certain guild with illegally interfering in the conduct of its affairs.[52] In all these cases it is duly proven in court that the *muhtesib* "traditionally" (a loose term probably meaning "as long as one can remember") had no role to play in guild affairs—which means, of course, also price policy, historically the most renowned function of the *muhtesib*. Taken together, this evidence probably indicates that in seventeenth-century Bursa we are witnessing the process of decline of the *muhtesib*, a noteworthy occurrence when coupled with the enhanced importance of the *kadi*.[53]

Other possible contenders for the role of judge in Bursa and in Ottoman society more generally were the governor, either the *mütesellim* or the *sancak bey*, and the so-called *subaşi*, or chief of police. The secondary literature on the Ottoman criminal system strongly suggests that it was indeed these functionaries who usurped the authority of the Ottoman *kadi* prior to the late sixteenth century and even more so thereafter. But I strongly doubt whether this was really the case in seventeenth-century Bursa—or at all. It is true that the absence in the *kadi* records of extensive evidence of the usurpation of the *kadi*'s authority does not necessarily prove that it did not occur. But the fact that it fails to be so much as mentioned in literally thousands of cases brought before Bursa *kadi*s in the seventeenth century is a telling one. My feeling is that had it existed, such a usurpation would have surfaced in the *kadi* records. The same goes for the *subaşí*; he is mentioned very often in the records as a police officer and prosecutor but never as a surrogate judge.

Another quasi-judicial institution that might potentially have detracted from the superiority of the *kadi* was the so called *teftiş*, a sort of law-and-order tour by a very high-ranking man of state of an area infested by robbers and criminals. He would come to the area assigned to him and question the local leaders about criminals in the region whom the law did not have the power to deal with effectively. He would then take these problems in hand and deal with them vigorously—meaning also not exactly according to the letter of the law. It must be borne in mind, however, that we are talking here about special and extremely rare drives that did not constitute a part of the normal and regular Ottoman judicial system.[54]

An important piece of evidence about the judicial monopoly of the Ottoman *kadi* in the seventeenth and eighteenth centuries is to be found in the *Şikayet Defteri* (*Book of Complaints*) mentioned in the introduction. As indicated, the number of complaints is so large and the coverage in terms of social groups and topics so wide that I venture to take this material as a meaningful statistical universe, in the positive as well as the negative sense. This means that a type of grievance not found in the register apparently did not exist in real life, at least not on a massive scale. And while there are several hundred complaints against wrongdoings committed by governors and *subaşí*s, there are very few complaints relating to the usurpation by them of judicial authority. I take this to be evidence that on the whole they did not pursue this line of extralegal activity.

By the same token, in those few cases appearing in the *Book of Complaints*, such adjudication by officials is clearly perceived as illegal (see chapter 5). Moreover, there are some cases of grievances filed by elite groups—such as members of various military units or fiefholders—who had formerly enjoyed the privilege of adjudication before their superior officers and now claimed they were being subjected to the innovation of being tried before a *kadi*. In at least one case this was declared by the central government to be illegal.[55] in addition, although in a considerable number of documents contained in the *Şikayet Defteri* we read about large-scale disruptions of public order calling for major police and military activity, there is never recourse to the military authorities alone. If not actually the major one, the *kadi* is invariably among the addressees, and great deference is shown to him and to the *shari`a* on such occasions. One is left with the impression that this deference is not mere lip service. I find remarkable in this context the story told by Lawrence Rosen about the governor of the Sefrou area in Morocco in the early twentieth century who wanted to force the local *kadi* to sign an illegal transfer of land. When the city's populace heard that the governor was about to arrest the reluctant *kadi*, they facilitated his escape, whereupon the governor marched the leading *ulama* of the town in a humiliating procession to jail.[56] It is difficult, if not impossible, to visualize an Ottoman governor meting out such treatment to a *kadi*.

Seventeenth-century Bursa presents us not only with the increasing importance of the *kadi* but also with the budding appearance of a public prosecutor. Heyd reminds us here that Islamic law does not include the function of public prosecutor. He adds that in the Ottoman Empire itself in the period he studied, and in cases of *had* violations, trials were brought to court by a wide variety of functionaries—*subaşi*s, tax farmers, *voyvoda*s, night watchmen, an *imam*, a *muhtesib*, or some type of military official.[57] Thus, the situation in seventeenth-century Bursa evinces a certain amount of change. In the first place, with very few exceptions, the only government official that brings cases to court in Bursa is the *subaşi*. All the other functionaries on Heyd's list simply disappear. It remains for the *subaşi*, as chief of police to bring to court, for example, the large number of prostitutes apprehended in various parts of the city.[58] The violation here is, of course, *zina* (fornication), which as a "law of Allah" is for the state to enforce. But in addition, the *subaşi* is found bringing to court cases involving the laws of men, such as murder. The surprising thing is that in some of these murder cases there is no hint that the murdered person was without relatives able to pursue the case in court.[59]

Let us now look at the type of law enforced in practice in Bursa and its region in the seventeenth and eighteenth centuries, particularly insofar as the relations between *kanun* and *shari`a* over time are concerned. On the whole it is quite clear that while the concept of the *kanun* may have declined somewhat, in practice there was more *kanun* after the sixteenth century than before, simply because the *kadi*'s role was enhanced and part of the *kadi*'s function derived from the *kanun*. Even logically it is somewhat difficult to speak about the decline of the *kanun*, although ostensibly it might look that way. If we bear in mind that the truly original contribution of the *kanun* to the penal system was the introduction of fines, then there is something in this argument, because I did not come across such penalties in seventeenth-century Bursa and its region. Nor have I seen any sign that torture was used or even hinted at, and I tend to conclude that this part of the *kanun* never crossed the threshold of the *kadi* court in the central region of the Ottoman Empire.

But the issue is really much more complicated. What we have is a kind of symbiosis or compromise between *kanun* and *shari`a*. It is impossible to talk about the decline of the *kanun* because, as we have seen, the penal law of the *shari`a* is built into the *kanun*. Thus, when a *kadi* of Bursa allows the relatives of a murdered person to decide the fate of the murderer,[60] as he does on several occasions, is he acting according to the *kanun* or the *shari`a*? The only possible answer is that he is acting according to both. In that sense, certainly, the *kanun* may be said never to have declined. It might be claimed that from the viewpoint of intention, the *kadis* thought in terms of the *shari`a*. But this would be much less credible in all those cases in which the *subaşı* brought to court people whose crimes were not particularly severe in themselves but who were described in court as habitual criminals. Many of these criminals were sentenced to death by the *kadi* merely because of their criminal nature. This kind of problem is not mentioned in the *shari`a* manuals but is expressly dealt with by the *kanun*. In this respect, the *kanun* truly lived on after the sixteenth century. I will, however, show later that when seen from the point of view of the *mufti*, this *kanun* innovation was accommodated into the *shari`a*.

This part of the penal code, current in Bursa and its region in the seventeenth and eighteenth centuries, is clearly associated with the concept of *sai bil' fesad* (fomenting evil in the world). In classical Islam, starting with the Quran, the concept was used mainly in connection with highway robbery. It is Ménage, in editing Heyd, who I think deserves credit for noticing that the Ottomans broadened the original concept a great deal by applying it to habitual highway robbers.[61] In fact, many documents from the Bursa court records indicate that the Ottomans applied the concept to all sorts of public offenses, whatever their nature, provided the criminal was a habitual one. What we seem to get here in the final analysis is a certain development in Islamic legal thought—a burgeoning concept of criminal record. Another interesting point here is that this broadening of the concept of *sai bil' fesad* does not seem to be decreed by the government. It seems rather to develop from below—a kind of customary development of an article contained in the *kanun*. Also, I find it most remarkable that the evidence for the existence of such criminal record comes not from the files of the state police but rather from the witness of a long line of trustworthy Muslims. Again, this extremely important role assigned to the populace in the Ottoman legal process is noteworthy.

Another appropriate context in which to analyze the relations between the different systems of law in Bursa is the handling of sexual offenses mentioned in the *kadi* records. As noted earlier, a large number of cases involve prostitutes, all said to have been apprehended in the act of committing the crime. The relevant penalty for such a violation is, of course, the *had* penalty of stoning to death (if the violator is or has been married) or at least one hundred strokes. But none of the cases ends with such severe punishment. In most cases the culprit is banished from the neighborhood or gets the *tazir* (discretionary punishment by the *kadi*), which is never specified exactly. This kind of treatment is again a sort of compromise between custom and *shari`a*.[62]

A type of penalty meted out by *kadi*s in Bursa that is connected neither with the *shari`a* nor with the *kanun* is the sentence to serve as an oarsman (*kürekçi*) on a galley of the Ottoman navy. Exactly when and how this punishment came into existence is unclear, but it was probably during the sixteenth century, when the Ottomans were enlarging their navy and were severely short of manpower. Because it was clearly a type of punishment ordained from above, there is some justification in treating it as *kanun*-linked. It, too, did not decline in the seventeenth century; in fact, it was used quite extensively and was meted out in many kinds of circumstances and for many kinds of offenses. Thus, three years as *kürekçi* were inflicted on three robbers who were apprehended while attacking a caravan.[63] In another case a gypsy received five years as a *kürekçi*, after being convicted of attempted rape and robbery, a group of witnesses having attested that such was his usual behavior.[64] In a third example, a man who stole a horse did not suffer the cutting off of his hand—the *had* penalty—but was sentenced to an unspecified time as *kürekçi*.[65]

In the context of the relations between the *shari'a* and non-*shari'a* fields of law within the Ottoman legal system, it is appropriate to touch on an additional area of Islamic law that in modern Western terms would be classified as penal law, although it is not so classified by Islamic law itself. I refer here to the prohibition on interest charging—a well-known prohibition in Islamic law, though its transgression was not a *had* violation. Going far beyond the *hila* (device) literature that allowed hidden interest charging in the pre-Ottoman period, Ottoman law flagrantly and openly violated that prohibition by allowing such loans. Contrary to classical Islam, this was done not through that *hila* literature, but openly and explicitly by merely avoiding the formal term *riba* (interest) and substituting for it less direct terms, such as *murabaha* and *rabh*. By now it is well known that charging interest was extremely widespread. In seventeenth-century Bursa, for example, almost no one in town was free from involvement in credit relations, either with individual moneylenders or with religious endowments specializing in that sort of activity. Cases involving moneylending were freely discussed in court, without anyone's ever mentioning its possible illegality.[66] The major institution through which the society under study engaged in credit relations was an arrangement called *istiğlal*, a classical Islamic term that in the Ottoman context was given a whole new meaning. In our documents *istiğlal* is an interest-bearing loan wherein the borrower receives money for a year and in exchange "sells" his house to the lender for the same period of time; he immediately gets the house back on a lease from the "buyer"; and the rent is, in effect, the interest on the loan. This institution was extremely popular in seventeenth-century Bursa,[67] and all the signs indicate that it was quite as widespread in eighteenth- and early-nineteenth-century Istanbul.[68] The *istiğlal* may look like an ordinary *hila*, or device to get around the legal prohibition against interest, and possibly it originated as such. But to my mind, it would be a mistake to view it as a device in the period and place under review. The fact is that many documents in our sources not only lay bare quite explicitly the elements of the formal transaction but proceed to decode it fully and specify what is really meant by each term.[69] These documents also clearly show that if loans were not returned, such houses were sold on the market as behooves an item of collateral, the loan being deducted from the price realized.[70]

There were some additional institutional arrangements for money loans in which the payment of interest was even more direct. One such arrangement was *devr-i şar`i*, which, according to the context in which it appears in the documents, simply meant an interest-bearing loan. In a great many documents people claimed they had got money without *devr-i şar`i* and refused to pay any sum over the amount loaned.[71] As opposed to this, some documents specify that a loan naturally carries a yearly addition, known as *devr-i şar`i*. In one example we read that a 3,450-piaster loan by a merchant to an orphan consisted of the original sum (*asli mal*) plus the yearly increment (*ve ba devr-i şar`i bir senelik nama*).[72] The parties did not call it interest, but they were frank about the fact that an amount was paid in addition to the original sum. It would be quite unreasonable, to my mind, to claim that they were not fully aware that this addition was equivalent to *riba*, or interest. After all, it is the addition, not the concept of *riba* per se, which is the crux of the classical Islamic prohibition of interest. Here it was exactly the addition that was not concealed. In that sense it was much more than another chapter in the device literature.

It goes without saying that the government knew about the charging of interest and approved of it. One may recall that charging interest (of no more than 10 percent) is allowed in the Süleymanic *kanun*. In addition, the government was aware that the institution was very popular and lent it legal support. Thus, several cases in the *Book of Complaints* of 1675 mention interest. In one example a manager of cash *waqf* complains he has given someone twelve hundred piasters in a legal loan (*muamele-i şariye*) but, that the borrower now refuses to repay the original sum plus the interest (*asl-i mal ile muamele-i şariye*). He asks for, and receives, an imperial order supporting his claim.[73] If we recall Baber Johansen's aforementioned suggestive remark that the prohibition on interest symbolizes the basic spirit of Islamic law as a law of small proprietors, in which the state intervenes only slightly in the affairs of the subjects, then possibly we have here another clue as to the spirit animating Ottoman law. Ottoman society was one based less on the equality born of face-to-face acquaintance, and the state was strongly integrated into the social structure as an employer and as a cultural model. Here we have spoken only of the way in which interest was integrated into the practice of the court. In the next chapter we shall see that it was also accepted on the level of thought of the religious-legal scholars, which in my view makes it a virtual addition to the shari`a.

This whole discussion of the place of interest in Ottoman society is also important in showing that there was nothing mechanical about the decline of the kanun. The creation of the Ottoman legal system in the seventeenth and eighteenth centuries was a process of bargaining and negotiation by social forces pulling in all directions. Certainly the state was one major factor here. Originally the legality of interest may have been connected with the kanun. But in the period under study it was not seen as part of the kanun; it was simply there. To my mind it is a classic example of a symbiosis between kanun, shari`a, and popular custom.

The main topic of this chapter is the rise of the shari`a court and the growing importance of the penal code of the shari`a. It may be interesting to see how generalized this development was within the Ottoman Empire. First, Galal El-Nahal wrote a fine study that confirms my findings with regard to seventeenth-century Egypt.[74] A more recent study on eighteenth-century Aleppo[75] confirms my main argument that far from declining or becoming marginalized, the shari`a and the kadi and his court were pivotal to the entire structure of Ottoman law: "Of the judicial courts that enforced the law in the city none approached the qadi's importance. Although commonly known at the time as shari`a court . . ., it enforced state and customary law as well as Islamic law. With its comprehensive jurisdiction, plurality of public function, and official standing as the chief court of the land, it dominated the legal scene."[76]

I claim that in Bursa the role of the kadi was even more pivotal than in Aleppo. The evidence in Aleppo attests that the governor played a substantial role in judicial affairs. He had a full-fledged court that brought people to trial. This court was a byword in Aleppo for oppressive and whimsical procedure, whereas the record and prestige of the shari`a court seem to have been quite good, especially by comparison. That the governor's judgment was harsher than that of the shari`a is clear from a law current in Aleppo whereby entire neighborhoods were liable for the extralegal activities of criminals or prostitutes.[77] Of interest is that in Aleppo the kadi seems to have enjoyed a somewhat narrower range of authority. Although he heard and passed judgment in cases involving the death penalty, when it came to cases of *sai bil' fesad* (fomentors of evil) he referred such cases to the governor, who dealt with them according to the principle of "administrative justice," *siyaseten*.[78] There is no sign in our sources that a comparable governmental court or judicial activity was extant in seventeenth-century Bursa; the *kadi* in Bursa handled without much ado cases classifiable as *siyaseten*. I interpret the difference between Bursa and Aleppo as reflecting the difference between the Ottoman core area and the outer provinces, where universalistic and bureaucratic processes were weaker than at the center.

An unexpected affirmation of the thesis presented here regarding the paramountcy of the *kadi* in the Ottoman legal system is found in a recently published study by Rudolph Peters on nineteenth-century Egypt.[79] Peters analyzes 129 *fatwa*s concerning the Egyptian criminal law in the period prior to 1883—that is, before the introduction into Egypt of the French penal code. He is surprised to discover that the penal code in pre-1883 Egypt was, in effect, the *shari`a*. In seeking an explanation for this paramountcy of the *shari`a* he suggests that the Egyptians were simply following the Ottomans: "In the Ottoman Empire the office of the qadi was a strong one and the Shari`a, supplemented by secular legislation, was almost universally and carefully applied."[80]

To conclude, it seems that for the most part the penal law current in the central region of the Ottoman Empire in the seventeenth and eighteenth centuries was a mixture of *shari`a*, *kanun*, and customary law, with the *shari`a* as the superior element—at least quantitatively. But there is no sign that the *kanun* was pushed aside culturally, ideologically, or practically. Rather than a coherent drive against the *kanun*, those parts of the penal code that may simply have been more resonant with local sensitivities were more strongly asserted. It is clear, however—and Heyd himself underscores this point—that the late seventeenth-century emotional spurt against the *kanun* was short-lived. Needless to say, non-*shari`a* taxes went on being levied, and there is increasing evidence that the juxtaposition of *kanun* and *shari`a* went on as before.[81] The crucial additional feature was the important place of the *kadi* and his court in the Ottoman core region's judicial system, beyond that in any previous Islamic state. It is in a sense paradoxical that the powerful and centralized Ottoman Empire should have delegated such important authority to the *kadi* and his court. To my mind, it is ultimately explained by the fact that Ottoman bureaucracy was based on universalistic principles to a much greater extent than is usually realized—a topic that is dealt with in detail in chapter 5.

All this represented a major change from the fourteenth and fifteenth centuries, when the legal system in this region was characterized by a multiplicity of conflicting judicial bodies and enforcement authorities. The explanation for the change can be sought in the growing bureaucratization of the state, coupled with the Ottomans' need for Islamic legitimation, topped by the dynasty's efforts to keep a proper balance between conflicting sectors of the growing bureaucracy—in particular, the religious clerics and the civil bureaucracy. It is a typical combination of factors that are partly objective and partly subjective, partly materialist and partly cultural (here meaning especially old Near Eastern norms about the way a ruler should keep his officials at bay). This combination is a nice exemplification of theories (such as that of Philip Abrams) claiming it is futile and wrong to isolate objective causation from individual experience and perception. The factors are intimately intertwined: without growing bureaucratization the Ottomans would probably never have adopted this typical ancient Near Eastern imperial perspective, nor would Süleyman the Magnificent have adopted the posture and claim of a messiah, as Cornell Fleischer shows (see chapter 5).

3. THE *FETVA* IN THE
LEGAL SYSTEM

THE *FETVA*, a legal opinion given by a professional jurist, is a specifically Islamic legal institution that played a certain role in the development of Islamic law and, more specifically, in the adjudication process of every subculture within Islam. Islamic legal production can be arranged along a continuum, or hierarchy, from the theoretical to the practical. The highest level is occupied by the jurist, the writer of legal manuals; the lowest level is occupied by the *kadi*, or judge, whose legal role is to pronounce on what the law has to say concerning an actual human situation. The *mufti* stands between them and is probably somewhat nearer to the jurist. He relates not to people and their specific dilemmas but to theoretical problems posed to him, his role being to state the position of Islamic law concerning such questions. Whereas in some other Islamic societies *muftis* were legal advisers to people in general, a *mufti's* main role under the Ottomans was supplying litigants with legal opinions to be used in court. Whereas the *sicill*, the *kadi* records, represent the practice of Islamic law, the opinions of the *muftis* represent what the religious scholars thought about the relation between that practice and Islamic law in theory. In the specific legal system under study here, the importance of the *mufti* reached unprecedented proportions. Because the *mufti* played the role of jurist, analyzing the intellectual product of Ottoman *muftis* is the closest we can get to a semi-official statement of the law in this polity—which is the main justification of the *fetva*. No less important is the fact that as Baber Johansen has claimed, it was mainly through the work of the *muftis* that legal change was accommodated into the *shari`a* in the middle Islamic period.[1] Comparing such statements of the law with the actual process of adjudication can throw considerable light on the major issue of the present study: the relation between the law in theory and the law as actual process. Analytically, the question of the role of the *fetva* constitutes an important element in the debate over the Weberian theory and the anthropological models presented in the introduction: the more important the role of the *fetva*, the more important the role of theoretical, faceless, context-free considerations in the process of adjudication. This is because the *fetva*, at least in the culture area under study here, was a question submitted to the religious scholar free of identifying details such as place, the names of the litigants, and so on. The scholar in question, the *mufti*, was specifically charged with giving a religious legal answer. In the area under study, such *fetvas* were usually requested for use in court; but in Islam in general this was far from being universal. In many instances people came to court armed with theoretical *fetvas* supporting their case, and the *kadi* was supposed to weigh the *fetva* as one component of the case. He was, however, by no means obliged to rule in favor of the *fetva* bearer, especially because the *fetva* had been issued on an expressly theoretical basis. At best it matched the facts as the bearer of the *fetva* saw them. It was still the role of the *kadi* to decide whether the facts narrated by the *fetva* matched the case in hand as he saw it. So the question of whether the *fetva* in the Ottoman context was an important legal institution, quantitatively speaking, and whether it exerted a palpable influence on the judicial process is an entirely empirical one, to be resolved by reference to actual Ottoman court cases.

One more initial question has, however, to be raised that does not directly concern the actual judicial process. A major political and administrative development that took place in the Ottoman Empire is, at least outwardly, connected with the institution of *fetva*. The reference is to the rise of the *mufti* of Istanbul to the position of *şeyhülislam*, the chief religious dignitary of the state in charge of nominating all religious officeholders in the land. It is obvious that this last function was the main one in the role of this dignitary. But the question is still open about whether the function of issuing *fetvas* had anything to do with this rise to greatness. In this chapter I claim that such a connection did indeed exist, which makes the *fetva* an important institution not only on the level of the humble provincial *kadi* but also on the level of the state itself. It must be emphasized immediately that even when the office of *şeyhülislam* reached its peak with the appointment of Ebu Suud Efendi (d. 1574), he remained a *mufti* all the while, theoretically even an ordinary *mufti*.

It seems highly unlikely, however, that political considerations, if not bowing to alleged superior knowledge, did not cause special weight to be given to the opinions of the man holding the key to all *ilmiye* nominations. Some hints of this exist in the available material. Thus, a study of the town of Kayseri extensively cites cases using *fetva*s, but underscores the fact that *kadi*s were not particularly impressed by them.[2] The same is not true of seventeenth century Bursa, where *fetva*s were viewed with the highest reverence. The fact that every *fetva* bearer in Bursa, without exception, won his case is only one expression of this reverence (in no case did both parties to a lawsuit present *fetva*s.) Perhaps it is in this light that we should view what seems to be the freak opinion of some Grand Muftis that a *fetva* was an absolutely binding document.[3]

An inspection of actual records in Ottoman courts of law reveals that the *fetva* was, in fact, very widely used. *Fetva*s by the hundreds are mentioned, often cited verbatim in the court records. Various parties to trials in seventeenth-century Bursa produced *fetva*s in court—all without exception issued by the Grand Mufti of Istanbul, the *şeyhülislam*. Most relate to agrarian matters, and most also invoke the *kanun*. In one case, a villager in the vicinity of Bursa sold a piece of arable land without obtaining the prior consent of the manager of the endowment to which it belonged. The latter produced two *fetva*s of the *şeyhülislam* and won the case.[4] Similarly, two women complained before the *kadi* that their father had died without leaving any male offspring. According to the *kanun* they had a prior right over the land. They won the case, again using a *fetva* of the *şeyhülislam*.[5] In a third case, a fiefholder in a region close to Bursa sued another Bursa citizen on the claim that more than fifteen years earlier he had been a villager in his fief. The defendant produced a *fetva* of the *şeyhülislam* to the effect that a claim is not valid after fifteen years have elapsed.[6] Cases are not confined to agrarian matters. Some *fetva*s deal with the legal status of non-Muslims,[7] and several deal with questions relating to religious endowments. Thus, a *fetva* of Şeyhülislam

Abdulrahim is cited in support of a demand that people holding endowment property on lease pay their share of the *avariz* tax imposed on the neighborhood.[8]

Bursa *kadi*s in the seventeenth century sometimes used early *fetva* collections, especially those of Ebu Suud Efendi, the great sixteenth-century *şeyhülislam* who was active in shaping the legal forms of the agrarian *kanun*, as a reference in matters relating to agrarian law. In one case a woman sued two men, claiming that land owned by her was being held illegally by them. The defendants claimed that they had not only inherited the land lawfully but had held it for more than ten years. In his verdict the *kadi* cited a *fetva* collection by Ebu Suud to the effect that whoever had held a plot of land for ten years decidedly had the right of possession (*hak-i karar*).[9] Large numbers of such agrarian *fetva*s later found their way into the *fetva* collections of these seventeenth-century *şeyhülislam*s, and several of them were also published in the nineteenth century; it can therefore be surmised that the *fetva*s appearing in the collections are copies of actual *fetva*s issued out to people requesting them.

As noted earlier, in seventeenth-century Bursa the party presenting a *fetva* in court always won the case. Exactly what this means is not necessarily self-evident. Because I did not get the impression that *kadi*s in Bursa were immediately swayed in favor of the *fetva* bearer without weighing the evidence, I am more inclined to the conclusion that *şeyhülislam*s issued *fetva*s only after considerable pondering. Thus, an old theory that a *mufti* would without much ado issue patently conflicting *fetva*s, even to parties in the same lawsuit, is completely belied by the material at our disposal. And in fact, neither in Bursa nor in any other comparative case dealt with in this study was more than one *fetva* presented in a single lawsuit.

In the *kadi* records of eighteenth-century Istanbul, too, one often comes across *fetva*s as part of the legal process. Thus, a *fetva* of Şeyhülislam Ali Efendi constituted authority in the question of whether a man could stand surety for a limited period of time.[10] Another *fetva* of the same *şeyhülislam* served as authority for the verdict given by the *kadi* in a murder case of someone who had no legal successor; the plaintiff—that is, the *subaşi* (police officer), claimed that in such cases it was for the sovereign to decide whether the punishment of retaliation (*kisas*) was to be carried out or whether the sentence should be commuted to payment of blood money (*diyet*).[11]

*Fetva*s are also found in the *kadi* court records of sixteenth-century Ankara. Here they relate to matters of civil law, to questions of personal status, and to agrarian issues. Some *fetva*s bear the signature of a *mufti* named Mustafa.[12] As there was no *şeyhülislam* by that name at the relevant date, it is obvious that sixteenth-century Ankara, unlike seventeenth-century Bursa, had an active *mufti* of its own. Seventeenth-century Kayseri fits this pattern as well: *fetva*s were extensively used as part of the process of adjudication, and they were as a rule issued by a local *mufti*.[13]

It is thus clear that a large number of *fetva*s were used in Ottoman courts and that the institution was an important component of the legal system. But is it really possible, as hinted previously, to trace a rule whereby the *şeyhülislam* as *mufti* was in actuality the *mufti* of the central area, the area being studied here? If this were established, it might be possible to conclude that the place of the *fetva* in the legal system prevailing in the central area of the Ottoman Empire was substantially more elevated; for, as already stated, it is highly likely that a *fetva* by the *şeyhülislam* counted for more than a *fetva* of a provincial *mufti*—politically, if not formally.

Is it possible to establish that in reality the *şeyhülislam* was merely the *mufti* of the area under study here and not of the entire empire? To investigate this point, I have compared the *fetva* collections by *şeyhülislam*s with some of the provincial *fetva* collections that are available in order to trace differences in subject matter—differences that could be "placed" geographically. The example of a provincial collection from which I have drawn mainly, though not exclusively, is that of the seventeenth-century Palestinian *mufti*, Khayr al-Din al-Ramli.[14]

When one compares the central collections to a provincial collection such as Khayr al-Din al-Ramli's, a number of differences immediately emerge. For example, the most fundamental rule characterizing the central collections is the thorough obliteration of all traces of identifying context. This pattern is not followed in the *fetva*s sent to al-Ramli, many of which include the place of origin and, more rarely, the year. This has a methodological significance that I will discuss in a minute, but it also possesses judicial importance. It means that the element detected in the central area, the judicial-theoretical weighing of cases without the influence of a personalizing context may have been weaker in areas lying farther afield. From a methodological point of view this contextuality is important because it reveals that most of the *fetva*s were sent from the area of Palestine and only a small minority originated in Lebanon and Syria. It would probably be safe to conclude, tentatively at least, that most of the questions addressed to Khayr al-Din al-Ramli were sent from Palestine.

There is an additional important point concerning the difference between al-Ramli's collection and the central ones. In the central collections it is possible to discern some socioeconomic institutions that, as far as we know, existed only in the Turkish culture area. And in the Palestinian *fetva* collections there is mention of institutions special to that region. A conspicuous example of the former is the institution of *icarateyn* (double rent) of *waqf* (religious endowment) real estate, in which the lessee pays a large sum of money as down payment and then a very small sum per month. This type of rent existed in the central Turkish area of the empire and finds expression only in the central collections. Another example of difference is the main agricultural tax prevailing in the empire, a tax levied as a proportion of agricultural produce. In Anatolia this tax was referred to as a tithe and was indeed something like one-tenth of the produce. As opposed to this, in Palestine the tax was referred to as *qasm* and was usually a quarter or a third of the produce. Again, this difference is reflected in the collections: in the central collections the *qasm* system is never mentioned, only the tithe; and in the Palestinian collections, only the *qasm* is ever mentioned. All these may be trivial facts in themselves, but they reveal something of considerable methodological importance about the geographical division of labor among the central and provincial *fetva* collections.

It stands to reason, then, that the *fetva* collections composed by *şeyhülislam*s contain questions sent only from the Turkish culture area of the state, or from an even more limited area such as that between Bursa and Edirne, because we have seen that Ankara and Kayseri actually had *mufti*s of their own. Geographical factors such as distance from the capital must have played a crucial role in the decision as to whether it was the *şeyhülislam* who was to be the *mufti* or whether the city was too far from Istanbul and needed its own *mufti*.

Proper elaboration of this point calls for a specialized study that has not so far been undertaken, but one gets the impression that there was an important difference in the legal and political approach of central as opposed to provincial *mufti*s in the empire. For example, Baber Johansen, who studied the views of Syrian and Palestinian *mufti*s in the Ottoman period, found that they held *mufti*s to be above judges, legally speaking—that is, a *mufti*'s interpretation of the law was considered superior. A *kadi*'s judgment could be put before a *mufti* for review, and the *mufti* could find it deficient and declare it null and void. Hence, *mufti*s of the Ottoman period, in Johansen's words, "encourage the plaintiffs to bring one and the same lawsuit before a second, third and fourth judge, each time they can produce new evidence and each time they want a decision concerning a new aspect of the case in question." It is for this reason, according to this view, that lawsuits can be dragged on indefinitely, literally for decades. At any given moment the *mufti*s may interfere and prevent execution of the verdict or decision.[15] None of these views of Syrian and Palestinian *mufti*s were shared by Ottoman *şeyhülislam*s in the period under study, nor were they found in actual law records as something that really took place. It is true that a *kadi*'s decision was not considered sacred and immutable; nor was it even irreversible, in the event that it was later found to be based on considerations that could be said to be flagrantly illegal. But it was definitely the case that in the core area of the Ottoman Empire it would take the authority of the sultan to reverse it. My impression is that this actually happened only on rare occasions. What took place in provincial courts in this regard is still unknown. In the court records of seventeenth-century Bursa no *kadi* was ever asked to reconsider a case formerly decided by another *kadi*, and no single case among the many thousands I have read dragged on beyond one or two hearings. This information may not be complete, but it is a fair representation of what is currently known.

Moreover, the views of Ottoman *şeyhülislam*s diverged drastically from those of the Syrian *mufti*s and were not found to express legal superiority over *kadi*s. A possible explanation for this difference of opinion may prove relevant and important to the general argument of this book—it is quite possible that Arab *mufti*s in the Ottoman Empire had good reason to assign greater importance to local *mufti*s over the foreign, Turkish-speaking *kadi*, who was not only nominated by Istanbul but was as a rule also a member of the Ottoman social elite. Ottoman *şeyhülislam*s obviously viewed the legal situation from the standpoint of the central government. It was responsible for law and order, a scheme of things in which the judge's prestige must rank first. But it should also be recalled here that by the seventeenth century the career path of *şeyhülislam*s was so structured that for most of their professional lives such *şeyhülislam*s were actually *kadi*s, not *mufti*s.[16] This was in

complete contrast to the Syrian *mufti*s, who were not at all part of
the Ottoman establishment either administratively (in terms of
career path) or culturally, because they received their education in
the University-Mosque of Al-Azhar. Neither culturally nor socially did the Arab *mufti*s have any reason to admire the bureaucratic
world of the Ottoman *kadi*, in which they had little share. This
difference clearly highlights the distinctly bureaucratic-adminis-
trative nature of Ottoman law, perhaps particularly so in the central area of the empire.

   An important legal aspect of the *fetva* collections that has
not been dealt with up to this point is this: by no means were all
the *fetva*s in these collections originally used to support cases in
trials before the *kadi*. There are clear signs that people made use of
the institution of the *mufti* for both legal and semilegal matters
that were not brought to the court. Thorough investigation of this
point in *fetva* collections may yield interesting and important
results and can surely lead to the conclusion that the recent ascendancy of the *sicill* (*kadi* court records) as the main source for the
social history of the Middle East has by no means made the *fetva*
collections a superfluous and redundant source. Here we must
limit ourselves to the discussion of only a small sample of such
cases. The point can most fruitfully be investigated in the provincial collections, exactly because of their less theoretical legal
structure, which finds expression in the highly detailed, empirical,
and factual nature of many of the *fetva*s in the provinces. In the
central collections we see only the bare skeleton of a legal problem; rarely is there a flesh-and-blood story. While this probably
yields a higher level of abstraction, a way of putting cases to the
mufti in as theoretical a manner as possible, and is a difference
that makes sense legally and bureaucratically, the social historian
has much less reason to rejoice: there are rarely facts that can be
placed contextually in time and place. It is consequently in the
provincial collections that one has to seek for legal material that
bears the mark of being dealt with uniquely by the *mufti*. In one
document al-Ramli is asked a question about a group of peasants
who have been summoned to court in a criminal case, the exact
nature of which is not specified. They refuse, saying: "We shall not
go according to the *shari`a*; we shall go by the customs (*da`ai'm*) of
the Bedouins and peasants."[17] Muhammad Khalili (also a seventeenth-century Palestinian *mufti*) cites a similar document,[18]
imputing to the peasants a very regular adherence to customary
law and concomitant shunning of the *shari`a* and *kadi* courts, to

the point that their being orthodox Muslims is called into question. The two documents seem to refer to something quite well known in the nineteenth century, the so-called *shari`at al-Khalil*, a kind of customary law widely used in the Judean Mountains and briefly described by the members of the Palestine Exploration Fund.[19] Save for the fact that in the seventeenth-century *fetva* there is no mention of the term *shari`at al-Khalil*, the reference is probably to the same customary law. From the point of view of the present study the information is important: because these peasants refused to go to court, this *fetva* was not procured as part of a trial procedure. Exactly who might have sought such a *fetva* is not entirely clear. The same problems are inherent in the *fetva* given by al-Ramli[20] concerning the behavior of various Bedouin tribes who were not following current orthodox modes of behavior. But it seems quite obvious that the *fetva* was not originally used as part of a legal process before the *kadi*.

A major evasion of the *shari`a* court is also complained about in a question presented to Khalili dealing with a problem alleged to be common in the regions of Jerusalem, Hebron, Gaza, and Nablus, as well as in Syria and Egypt. This problem relates to the property of underage children whose fathers have died. Such properties were being seized by relatives of the deceased without the court's being allowed to nominate a legal guardian over the children.[21] Such a question, which obviously discloses important social information, was naturally not asked as part of a trial before the *kadi*. It is quite clear that whoever brought this question before the *mufti* wished to use his legal and moral authority to rectify a widespread legal wrong that could not be rectified by the court of the *kadi*. It is thus obvious that in provincial areas the *mufti* had important sociopolitical functions, which are obscured at present by the lack of systematic research into this topic.

Another source that sheds important light on a semilegal function filled by the *mufti*—this time the *şeyhülislam* himself— is the *Şikayet Defteri* (*Book of Complaints*), which is dealt with on its own merit in chapter 5. Contained in the *Şikayet Defteri* are citizens' complaints about a variety of wrongs, sent in 1675 to the central Ottoman government. It turns out that a substantial number of these complaints were accompanied by a formerly secured *fetva* of the *şeyhülislam* supporting the case, which was intended to convince the central government to issue a certain order. In one complaint a group of citizens from Istrumca protest that the governor of the province seized some of them as supposed killers of a man whose body had been found in a mosque. Because the governor had no shred of evidence against them, they were able to secure a *fetva* supporting their case.[22] In another case inhabitants of a town in the Morea complain that the local governor extorted *diyet* (blood money) from them for a murdered man whose body was found in the area. This was plainly illegal, and again a *fetva* of the *şeyhülislam* supports the case.[23] Because these complaints were aimed at securing a sultanic order, it is clear that the *fetva* was not intended to be used in court. Yet in these and many other cases recourse to the *şeyhülislam* was made on the basis that the issue at stake was legal in nature. The central government was called upon to intervene to rectify a wrong done by usurpation of legal authority.

Still, there are many cases in the *Şikayet Defteri* where *fetva*s were requested in support of quasilegal disputes within the administration itself. Thus, a tax farmer might arm himself with a *fetva* of the *şeyhülislam* when asking for an order against the actual collector.[24] Disputes between fiefholders and tax farmers were also a context in which *fetva*s were issued.[25]

ŞEYHÜLISLAM EBU SUUD EFENDI AND THE *MARUZAT*

A very unusual, even bizarre, but at the same time extremely important chapter in the history of the *fetva* institution and in Ottoman legal history in general relates to the *fetva* collection authored by Şeyhülislam Ebu Suud Efendi and known by the name *Maruzat*.[26] Besides being an important chapter in the history of the *fetva* institution, it is also important in the relations between law and the state in the Ottoman Empire, being in a sense the climax of the bureaucratizing drive of the Ottoman polity in the province of the law. Certainly no topic dealt with in this book expresses as lucidly the nature of the Ottoman state as *Rechtsstaat*. In a way, therefore, this section should be viewed as an extension of chapter 2.

Outwardly the *Maruzat* is a plain-looking *fetva* collection, but it seems to me that its true nature has not so far been adequately revealed.[27] The document constitutes part of a *kanunname* but is structured like a collection of *fetva*s. What it was originally meant to be is not clear, but legally the document certainly has to be classified as a *kanun* rather than as a *fetva* collection. However, it is not a *kanun* in the regular sense; it is a *kanun* legislation within the *shari`a*—an area in which the Ottoman state never before or after dared to intervene in this way. In a sense it could be called the ultimate *kanun*, being one that did not content itself with regulating areas of life alongside the *shari`a* but crossed the line and set administrative laws within the *shari`a*. In that sense it is a shocking episode, as much as it is a unique one in the legal history of the Ottoman Empire. Yet substantively the document did have a lasting effect in several areas, as I will show.

In a regular *fetva*, we have a situation in which a *mufti* receives a question about which he is asked to state the opinion of the *shari`a*, the law of Islam. (The same is true of a case coming up for decision before a *kadi*.) Sometimes he may answer with a laconic yes or no without raising the issue of whether the answer is fully commensurate with the *shari`a*. Usually we are not given a complicated legal argumentation. Again, the same applies to what *kadi*s in the area of study usually did. Sometimes, in complicated cases, especially when there was no consensus among the legal scholars of Islam, the *mufti* or *kadi* might cite opinions of traditional scholars of note on the matter. They are likely to mention conflicting opinions and to state which of these opinions is the "strong" one—which is usually the one they prefer. Occasionally, for a stated reason, they may prefer the "weaker" opinion, or tradition (in my own research such a situation arose only very exceptionally). In this sense, the *kadi* court in the area being studied might rarely operate under a somewhat similar cultural assumption as, for example, it does in Morocco according to Lawrence Rosen's description.[28] It is this fundamental design of traditional Islamic law and thought that Ebu Suud was targeting—not universally, it is true, but only in some areas apparently considered problematic at the time, though we have no independent information on this point.

Ebu Suud used the authority of the sultanate to innovate, even to legislate, within the *shari`a*. But the episode and the act seem much less shocking, to my mind, when we look at it in the light of Wael Hallaq's discovery that the old theory on the closure of the gate of *ijtihad* (individual interpretation) in late classical Islam was an interpretive mistake of Western orientalists, born probably of the tremendous reverence with which later Muslim generations viewed the ancient sages and their consequent reluctance to recognize that living scholars were up to the standard of the ancient ones.[29] It is not, therefore, really surprising that some of the traditional Ottoman sources relate to the work of Ebu Suud as *ijtihad*, and I fully agree with Richard Repp that such scholars quite simply had in mind the meaning of "individual interpretation" rather than the literal "exertion."[30] I believe this episode confirms Hallaq's important study and enhances my argument that the special pecularities of the *shari`a* under the Ottomans were viewed by contemporaries as a natural development within the *shari`a* itself.

All this is reflected in what we actually read in the *Maruzat*. The first question in the *Maruzat* deals with prayer. It tells us about a village that does not have a real mosque and whose inhabitants pray in an open space. The question is whether the *kadi* can force them to build a mosque. The answer is that not only must the *kadi* force them to do so, but that a sultanic order to that effect has been issued (the year is 944/1537–38).[31] It is noteworthy that the order is directed not merely to that particular village but to all villages in a similar situation. Another *fetva* addresses the question of whether it is permissible for a prayer leader to nominate a substitute when he is absent. The answer is in the affirmative, adding that in fact an order permitting such substitution has been issued by the sultan.[32]

A further question addressed to Ebu Suud deals with marriage. The question points out that there is a discussion among the classical scholars as to whether a grown woman can marry herself to someone without the consent of her guardian. While many of the traditional scholars have approved of this practice, Ebu Suud says that an order making it illegal has been issued and that *kadis* are henceforward not free to choose their own solution.[33] This issue is further probed by a question about a *kadi* who insists that he has the right to make his own choice among the traditional interpreters. Ebu Suud says such a *kadi* has no choice but to accept the crystal-clear decision of the sovereign because the *kadi*'s authority derives from that of the sovereign.[34]

Ebu Suud does not desist from trying to set hard and fast rules even within the penal law of the *shari`a*. The specific question is one that must have represented a pressing practical problem and must have stirred deep emotions at the time: who is responsible for the payment of blood money for a murdered person whose body is found in a house? Is it the owner or the actual occupier (lessee)? The "strong" view among the scholars seems to have been that the owner was responsible. But Ebu Suud says this stronger position did not appear reasonable to him; as a result, he persuaded the sultan to issue a decree making the lessee of the house solely responsible for paying blood money in such circumstances.[35]

Another important question dealt with in the *Maruzat*, also quite obviously a practical rather than a theoretical one, relates to the statute of limitation. Ebu Suud notes that the issue was discussed in former times but remained undecided among the scholars. He then goes on to say that the sultan's decision is contained in a decree of 957/1550, which set an obligatory statute of limitation of ten years in all matters other than those pertaining to sown lands, in which the limit for filing suits was set at fifteen years.[36] In these two *fetva*s, in particular, Ebu Suud shows himself capable of *ijtihad*. Because we know that he had a tremendous influence on the sultans of his time, the initiative in these matters was clearly his. But he might have persuaded the sultan to issue an order and then left the sultan to bear the brunt of legislating against a clear *shari`a* tenet. But Ebu Suud encapsulates these orders within the bounds of his own *fetva*, thereby lending it his own scholarly and religious authority. To put it differently, Ebu Suud seems in these *fetva*s to take responsibility for innovation within the *shari`a*, which he might have avoided without shirking his duty as a *şeyhülislam*. He clearly seems to be unbothered by the issue of innovation.

The *Maruzat* is, then, extremely important as a cultural-ideological document because it reveals the aims cherished by the Ottoman state concerning the actual working of both the *shari`a* court and Islamic law itself. In a way this document goes to the very heart of one comparison pursued in this book, that between the Ottoman Empire and Morocco, because it deals with the topic of judicial discretion that is so central to Rosen's analysis. And it deals with the topic in a way that shows that the Ottoman Empire indeed viewed this discretion as exaggerated and tried to curb it. In the methodology of the classical *shari`a*, which allows the *kadi* a legitimate choice and discretion among several possible solutions, Rosen sees a characteristic feature of Islamic law—one that explains why the *kadi*'s task is merely to get people back on the negotiating track.[37] It is exactly that looseness that Ebu Suud is trying to limit. In that sense the *Maruzat* is highly symbolic of the argument I am trying to establish in this book.

But culture and ideology, important as they are to an understanding of the nature of Ottoman law, are only one aspect; there is also the question of the living law. For example, if the *Maruzat* had remained a dead letter, merely a theoretical document, then we would have to reduce considerably the importance attributed to it. Therefore, it is important that evidence suggests that at least part of the innovations of Ebu Suud were extremely well accepted, especially the ones relating to the statute of limitation and the attribution of penal responsibility to the occupier rather than the owner of a house (see the following section on *muftis'* opinions).

A COMPARATIVE VIEW OF THE
OTTOMAN INSTITUTION OF *IFTA*

If it is my purpose in this study to show that Islamic law was never entirely immutable, this purpose can be shown in the context of the *ifta* institution as well. In this section I will show that the bureaucratization of this institution proceeds with the bureaucratization of the state in general and the bureaucratization of the *shari`a* courts in particular. This can be discussed on two levels: that of the citizens who use the *ifta* institution in everyday adjudication, and that of the status of the Grand Mufti within the state hierarchy.

Let us look first at the Grand Mufti, the *şeyhülislam*, in the Ottoman state. The rise of this officeholder from relative obscurity to the head of the entire religious establishment of the empire is one of the most notable bureaucratic changes of the sixteenth century. The question is how to interpret it, and here I partially disagree with the interpretation offered by Richard Repp, despite his painstaking study on the rise of this officeholder.[38] Repp suggests that the *şeyhülislam* rose from the role of mere *mufti* of the capital to that of head of the *ilmiye* (the learning institution) because the Ottomans had a bad conscience about their extremely secular policies at the end of the fifteenth century and sought to compensate by enhancing the importance of an officeholder known for Islamic spirituality. There is no positive evidence to back up this suggestion, however; and I suggest that a no less likely explanation is that as bureaucratization of the state grew, the Ottomans increasingly valued the role of the officeholder supplying the sultan with political and legal advice at the highest level. There is ample evidence that the sultans not only had recourse to such advice but also followed it almost to the letter throughout this period.[39]

During the sixteenth century, the Ottoman institution of *ifta*, especially that part of it connected with the *şeyhülislam*, underwent considerable bureaucratization. Heyd's study on the Ottoman *fetva* sheds some light on this process. In the beginning, the process of *fetva* issuing was quite simple and the work load small. A story relates that one *şeyhülislam* had a basket hung from his window into which people put their questions and received their answers. In the course of the century this work load increased enormously—even if one views with suspicion the legendary total of 1,413 *fetva*s a day issued by Ebu Suud Efendi. The more realistic figure of two hundred to four hundred *fetva*s twice a week, which is the current estimate of the *şeyhülislam*'s workload in the seventeenth century, still indicates an enormous growth in the demand for the services of the *şeyhülislam*. Small wonder that there developed a substantial bureaucratic apparatus to handle *fetva*s issued by the *şeyhülislam*, from draft writers to writers of fair copies as well as at least one legal expert.[40]

Very different from this was the nature, structure and function of the institution of *ifta* in traditional and modern Yemen, studied by anthropologist Brinkley Messick.[41] And again, it is significant that the differences between the *ifta* in Yemen and the Ottoman Empire are systematic and intimately linked with the differences in the political structure of the two areas. Politically, we are talking about a centralized bureaucratic empire in the case of the Ottoman Empire and a small frontier princedom in the case of Yemen. That this was reflected in the differences in the structure of the *ifta* institution between the two states is not self-evident, but it is of importance for an understanding of Islamic societies more generally.

What then were the characteristics of the *ifta* institution in Yemen? In the first place, it is clear that the *ifta* there was much less institutionalized. For example, *fetva*s were never presented in court as part of the adjudication process; they were merely asked for by individuals to help them arrange their lives.[42] By the 1930s there was little demand for the services of *mufti*s in Yemen, and they spent most of their days reading.[43] Earlier, the office was even less structured, for there were no specialized *mufti*s: "Prior to the nineteenth century, the giving of fatwas was an informal activity of leading scholars. 'He studied, he taught, he gave fatwas'. . . is a summary statement of what a scholar did."[44] The most outstanding scholar in a certain area and time was also the natural *mufti*. This amorphous nature of the institution is possibly even the background for the appearance of a learned man like Shawkani, an eighteenth-century scholar who had the courage and intellectual capacity to reject explicitly the notion of the so-called closure of the gates of individual interpretation, and offered his own interpretation of Islam. Messick himself observed the amorphous nature of the *ifta* in Yemen: "Yemen has had only indirect experience of such public institutional elaborations of the office as occurred in Mamluk Egypt . . . and in the central provinces of the Ottoman Empire."[45]

THE LEGAL VIEWS OF OTTOMAN *ŞEYHÜLISLAM*S

If the *kadi* was clearly the centerpiece of the Ottoman legal system, there are nevertheless some other major elements that deserve mention for the sake of completeness. One of them is the role of the *şeyhülislam*—that is, the head of the *ilmiye*, the Islamic institution of the empire from about the third quarter of the sixteenth century, and also the *mufti* of the capital. Earlier I spoke of the role of *fetva*s issued by the *şeyhülislam* in trials before *kadi*s in the empire. I also mentioned some other possible uses of such *fetva*s; but I have indicated that contrary to other subcultures within Islamdom—for example, Yemen—in the case presently under study, the main use of the *fetva* was as part of the judicial process that unfolded before the *kadi*. Moreover, as we have seen, the *kadi* court records are replete with *fetva*s used by litigants. Furthermore, without any exception, the *mufti* whose *fetva*s are cited in the court records of Bursa and Istanbul was the *şeyhülislam* himself, who thus appears to be the *mufti* of the entire Istanbul area rather than merely of the city itself. While *kadi*s were under no obligation to rule in accordance with a *fetva*, this nevertheless happened in the vast majority of cases. What emerges quite clearly is that *fetva*s of *şeyhülislam*s constitute a realistic historical source for socioeconomic as well as legal history. Hence, the *mufti* was a link between reality and the world of Islamic scholarship. The opinions of *şeyhülislam*s can therefore be investigated in order to discover what the exponents of Islamic learning really thought about the world of reality. In addition, the views of these *şeyhülislam*s, though strictly speaking private views, are, as we have said, the nearest thing we have to an official view of the law as seen by the government. Bearing in mind that Ottoman *şeyhülislam*s were, politically speaking, members of the innermost councils of the state, it seems justifiable to regard their views as politically and ideologically important. If the Ottoman sultan wanted to effect a change in legal policy, he had to go through the *şeyhülislam*s.

My main interest in studying the views of the *şeyhülislam*s is to trace changes in Islamic law in the middle period. There are two elements in this interest: first, to find out what they thought about the practice of the court and second, to trace in their writings changes in the *shari`a*.[46] A cursory glance at the several *fetva* collections of Ottoman *şeyhülislam*s that have been published may lead one to the conclusion that we have here one more faithful version of what we may call a *shari`a* manual. The best known and most widely used such manual in the Ottoman Empire was Ibrahim al-Halabi's *Multaqa al-Abhur*, composed in the sixteenth century. That book is a typical product of the theoretically inclined *madrasa*; neither the weights and measures nor the types of coins mentioned in it belong to the sixteenth century, and the book is therefore of little or no use to anyone but a historian interested in the intellectual world of the *madrasa*. But a more careful look at the *fetva* collections reveals that the match between them and the *shari`a* manuals is far from perfect. All the collections contain chapters that do not appear in the manuals for the very reason that they deal with fully contemporary issues. And some of these chapters contain quite flagrant violations of, or additions to, the *shari`a*—although, of course, this is never openly admitted. These small diverging chapters reveal the *fetva* collections as realistic sources that reflect more or less fully the legal universe of the *mahkama*, the court. With regard to the remaining portions of the collections, here, too, there is a rough match between the collections and the real, living law. However, both collections and the *kadi* records go by the *shari`a*, so it is impossible to tell whether a collection's point of reference is *shari`a* manuals or real-life problems. Hence, it is the diverging chapters in the *fetva* collections that make the difference and deserve to be studied more carefully.

A modern researcher who has studied the *fetva* in Yemen as a mode of interpreting the world has commented that the *mufti* and the *kadi* are antidotes in a hermeneutic circle.[47] While the *kadi's* interpretation is closely related to the real world, those of the *mufti* are more related to the *madrasa*, the school. On the basis of the diverging chapters of the *fetva* collections of *şeyhülislam*s in the Ottoman Empire, I would say that these *mufti*s were much closer to *kadi*s in their way of perceiving the world than were their counterparts in Yemen according to Messick. In the opinion of the *mufti*s there is no criticism of the prevailing legal system, though there is no slavish acceptance of it either. They accept it calmly and see themselves as an integral part of it. In fact, when one notes the degree to which actual law conformed to the shari`a, in comparison with other Islamic countries, these ulema had little to complain about.

It is noteworthy that most fetva collections known to have attained public currency and influence are from this period. These are mainly collections that were published, not just formally by being completed by the author and copied anew, but published in the real sense, though still by traditional scholarship. Nor was it just the collection of the illustrious Ebu Suud that was published, but also those of the much more pedestrian Ali Efendi or Abdallah Efendi, muftis from the so-called period of decline. Apparently the Ottomans of this period at least did not view these ulema as decadent and devoid of intellectual importance. I am using in addition the fetva collection of Ebu Suud (not to be confused with the Maruzat, discussed above) published just a few years ago in a semi-scholarly edition. In general, Ebu Suud's collection compares unfavorably with the later collections, which seem larger, richer in material, more varied, and more interesting.

The first question that I wish to discuss is this: what was the relation of the şeyhülislams to the penal law prevalent in the central area of the empire in the seventeenth and eighteenth centuries? It is sometimes alleged in connection with these şeyhülislams that they failed in their collections to take notice of the kanun and dealt merely with shari`a penal code. This is not entirely the case. It is true that the term kanun is not found in penal contexts—an omission that unquestionably expresses some resentment toward the kanun. But it nevertheless seems that the collections reflect judicial reality, which as we have seen was mainly based on the shari`a, although it included also elements from the kanun. Let us consider some examples. When dealing with hudud matters such as theft, false accusation of fornication, and wine drinking, the fetva collections invariably prescribe the Islamic penalties without any departure from the norm.[48] Highway robbery, too, is always punished by the canonical penalty of cutting off a hand and a leg.[49] Noteworthy is the treatment of zina (fornication), in view of the unusually severe penalty imposed on violators. And yet the muftis invariably prescribe the penalty of death by stoning in cases in which the lawbreaker is a muhsan (one who is or has been married).[50] As noted earlier, in seventeenth-century Bursa the actual treatment of violators of this law—invariably prostitutes—was much more lenient, and it does therefore seem possible that on this extreme point the *muftis* were expressing somewhat theoretical views. It is also possible that prostitutes were taken somewhat less seriously than other people. The *fetva* collections deal quite extensively with cases of murder; they invariably prescribe the penalty of *kisas*.[51]

The problem known in *shari`a* codes as *kasama*—that is, the swearing by a group of people that they had nothing to do with the killing of a person whose body has been found in the neighborhood—is treated in the *fetva* collections exactly as it is in the *shari`a* manuals. This law holds the people of the vicinity responsible for blood money even if they are able to exonerate themselves of the more serious charge of murder. I have previously shown that Ebu Suud Efendi innovated in this area by ruling that when a body was found in a rented house, the lessee rather than the owner was responsible for the blood money. All relevant cases appearing in the *fetva* collections go by the new rule laid down by Ebu Suud.[52] Neither in the *fetva* collections nor in the court records of the area under study is there any trace of the early *kanun* insistence on the absolute obligation of the people of the neighborhood to find the culprit at all cost; such traces were found in eighteenth-century Aleppo (a point I will discuss later).

A very unusual and rare kind of punishment found in the *fetva* collections is *teşhir*, exposure to public ignominy, specified both in the *shari`a* manuals and in the *fetva* collections only in connection with false witnessing.[53]

A large number of *fetva*s deal with serious violations that are not, strictly speaking, *hudud* in the technical sense because *hudud* covered only five specified types of crimes. In one unusual example, Abdallah Efendi Yenişehiri relates a story about a Muslim village whose inhabitants one day in the year held a festival and picnic where men and women gathered together without any segregation, disregarding the prohibitions against such behavior (a prohibition that, by the way, seems to lack legal basis in *shari`a* manuals). Asked to name an appropriate penalty, the *mufti* replied that the violation is indeed a grave one, to be punished by *tazir şadid*—that is, strong discretionary punishment to be decided by the *kadi*.[54] Other violations in this more or less residual category were curses by ordinary citizens against *ulema*, curses against ordinary citizens involving allegations of disbelief, etc.[55]

An important and interesting chapter that appears in only one *fetva* collection (that of Abdulrahim Efendi) deals with one kind of homicide that does not entail penal responsibility: when a man discovers his wife in the act of adultery and kills her or her accomplice. In all such cases the *mufti* exonerates the husband from any responsibility if he swears the woman was a voluntary participant in the affair.[56]

Were the *mufti*s in all these cases applying the *shari`a* or the *kanun*? It is impossible to answer this question because, as noted earlier, in all these cases the *shari`a* was integrated into the structure of the *kanun*. A *mufti* might have had in mind merely the *shari`a*, but he was nevertheless stating the legal situation also according to the *kanun*. It might be claimed here that if they were also thinking in terms of the *kanun* the *mufti*s might have imposed additional penalties that were specific to the *kanun*—which they never did—and this is probably meaningful. But the *kanun* is there. And it is possible to push elucidation of this point a little further if we recall that one section of the so-called penal law current in the area under study was specifically an addition of the *kanun* to the *shari`a*. This section is the one connected with the concept of *sai bil' fesad*, habitual criminality, even if the nature of the crime is not of the utmost gravity. We have seen previously that this part of the *kanun* did not fall into abeyance after the sixteenth century.

The *fetva* collections show that Grand Muftis of the seventeenth and eighteenth centuries were fully aware of the concept of *sai bil' fesad* and that they, too, saw it as part and parcel of the current penal law, non-*shari`a* in origin though it may have been. Thus one *fetva* speaks about Zeyd, *şaki* and *reis-i eşkiya* (robber and leader of robbers), something he used to do habitually, which made him a *sai bil' fesad*, fomentor of evil in the world. The *mufti* prescribed for him the death penalty in this case, although by the *shari`a* the man deserved to be punished only by cutting off a hand and a leg.[57] A number of *fetva*s explicitly and specifically emphasize the fact that *adet-i mustamirre*, a continuous habit, was important in deciding the penalty. Declaring a culprit *sai bil' fesad* invariably entailed the death penalty, even for relatively light offenses.

In most such cases the *mufti* would add that the accused was to be put to death by order of the sovereign.[58] This does not to my mind mean that the *mufti* disclaimed responsibility for the verdict, the matter not being a *shari`a* affair in the strict sense. (We have seen that the *kadi* of Bursa in the seventeenth century passed the death penalty in such cases with equanimity.) To my mind the order of the sovereign was merely mentioned because most, if not all, of these *fetva*s were probably put to the *mufti* by the central government itself, which had apprehended a well-known criminal that it wished to put to death in a legal fashion. Other cases may have been put to the *mufti* by judges in remote places.

There are some other examples of cases that led Ottoman *mufti*s to admit new solutions to the *shari`a*. For example, a group of violations is mentioned by the sources that, strictly speaking are not deserving of punishment in Islamic ethics because they are not so much as mentioned by the *shari`a* manuals, but Ottoman sensitivity viewed them in a completely different light. One such major category in the *fetva* collections is the forging of money. It is not surprising that in a bureaucratic state like the Ottoman Empire the official coin was considered one of the most sacrosanct emblems of authority and sovereignty. Coin forgery became an issue particularly after the end of the sixteenth century, when the Ottomans opted to solve a major monetary crisis by issuing debased coins (that is coins containing less silver than they had contained previously and that the public assumed was contained in them). Such an operation managed to deceive the public for a short while only and frequently resulted in severe riots, often by soldiers who received their pay in these debased coins. Obviously in such circumstances coin forgery was perceived as a particularly severe crime; and because it was widely practiced, there are quite a few *fetva*s relating to it. One such *fetva* is of particular importance, for in it the *mufti*, Feyzullah Efendi, goes to great lengths to detail his feelings concerning the legal problems entailed in the issue.[59] The question posed to him is about a man who has forged Ottoman coins, thereby cheating the citizens and causing losses to the treasury. The question is whether it is legal for the sovereign to order the execution of this man. Rather than giving the usual and expected affirmative answer, Feyzullah Efendi launches on a detailed exposition that is surprising for its sensitivity to the fine points of law. He says he has searched the law manuals and found nothing whatsoever on money forgery. Consequently, it is impossible for him to issue a *fetva* authorizing the execution of a money forger. However, because the offense is unquestionably despicable, if the sultan wishes to issue a death warrant, there is no harm in it (*be's yoktur*).[60]

Such a disclaimer is completely missing from other similar *fetva*s,[61] as well as from *fetva*s dealing with other grave cases not dealt with in the classical *shari`a* manuals. An example is the case of a person said to have leased from the government the right to collect a certain tax. This man extorted money from the people "illegally and against the [sultanic] order." The *mufti* unhesitatingly authorized execution.[62] The same *mufti* was asked whether it was permissible to put to death a person involved in sorcery and here too his answer was in the affirmative.[63] Most cases in this category involved abhorrent versions of more ordinary crimes. An example is a robber who, when ordered to come to court to face charges, attacked the court and beat the *kadi*, a crime declared deserving of the death penalty.[64] In another example two robbers broke into a house and took property but also raped and injured the woman living there. They, too, were said to deserve the death penalty *siyaseten*—that is, by the administrative justice of the sovereign.[65] A further example is a man who sodomized and then killed a seven-year-old boy. He, too, was said to deserve being put to death *siyaseten*, thereby overruling the *shari`a* law permitting the boy's next of kin to commute the death penalty by accepting blood money.[66]

The importance of this whole point (seeing as particularly abhorrent acts that were not so treated by the *shari`a*) goes much beyond the formal aim of the previous analysis. Basically this point disproves the claim that Islamic law did not know the concept of theoretical principles. True, the law did not know what to do with a new kind of social behavior considered gravely immoral. But the concepts of *tazir* (discretionary punishment) and *siyasa* (administrative justice) were serviceable substitutes ready at hand. Effectively, there was an addition to the body of what we may call classical *hudud*.[67]

My enumeration of the fields of law covered by the *fetva* collections is intended to show the far-reaching match existing between them and the real law of the courts, as well as to point out that this law was basically eclectic, with the *shari`a* playing the leading role, though without the disappearance of the *kanun*.

Another topic I would like to analyze, which concerns the opinions of *şeyhülislam*s, is that of interest taking. We have seen that interest charging was a major innovation in Ottoman law, albeit an undeclared one. To be more exact, it made its way into Ottoman law after becoming a major component of the economic activity of Ottoman towns and cities in the area of this study. Thus, in seventeenth-century Bursa most people were involved in credit relations, for the most part based on interest charging, and it made little difference whether it was rich or poor man. Moreover, seventeenth-century Bursa included an important social group of professional moneylenders, people who had in their estates long lists of debtors. To top all this, Bursa had one type of *waqf* institution entirely devoted to supplying credit to the public. This is nothing less than a primitive banking institution. A survey register from the second half of the seventeenth century showed over 250 institutions of that type in a town of some thirty thousand inhabitants. Let us look at the legal aspect of the institution. Interest-bearing loans took several practical forms, of which the most widespread was the so called *istiğlal*, a concept extant in classical Islamic law with a completely different meaning.[68] In the present context, *istiğlal* means a loan containing several additional components. When a man received a loan, he immediately sold his house to the creditor—usually an endowment, but not necessarily so—whereupon the new owner leased the same house to the borrower for a year. If the creditor repaid his loan after a year, he could reclaim his house; if he failed to do so, the parties might continue with the lease or the house could be sold on the free market and the loan be repaid from the proceeds of the sale. (see the discussion of *istiğlal* in chapter 1). From this it is clear that the sale was really a form of collateral and the lease a means of concealing the interest involved in the transaction. Thus, the *istiğlal* was really nothing other than the traditional legal device, *hila*, to conceal an interest-bearing loan in classical Islam. But it must be borne in mind that in the Ottoman case the discussion of *istiğlal* and similar topics was not relegated to specialized literary genres, clearly secondary from a legal ideological point of view. They were dealt with by the most important scholars and in the most highly esteemed *shari`a* books. Within these books themselves these topics are dealt with as ordinary organizing chapters of the *shari`a*. All this seems to be a far cry from the status of *hila* literature in classical Islam.[69]

Furthermore, we must recall that the whole institution of cash *waqf* in the Ottoman Empire was based on interest charging that was direct, not concealed: the foundation documents of such institutions never use roundabout terms but always specify that the money is to be given out on interest, using the terms *muamele, istirbah,* or *murabaha*. These terms existed also in classical Islamic law but usually with completely different meanings; Ottoman society simply borrowed and adapted them to a new use.[70] The Ottomans' use of obscure terms to denote interest charging may indicate that they had a bad conscience about this practice; nevertheless, the documents are lucid and specific, clearly stipulating the exact annual percentage that a certain loan was supposed to fetch. Whatever the term used, a more explicit mode to describe interest charging cannot be envisaged.

What did the Ottomans have to say about the institution of cash *waqf* from an ideological legal point of view? The issue exploded in the sixteenth century in a very heated public controversy involving the law and Islamic morality, in which the most illustrious religious scholars of the land took part. The approach taken in this debate by the scholars close to power reveals something of the Ottoman center's approach to the law as a discourse. The whole controversy was researched by Jon Mandeville, whose excellent study is the basis of what follows.[71]

To begin with, a somewhat disturbing point in this controversy is that it was not conducted about the issue of interest charging but about the apparent side issue of the legality of the cash *waqf* itself. A very basic rule of the law of *waqf* in Islam is the durability of the property endowed; hence, the ancient objection to moveable property—for example, money—as *waqf*. Interest as such is mentioned only in passing, at the very end of the last verbal exchange. The solution may lie in the fact that for the people of the sixteenth century, religious endowments were no less central to their lives than interest-bearing loans; and because endowments were the logical prior issue, they debated over that issue—the cash *waqf*. They evidently knew that cash *waqf* and interest charging were Siamese twins: no such *waqf* could exist without interest; how else would such an institution secure income that could be spent? The cash *waqf* is apparently a socioeconomic innovation of the Ottoman period—it makes its first appearance in documents of the fifteenth century. It then grows slowly to become during the sixteenth century more important than other types of *waqf*. There is no question but that the top Ottoman *ulema* knew about the rise of the institution because founding deeds came for confirmation before these people as *kadis* of Istanbul.[72]

Such was the situation until the mid-sixteenth century, when an important scholar brought the issue to a head by issuing a *fetva* declaring the institution illegal. The *şeyhülislam* of the day, the famous Ebu Suud Efendi, immediately replied with a *fetva* of his own, which read in part: "Although the citations of books seem to be against the permissibility of akce and filuri [types of coins] awqaf [endowments], it is also well known which sources of these books are true and sound. It is recognized absolutely that throughout the lands of the provinces of Rum cash waqf is popular and generally practiced, that most of the awqaf of mosques and welfare establishments are based on cash, that judges past and present relying on the aforementioned citations have ruled in favor of its permissibility, that up till now military judges and provincial governors have been ruling in favor of its validity and irrevocability, and no one has spoken out against this. The practice is perfectly sound and irrevocable."[73]

This is, of course, an amazing explanation in the context of a society based on a relatively rigid code of legality and ethics. What Ebu Suud proposes here is to accept the permissibility of a certain mode of behavior merely because a large number of people engage in it. And Ebu Suud was not alone in holding such incredibly liberal opinions. A letter of a Sufi scholar from the same period contains a very similar opinion and points out very explicitly that the institution is extremely popular and most charity institutions in the empire are based on it: "We were asked by two muftis about the cash waqf; one had permitted it, one had not. We followed admissibility, because it better suited the conditions of the people of our time in their religious and worldly affairs, as well as the opinions of the majority of the scholars of the time and their predecessors."[74] A *fetva* by the sixteenth-century *şeyhülislam* Ibn Kemal, cited by Omer Lutfi Barkan, asks what is to be done about a person who claims that all forms of hidden interest charging are no better than the deceiving of God. The *mufti* retorts that such a man deserves severe punishment, in the form of *tecdid-i iman*, or renewal of faith, a punishment proper for violations that border on heresy.[75] The only way to interpret such a severe stand toward a seemingly naive, religiously motivated opinion is that it was apparently very dangerous: it might lay a tremendous burden of guilt on people about being bad Muslims. Alternatively, it might lead to a reduction in the volume of credit, thereby causing harm to many people—including the *ulema* themselves—by damaging the economic status of the religious endowments. I for my part do not think that we should lay too much stress on the cynical or materialist explanation: that the pragmatic approach of the *ulema* was merely designed to protect their own economic interests. It seems to me that the cultural argument is more weighty—that religious endowments, among them cash *waqf*s, constituted the backbone of Ottoman civilization, to the extent that any potential harm to these institutions was viewed with horror. Why these institutions were so important to this civilization is a puzzle I intend to address in another study. It was by no means only the *ulema* who depended on these institutions, both materially and spiritually.

The importance of these views lies in their being opinions of the overwhelming majority of scholars—indicating that eminent Ottoman religious leaders in the sixteenth century were not primarily detached religious theoreticians, but men of state with public and societal responsibilities and commitments. It will be interesting now to find out how the *şeyhülislam*s of the seventeenth and eighteenth centuries related to this problem. Because this is the so-called period of decline, one might expect that the highly pragmatic approach current in the sixteenth century would give way to a more rigidly ideological approach. However, nothing of the sort seems to have happened. And, as I shall argue later, this is just another weak point in the whole decline theory.

But to come back to the *fetva*s about credit relations in the collections under study. As it turns out, questions on interest and interest-bearing loans take pride of place in the collections; they are by no means hidden away in a chance question. Some of the collections even devote special chapters to this topic. These chapters are sometime misleadingly small: if we take into consideration all the credit documents scattered in the collections, their number is quite large. The *istiğlal* type of loan, which was the main mode of linking cash *waqf*s and clients, appears very frequently in the collections. Thus, in one *fetva* we hear of Zeyd who gave Amr a loan of one thousand piasters, in exchange for which Amr sold him his house in *istiğlal* and immediately leased it back from him. After a while there was a fire, and the value of the house was reduced. Who is to bear the damage caused? The answer is that the damage is to be borne by the lender, who was during that year the legal owner of the house.[76] This type of loan, along with its special name, appears in scores of *fetva*s, and there is no doubt that both *kadi*s and *mufti*s knew it was a veil behind which interest charging was hidden.[77] They therefore must also have known that the "sale" in these transactions was in effect fictitious. Nevertheless, a transaction has to be kept to the letter, whatever the substance behind it.

This is a feature supposed by Weber to be entirely missing from Islamic law. Yet it is the approach of Ottoman *şeyhülislam*s to the *istiğlal* type of contract. And this is just another good example of the high degree of legalism detectable in Ottoman law. Several *fetvas* reveal that because the sale was not a real one, people had the tendency to skip some semi-ceremonial parts of the sale that were obligatory according to Islamic law—for example, the actual physical handing over and receiving of the object sold. A number of *fetvas* reveal that in the eyes of the *muftis* such omissions invalidated the entire transaction, thereby also showing that the exact letter of the law, not just or even mainly the social relations behind it, was crucially important for them.[78]

The *istiğlal* is still within the bounds of the traditional *hila* literature. Yet in many *fetvas* the cash *waqf* and the interest are fully described. I found only one question dealing squarely with the legality of the institution itself.[79] Other relevant *fetvas* deal with specific points within the institution. This is a typical *fetva*: "Can Zeyd, the manager of a cash *waqf*, the [founding deed of which] stipulates that the money will be given for interest (*istirbah*) of 10 percent, give it with interest of 15 percent, with the consent of the *kadi*, if the economic status of the institution has weakened? Answer: He can."[80] Although this document uses the term *istirbah* instead of the more genuine *riba*, *istirbah* is almost as direct a term—again, when read in the context of what these people were saying about it. And on the whole it is quite clear that interest is here described without any effort to hide it, whether by financial trickery or language juggling. The founders of cash *waqfs* were often cautious people, who entered into the founding deeds all sorts of security measures to prevent loss of their *waqf*. The outcome is a large number of *fetvas* where the subject is an allegation of mismanagement of *waqf* funds. Thus, it was charged in the case of one manager who had lost *waqf* money that he was supposed to lend the money in the presence of witnesses, which he had failed to do. As an outcome, he was made responsible for the loss and asked to pay for it out of his own pocket.[81] In another case the manager was charged with violating the founder's stipulation that the money should be lent only on the basis of surety and collateral.[82] It is evident, then, that the approach of the *muftis* to the cash *waqf* and to the interest embedded in it continued in the seventeenth and eighteenth centuries to be as pragmatic and liberal as before.

One particularly important *fetva* that can be cited in support of this conclusion comes from the eighteenth century, and it reads:

Zeyd, who is a self-styled scholar in a town, claims that cash *waqf* is religiously forbidden (*haram*) and that those who establish them will go to hell, and that profit (*rabh*) accruing from a loan (*devir*) is forbidden, and he prevents those who take [such profits] from praying in the mosque. Consequently, there is fear that most mosques in this town will be deserted and that commotion and disorder (*ihtilal*) will take place among the people and that words such as these may cause a civil war (*fitna*). What is to be done about Zeyd?

The *mufti* answered this question by saying such a man must be strongly reprimanded and ordered to desist. If he does not comply, he is to be put in jail until he does.[83] That the institution of cash *waqf* was still so popular in the mid-eighteenth century is in itself quite remarkable. It may well be that rather than declining, the credit institutions of the Ottoman Empire developed even further in the eighteenth century. But for our purposes the more important point in this *fetva* is that we see the same view as the one evinced by Ebu Suud in the sixteenth century: in the minds of the Grand Muftis the highest priority is that of public order and tranquillity. It is the approach of an imperial bureaucracy in charge of law and order; it is not purely the theoretical view of the *madrasa*, but the pragmatic view of the politicians and bureaucrats of the forum. So it is still true in the eighteenth century that the most important aspect of the high Ottoman *ulema*'s social identity is that of public duty. Is it too fanciful to sense here far-off signs of nineteenth-century developments, when the *ulema* would be more or less with the government rather than fighting reforms to the bitter end?

While the *muftis'* liberal approach to interest-bearing loans can certainly be seen as part of their pragmatic approach to questions of customary law—in itself to be interpreted as evincing political responsibility by a group forming part of the state's bureaucracy—it is also a simple enforcing of the *kanun*. We can recall that the *kanun* of Süleyman contained an article laying down that it is illegal to charge interest of more than 10 percent.[84] This *kanun* is sometimes reflected in the *fetva* collections. Thus, a *fetva* of the seventeenth-century *şeyhülislam* Minkarizade says: "While an imperial order has been issued to the effect that no money is to be given in an interest-bearing loan (*muamele*) with an interest of more than 15 percent, what is to be done to someone doing this?" (The *mufti*'s answer was that such a man had to be severely reprimanded).[85]

It is quite evident that the sultan in such an order merely extended the Süleymanic *kanun*. Such a general order may, in fact, be seen as *kanun*.[86] It can also be viewed in terms of the anthropological model used in this study: while permitting interest is a clear and major case of bargaining and negotiation in the creation of the typical Ottoman law of the eighteenth century, it is at the same time probably a derivation of formal, imposed law—not in itself an arbitrary invention but giving in to pressures from below.

It may be of some interest to compare the credit institution in the Ottoman Empire with that in classical Islam, not only because every possible comparison is important, but because it is known that credit institutions at the height of classical Islam were unusually developed. When one reads A. Udovitch's study on this topic, one gets the impression that in no other period in the premodern Middle East were these institutions as advanced.[87] At the top of this financial system we find international merchants who handled large-scale commerce, accepted money deposits, and issued letters of exchange that could be cashed in other cities. This is very close to full-fledged banking and far beyond the sophistication of the financial system in the Ottoman Empire, in which even *mudaraba* partnerships (designed to serve in international commerce) were very simple and usually local in nature.

But when it came to interest-bearing loans, the Ottoman Empire far surpassed classical Islam. Despite the development of commerce and finance, interest remained well below the ground in classical Islam. It was hidden mainly in agreements on higher prices for delayed payment, a transaction against which Islamic law has no recourse. Udovitch comments that "suppression of open interest was considerable."[88] Yet we have seen that nothing of the kind took place in the Ottoman Empire. How are we to interpret the paradox? I hazard the explanation that Ottoman society was more bureaucratic than Near Eastern society in classical Islam—more bureaucratic in the sense of being based less on communal, face-to-face relations. It is noteworthy that Udovitch has suggested that the prohibition on interest arose in social circumstances featuring close personal ties and long-standing intimacy between members.[89] He has shown that medieval Islamic society banned interest for deep cultural and societal reasons. In economic relations this meant an abhorrence of aggression, unfairness, and discord; and interest symbolized just that, because it introduced an element of inequality between the parties. If a society based on interest-free trade is socially characterized by localism, personal acquaintance, and kinshiplike relations, then I suggest that a society that freely featured interest charging had substantially fewer of these qualities. But again, I assign much importance to the tremendous place in Ottoman society of sultanic *waqf*s and other large *waqf*s, providers of charity on a grand scale to the urban population as well as focal points for a bureaucratic type of patronage.[90] If this is correct, it is a surprising first hint that the Ottoman political decision-making mechanism was, after all, open to influences from the business world.

Another legal area in which practical needs forced Ottoman high *ulema* to go along with the public in relaxing the initial rigidity of the *shari`a* is the law of *waqf*—or, more precisely, the law relating to the leasing of *waqf* real estate. It is only a realization of the extreme importance of the *waqf* institution in Ottoman society that makes me dwell on this seemingly minor issue. Such a realization may be gained first of all from the empirical fact that a great deal of the activity that went on, for example, in the Bursa *kadi* court in the seventeenth century was connected in one way or the other with the *waqf* institution. It is also indicative that in both *fetva* collections of the *şeyhülislam*s and in edited collections of *sicill* documents (*sakk mecmuasî*) the largest amount of space is devoted to the *waqf*. All this cannot be fortuitous; the *waqf* was evidently one of the central and most characteristic institutions of Ottoman society; hence, leasing *waqf* real estate was a law of high visibility.

Waqf is a religious endowment, a piece of property whose ownership is, in principle and law, endowed to God and that cannot therefore be permanently alienated—hence also the sensitivity of classical Islamic law concerning the leasing of such property and its limitation of leases to one year only. Yet in the course of Ottoman history strong forces developed that exerted pressures to relax this basic limitation. The law yielded, and this is another major case of a compromise between Islamic law and practical life in that state, another clear case of negotiation in making this law.

One version that purports to explain how the new law of *waqf* came about—and it may or may not be factually true—claims that it happened at the beginning of the seventeenth century, when Istanbul underwent a period of huge fires that consumed a great deal of the city's wooden houses. A large number of *waqf*s remained propertyless and with no means of renovation. Recourse had to be had to private investors, who could hardly be expected to invest large sums in properties they could lease for only one year. It was necessary to bend the rules a little in order to allow these potential investors to enjoy the fruits of their investments, and this is apparently how long-term rent, also called double rent, *icarateyn*, came into being.[91] In this kind of rent a lessee would lease the property in a long-term rental that involved two types of payment: a large initial sum at the beginning that was a sort of down payment, and then a small sum every month. If there were renovations to be made, the lessee would undertake to carry them at his own expense and deduct the sum from the down payment or the monthly rent. In fact, in the law that developed, it was considered incumbent on the lessee to carry out renovations, and the *waqf* manager had the right to evict him if he failed to do this.[92]

Leasing by *icarateyn* not only meant a long-term lease; it also meant that the lessee could pass on the property as inheritance to his sons. In this way, of course, it paved the way for what has been called the dismemberment of *waqf*s, although there are no real indications that such a major dismemberment took place in the central area of the Ottoman Empire; when in the nineteenth century the Ottoman state proceeded to dismantle the *waqf* institution, there seemed to be no shortage of large-scale institutions to be dismantled.[93] In any event, the *waqf* system could not do without the long-term rent, and *kadi* court records—for example, those of seventeenth-century Bursa—show that it became the major mode of leasing *waqf* properties. Hence, it is interesting to observe how the *şeyhülislam*s, repositories of Islamic ethics and law, viewed the matter.

A review of the chapters on *waqf* in the *fetva* collections shows that the *şeyhülislam*s accepted the long-term lease as part of the general scheme of things and did not raise fundamental questions about it.[94] They rather dealt with its various legal peculiarities. One such peculiarity—perhaps arising out of a bad conscience over the whole issue—concerned the limited right of inheritance of *icarateyn* properties. They were not subject to regular laws of inheritance and could be inherited only by children. Other heirs had no right to this part of the estate of the deceased, and a large number of *fetva*s show that this limitation was rather effective.[95] If the lessee had heirs other than children, the property reverted to the *waqf*. But in such cases a major legal issue arose because there was the likelihood that part of the investment in rebuilding or renovation was as yet unpaid by the *waqf* at the time of death. These investments were, of course, regular property belonging to all the heirs, and hence fertile ground for very complicated legal accounting of rights.[96] For us the important point is that the legal system under study was able to adapt itself and to adopt necessary innovations, even when these were against the basic design of Islamic law. Here, too, is additional proof that this legal system was at times based on refined legal distinctions that were adhered to precisely.

Another non-*shari`a* matter that appears in the *fetva* collections and that deserves to be mentioned at least briefly is the statute of limitation, which appears as a special chapter in all the *fetva* collections. All, without exception, affirm that the law as phrased by Ebu Suud Efendi in the sixteenth century became universally applicable.[97] We have seen that the *muftis* did not refrain from dealing with areas of law not forming part of the *shari`a* as traditionally understood. The *muftis* did this with equanimity and with excellent knowledge of extra-*shari`a* bodies of law. Both these points indicate that they viewed themselves as part of the state bureaucracy in charge of enforcing the law. But an interesting question about their intellectual and spiritual world that has so far remained undiscussed is, what were their opinions concerning the *kanun*? The truth is that there are very few references to this question in the collections; nevertheless, those that exist deserve a closer look. That the *muftis* accepted the *kanun* at least in part there is no doubt: all the collections contain chapters on the land law of the empire based entirely on the *kanun*. In this field there is no question of any decline of the *kanun*. But I suggest that land is culturally of secondary importance, less likely to give rise to strong emotions than criminal law or interest charging. So what about implicit references to the *kanun* in these more sensitive areas?

Despite the prevailing opinion that the *kanun* is not mentioned explicitly in the *fetva* collections, careful reading may yield a few such references. In the first place, as noted earlier, the *fetvas* sometimes use the term *sultanic order* as a substitute for *kanun*. Thus, one question asks about Zeyd, a fiefholder: does he have a right, after levying the traditional tithe on his peasants, to levy on them also the *çift* tax, which had been collected as of old, "according to the order and the register (*defter*)."[98] I doubt that an effort is being made here to avoid mentioning the word *kanun*. Apparently *sultanic order* was perceived as synonymous with the *kanun*. That the term *kanun* is never mentioned in the penal sections of the collections is easily attributable to the fact that in practice the current law was a mixture dominated by elements emanating from the *shari`a*, so possibly there was no objective need to mention the *kanun*.

There is, however, an interesting group of *fetva*s in which the *mufti*s do take on the *kanun* as an ideological problem, and these *fetva*s show that the extra- *shari`a* laws, including the *kanun*, were accepted implicitly, though probably somewhat grudgingly. In a head-on encounter the *shari`a* remained formally undisputed. Thus, in one *fetva* we read about a person who, when summoned to the *shari`a* court, retorted, "As long as the *kanun* exists, the *shari`a* has no place among us; let us deal with it according to the *kanun*."⁹⁹ Asked what to do with such a person, the *mufti* replied that this was a violation worthy of "renewal of faith"—that is, a grave religious offense. In another *fetva* the same *mufti* was asked about a group of people who said: "We do not recognize the *shari`a*; our *shari`a* is the governor of Alexandria."¹⁰⁰ Again the same punishment was meted out. An unmistakable resentment of *şeyhülislam*s against military governors is detectable in these documents, probably born of the natural competition between them over rights of jurisdiction—in the final analysis, over their respective places in the polity. This resentment in fact finds expression in a variety of *fetva*s. In one case we read about Zeyd, a *subaşı*, or chief of police, who beat a non-Muslim villager to death with a stick. The *mufti* reasons that the *subaşı* should be put to death by retaliation—that is like an ordinary murderer.¹⁰¹ In another case a man denounced someone to the authorities (*ehl-i örf*), believing it was he who stole things from his house but without real evidence to that effect. The officials then tortured the suspect so that he lost an eye. Asked if the denouncer was liable to punishment, the *mufti* answered in the affirmative.¹⁰²

All these and similar cases do seem to reflect a strong stand of the high *ulema* in defense of the *shari`a* itself and the position of the religious scholars as the sole upholders and enforcers of the law in the Ottoman Empire. Evidently, their approach is motivated by class position no less than by a pure cultural stand. But it is also indicative that *mufti*s could attack lay bureaucrats without fear of reprisal from the central government. I interpret this as an indication that in the minds of Ottomans living in the seventeenth and eighteenth centuries there was no association between officials and "the government." To my mind these opinions also support the thesis of *ulema* superiority in legal matters in this period:

there would be no point in fighting against a predominant opposite trend.

To conclude, this chapter has sought to find out whether there was a match between the semi-official statement of the law as pronounced by the *şeyhülislams* and the law as practiced by the law courts. And we have seen that this match was indeed far-reaching, enhancing my argument that the imposed element in Ottoman law was quite strong. It was not in any sense solely an imposed law because, as we have seen, there were crucially important elements that were plainly negotiated, such as the law of interest. But once negotiated, these new laws functioned rather coherently; there were no fresh negotiations each time. In the process of adjudication, the element of legalism is the predominant one.

This chapter has also shown that Islamic law under the Ottoman Empire was far from frozen and immutable. It was not merely the courts that accepted and adapted new solutions to legal problems, but also the religious scholars, guardians of the sacred law of Islam. While they were not raising the banner of change for the sake of change, they did not try to conceal new solutions in little publicized books intended for the expert. Nor did they seem to apologize for their need to come to grips with circumstances beyond their control. To my mind they seem to convey the impression that they lacked any inhibition whatsoever about these changes. I rather suspect that their supposed inhibition about introduction of changes may well be—to some extent at least—the creation of modern Western scholarship.

4. THE GUILDS AND CUSTOMARY LAW

SO FAR I have talked about *shari`a* and *kanun* as the basic elements in the Ottoman legal system. The discussion would not, however, be complete without taking stock of a major additional component that is based on entirely different considerations and principles yet constitutes as vital a part of Ottoman law. The main argument of this chapter is that guild law was not handed down by the Ottoman government to the populace; rather, in this field the Ottomans allowed a substantial measure of social and legal autonomy. The argument put forward here is that guild law was the one major component of Ottoman law that was not either imposed from above or by way of a sacred tradition.

This point is also important to my general argument for another reason: in the approach to guilds lies proof that the Ottoman approach to the civil society fell a great deal short of sultanism—which is characterized by suffocation, strangulation, and total centralization. This approach was, in fact, much more benign, much closer to the Weberian model of bureaucracy. My argument concerning the Ottoman guilds tends in this respect to concur with that of Halil Inalcik.[1] But to place this topic within the framework of my anthropological discussion, I must point out that though guild law was a product of the law as process, the Ottoman court related to it as imposed law. There was no free-floating bargaining; rather, the court made an effort to get to the bottom of past relations and rights. It never made any effort to mediate between guilds, only to find out which one of them was legally right.

In a way, guild law is the ultimate affirmation of the thesis I am trying to put forward in this study. It was plainly not handed down by the government (I hope to be able to establish this point); yet when it came to adjudication, it was applied as an imposed law. I interpret this as indicating that the tendency to legalism and formalism in Ottoman law was not in itself an imposition from above so much as a societal characteristic, a feature I shall analyze more fully in the next chapter. But let us look at the evidence.[2]

The point of departure for examining the Ottoman guild system was my investigation of the *kadi* court records of seventeenth-century Bursa.[3] The picture that emerges from the documents relating to that city is one of a quite autonomous guild system. The rules connected with the guild system tended to be attributed by all the parties involved to the old customary law of the city, never to a rule or set of rules ordained from above by the government. The involvement of the central government in the guild system was clearly seen as derivative, the government having been merely co-opted into involvement by the artisans themselves. Some of the guild rules that I found in Bursa were freely invented by guild members, but mostly the situation seems to have been somewhat more complicated. Guild rules, while emanating from the people themselves, were said to be legally binding because they existed as of old. Sometimes a rule was convenient to one guild but not to another. While such a rule was certainly not the outcome of the second guild's free invention, that guild nevertheless could not change it; for again, the rule was an outgrowth of the old customary law of the city. The interesting point is that this sacredness of the old and customary was not merely a sociopsychological tendency among the common people; the Ottoman government itself and the *kadi*s, too, subscribed to it and saw in it a totally binding legal norm. Indeed, judging by the case of Bursa, one is forced to the conclusion that Ottoman society was saturated from top to bottom by a sociopsychological ethos that may be termed a customary law mentality. There can be no doubt that in Bursa the entire guild system rested on this foundation.

When we turn our eyes away from Bursa, the first distinct point that we find difficult to reconcile with a theory of tight govermental control over the process of guild creation and functioning is the extreme heterogeneity existing in the Ottoman guild system. In various cities we find different names for the officeholders.

While the guilds of Bursa were closely connected with matters of taxation, those of Istanbul had nothing whatsoever to do with taxation;[4] consequently, the extremely complex institutional arrangements that developed in Bursa to handle tax problems were totally absent in Istanbul. Istanbul had a very elaborate and sophisticated method of controlling the number of shops in any occupation, a method called the *gedik* system, while nearby Bursa had nothing of the kind. And then we have the case of Damascus, where almost everything was again different. It seems highly unlikely that one mind was responsible for inventing such a heterogeneous guild system.

Descending from the level of generalities to some specific topics and places, the question is, to what extent were the autonomous guilds of Bursa representative or exceptional? Let us look first at the case of Ankara. One study dealing with the economic structure of that city in the early seventeenth century speaks about the "tight governmental control" under which the guild system of that city operated.[5] But this is not substantiated by any concrete examples. Investigation of the two volumes of Ankara court records that have been published reveal a very different picture.[6] In the first place, there are in these two volumes very few documents concerning guilds, which leads me to suspect that Ankara guilds were at a very low level of institutionalization. Moreover, my objection to the argument that Ankara guilds were tightly controlled is enhanced by the fact that we find in that town the same economic motive for the existence of the guilds detected in seventeenth-century Bursa. Thus, in one Ankara document we read:

> [The content of this document] is that Şah Mehmed and Haci Mehmed and others from the weavers' guild summoned [to court] Sakaoğlu Nasuh from the said guild and said in complaint: "Whenever cotton yarn comes to [town], the aforementioned arrives, pays an extra price, and takes it from its owner, and the other weavers remain deprived [of cotton yarn]. As of old, when cotton yarn came, we all bought it together. The aforementioned has now acted contrary to the old custom; we do not agree to this." The aforementioned was warned emphatically that when cotton yarn comes once more he should not buy it alone, but rather that it should be distributed among all. Whereupon the aforementioned took it upon himself to behave in the said manner.[7]

The importance of this document lies in the fact that we have here a typical guild agreement, the like of which occurs very often in the court records of seventeenth-century Bursa: a group of artisans tries to keep a certain measure of equality among their number by artificial legal means.[8] It is typical that the authority behind the legal act is not the government but the old custom. But here especially there is an additional point of interest. No mention is made of any formal guild structure; the economic function of the guild is in existence before the development of such a structure. In Bursa I never once encountered a failure to mention guild officeholders in a similar context. So in all probability we are facing an earlier stage of development of the guild system—a reasonable conclusion if we remember that Ankara was certainly much more economically backward than Bursa. The crux of this point for the purposes of the present study is that there are differences in the development of the guild system in various cities and that these differences are attributable to socioeconomic factors. Establishment of the guild system by governmental fiat should have brought about a more or less homogeneous system throughout the empire, whereas the system that actually obtains presents an extreme form of Geertzian "local knowledge."

Another locality that can profitably be drawn into the picture of the Ottoman guild system is the southern Anatolian town of Ayntab in the eighteenth century (present-day Gaziantep). C.C. Güzelbey published a number of collections of court records from this town in which guilds are quite frequently mentioned.[9] These documents portray an even greater measure of autonomy than that found in seventeenth-century Bursa. Thus, in one document we find the guild of the cotton weavers of Ayntab declaring in court, in the presence of a group of merchants (*bezirgan*), that from olden times there had been an agreement between the two guilds to the effect that the weavers should produce their fabrics in pieces of 23.5 zira each. But lately people have begun to produce in whatever fashion they like, with the result that the merchants are refusing to purchase their products. So the two guilds now declare that they are renewing their old agreement: the weavers undertake to produce fabrics only in the aforementioned measurements, and the merchants undertake to buy all the products of the weavers and through only one agent.[10]

In this agreement we have in a nutshell almost all the characteristics of the guild system that I detected in Bursa. First, we have here a free guild agreement—all its components being an expression of the free will of the artisans themselves—which is probably the most characteristic aspect of guild autonomy. Second, the production standard is attributed to the old custom, not to the government. Third, an important aspect of the document is that recourse was had to the court. It would be a mistake to see in this fact a formal state sanction of the agreement. The application to the court should be perceived in the context of the civil law. The situation is identical to that of countless cases in which we find two people coming before the *kadi*, notifying the court of a business transaction that has taken place between them involving deferred payment, and asking for a court document that will serve as a proof in the future should any problem arise. Some of the other guild documents cited in this section are also by their nature guild agreements.

Other aspects of the activity of the guilds in eighteenth-century Ayntab also indicate a situation of marked autonomy. This was certainly the case with regard to the nomination of officeholders. In one case the guild of hemp dealers declared in court that because they and the spice dealers shared some trade items, they resolved to nominate the head of the spice dealers' guild to head their own guild as well.[11]

Production standards were clearly not handed down by the government but again were the product of customary law. One document from eighteenth-century Ayntab deals with the production standards of the masons' guild. From the document it can be gauged that this was not a formally organized guild, for there is no reference to terms connected with guilds. Nevertheless, the document is a full-fledged artisan agreement in the sense specified previously. Members agreed on renewal of the old rules connected with building construction, as well as on new wage standards for hired labor. The last article of the agreement is the most interesting: the guild decided that members were to be fined thirty piasters for every contravention of the agreement. Thus, the autonomy enjoyed by this guild went so far as to have the authority to mete out punishments of its own.[12]

It seems that the authority of guilds in Ayntab to punish rule breakers—unquestionably the pinnacle of guild autonomy—was much more common than, for example, in seventeenth-century Bursa. In another Ayntab document in which a guild imposed punishments of its own, we read about the *şeyh* of the dyers' guild complaining about a fellow member who was alleged to have deceived people in matters of weights and measures. The *şeyh* demanded that this man be expelled from his shop. The court investigated the complaint, found it well based, and granted the şeyh's demand.[13] With this case we probably reach the limit of guild autonomy; meting out really serious punishments remained the prerogative of the government.

The guild system of Ayntab was similar to that of Bursa in that the guild's main function was to uphold a series of economic monopolies, all of which were an outgrowth of customary law. Thus, in a document of 1752 we find the şeyh of the cotton weavers, together with other members of the guild, complaining in court that in earlier times cotton yarn brought into Ayntab was purchased by members of that guild alone. They demanded that this old custom be enforced, and their demand was granted.[14] Another aspect of the same economic function was the distribution of raw materials. In a document of 1731 the *helva* (sesame sweet) makers claimed, and with justice, that they had always distributed among their members the raisins brought into the city for sale; but this year, somebody had purchased the entire stock available in the market. The *kadi* declared this to be contrary to the old custom and therefore illegal.[15] Similarly, in an order to the *kadi* of Ayntab in 1750 we read about a petition of the spice dealers, in which they complained about people violating their old monopoly of buying their special products in a centralized fashion through their şeyh, who later supervised its just distribution to all the members. They requested—and received—a sultanic order reaffirming this monopoly. As so often in guild matters, the government here confirmed the legal validity of the customary norm; it did not impose a norm of its own.[16] There is thus no doubt that the guild system in eighteenth-century Ayntab was as autonomous as that of seventeenth-century Bursa.

In eighteenth-century Damascus we observe a guild system not entirely dissimilar to that of Bursa.[17] There, no less than in Bursa, the customary law of the city, rather than the government, was seen as the legal basis for deciding on guild rules. In one case a tanner was forbidden to continue his occupation because he had not undergone the usual guild training. The justification for this was "custom and precedent," not a governmental law or decree.[18] In Damascus, as in Bursa, we find various restrictions on guild members (and on entire guilds) that aimed to protect the interests and privileges of other members (and other guilds)—and were justified as such in trials before the *kadi*. Thus, the tanners' guild brought a case against a tanner who worked at home rather than together with all the rest by the riverside. This was said to be harmful to the guild's interests and was forbidden as such.[19] Additionally, entire guilds in Damascus, as in Bursa, were bound to sell their products (those that constituted the raw materials of other guilds) to those other guilds at fixed prices as of old.[20] Finally, Damascus guilds were much like those of Bursa in matters of taxation. The term *yamak*, or assistant guild, so central in seventeenth-century Bursa, existed in the same sense in Damascus; and there, too, the term was connected with the payment of the army tax.[21]

It seems to me that even in Istanbul close inspection of the available documentation shows that the guild system enjoyed a wide measure of autonomy and that its legal basis was essentially customary law, not fiat from above. We might expect one of the main features of the Istanbul guild system to be to ensure total control of the city population by the totalitarian Ottoman government. For this, the guild system would have had to be all-encompassing, to include the entire artisan population of the city. But in fact, this feature never existed. Much of the material available on the guilds of Istanbul, especially that concerning the institution of *gedik*, deals almost entirely with the ways and means developed by the guilds to restrict admission into them. And there is no question that these rules and limitations were at least partially effective. Now, if the Ottoman government allowed a substantial part of the male population of Istanbul to remain outside the guild system, it must surely have thought it did not need the guilds in order to control the population. Moreover, contrary to current notions, the guilds of Istanbul, unlike even those of Bursa, did not constitute an administrative link to the government. In Bursa the government at least made use of the guilds to collect a certain tax, but not even this much was done in Istanbul. And in that sense Istanbul guilds were to a degree more autonomous than those of Bursa.

Production standards even in Istanbul were only rarely handed down by the government. An example that has survived does not really pertain to production standards in the full sense but to some ethical principles relating to the production of certain basic commodities, mainly foodstuffs.[22] In all probability, the government did not care much about the exact production processes of most products. In the documents cited by Osman Nuri, it is the guilds that complained about various violations of production standards. But the important point in all these documents is that members complained about harm being done not to state laws but to their own interests and traditional privileges.[23]

Important aspects of the guild were the rules pertaining to its head, whether he was called *kethüda* or *şeyh*. In Bursa I found that the head was elected by the members and received a formal confirmation from the *kadi*. Possibly in Istanbul the role of the government was slightly greater, but even so the measure of autonomy enjoyed by the guild was quite substantial. Although Nuri describes the *kethüda* as holding a semi-official position,[24] he adds that in most cases this officeholder was elected by the guild members themselves. This statement is followed by a number of decrees showing free appointment by the members and simple notification of this fact to the court.[25] Most interesting is a decree of 1697–98 in response to a complaint by three textile guilds. They claimed that since olden times it had been customary for them to nominate their own *kethüda* without outside intervention, but now the central government had nominated somebody over them. The sultan granted their request to regard the appointment as null and void and went on to say: "The one who has been chosen among the guild [members] themselves, [he is] to be *kethüda* with the help of the law court; even if a letter of appointment [to the contrary] has been issued by the government, it should not be acted upon."[26]

This is a document of far-reaching implications for our understanding of the legal role of the sultan and his legal relations with the civil society in the Ottoman Empire. Nor is it unique. In a document from the Vienna *Şikayet Defteri* we read about a complaint launched by the guilds of grocers and bakers. They alleged that some other guilds selling foodstuffs, who used to pay army taxes together with them, had now somehow managed to secure a sultanic order freeing them from that obligation. The plaintiff guilds asked the sultan to revoke the order as being contrary to the customary law and therefore illegal. And indeed, their claim was found to be true in principle, and the *kadi* was ordered to act accordingly.[27] While it is true, then, that the government had a certain say in *kethüda* nominations, there is also no doubt that the guild retained a wide measure of autonomy in the matter. More generally, the sultan himself admitted openly and formally that customary law (meaning here "known and established law," whatever its origin) was superior even to the sultan's order.

Some economic restrictions thought to be characteristic only of Bursa were, in fact, found in Istanbul as well. For example, in the case of the "just" distribution of raw materials and commodities among fellow members of the guild. Thus, in a document from the court records of eighteenth-century Istanbul we read of a complaint launched by the officeholders of the bottle sellers' guild of Galata against one of their number, the Jew Musa. The defendant had been importing bottles from Venice without the knowledge and involvement of the guild, something described as violating the custom of the guild. He was consequently forced by the court to relinquish the commodity to the guild.[28]

A major topic in the life of the guilds of Istanbul was the restriction of the number of independent businesses in each occupation. It is open to question whether such restrictions were in the interest of the government or of the particular guild. Government interest no doubt existed in some occupations, such as those dealing in gold and silver. When the Ottoman treasury was hard-pressed for precious metals to nourish the Ottoman mint (as very often was the case), free dealing in gold and silver was not in its interests. It is natural, therefore, that we often find in the Ottoman records severe restrictions on all kinds of dealing in gold and silver. But it seems that in the case of most other guilds the motive behind limiting the number of independent businesses was purely a guild interest. A good example of this is cited by Nuri in a document of 1786, taken from the *kadi* records of Istanbul. In it the members of the weighmasters' guild claimed that "since the occupation of Istanbul" there had been only seventeen shops in this occupation in the city, all of them in the vicinity of the wood market. They complained that a shop of this type had recently opened in another place, although there was no necessity for an additional shop.[29] Again, the prevailing rule seems to have been that laws relating to the guilds were the consequence of growth from below rather than an imposition from above.

Another economic restriction observable in Istanbul guilds was one stipulating what goods each guild could produce or sell. I believe this rule, too, had little or nothing to do with the government. In one document a declaration was made in court by two guilds producing silk fabrics: each undertook not to produce what the other guild was producing. This document was specifically referred to as a free agreement between the two guilds and hence had nothing to do with the government.[30]

One of the main findings of my study on the guild system of Bursa was the existence of guild agreements—that is, documents freely drawn up by the masters of a certain guild and specifically referred to by the members as "agreements." This is probably the epitome of guild legal autonomy because it depicts the guild as laying down rules that are, in effect, a kind of law. If a group of people is allowed to form its own law, that group is only a short step away from state recognition as a legal body. Islam, however, is well known for recognizing only individuals—or at least this is what we are often told. Be that as it may, the evidence at our disposal indicates quite clearly that Bursa was not unique in having guild agreements.

Though so near to the very nerve center of the Ottoman political system, Istanbul, too, had its guild agreements. The following guild agreement is taken from the *kadi* court record of Galata (Istanbul):

> The bearers of this document, members of the coopers' guild of Galata, their *kethüda*, Yakomo the son of Anton, and the non-Muslims so-and-so, and others, declared in court and stated their intention as follows: "Our matters and interests are [lately] in disarray in every respect and our order and organization are full of troubles and stoppages because many matters which had formerly been observed and maintained by guild members as of old, according to their customary law and habits, are not being observed and respected. We therefore made a contract and agreement and undertook a commitment (*kavl ve vifak ve misak eyledik*) to the effect that, henceforward, according to old and accepted customs of ours, when the masters of the said guild are performing works for each other for pay, they should not bring about stoppages and confusion in the work of the hiring master by doing work for another master before completing the contracted work and receiving the pay. And members of the said guild will not disrupt [their colleagues'] breadwinning by contracting work for less than the appropriate pay and less than what is customary out of wicked selfishness and vain greed and thinking evil of one another. And there should not be, on the part of apprentices and journeymen, behavior contrary to the old custom and the former habit, or the religious or state law. Should there occur on the part of apprentices and journeymen any behavior calling for discretionary punishment (*tazir*), this punishment will be carried out among the members of the said guild, according to the former custom. The apprentices

and journeymen should comply with the wishes of the masters and obey the elders."[31]

Unquestionably we have here a full-fledged guild agreement in the best tradition of seventeenth-century Bursa. Even more interesting is the fact that the guild retained the right of meting out punishment for breakers of guild rules. Such far-reaching authority was not found even in seventeenth-century Bursa. It is therefore possible that in certain respects the autonomy enjoyed by Istanbul guilds was no less than in Bursa.

One of the central points in the discussion about the Ottoman guilds is connected with the fact that in many matters the guilds had recourse to the *shari`a* court, which was, of course, the state's court. However, it seems at least partially erroneous to draw the conclusion that guilds were, as a result, drawing their entire authority from the state. The *shari`a* court was something over and above a mere state's court. It was an old and established Islamic institution, drawing its legitimacy partially from that source. When two guilds were engaged in a dispute and turned to the *kadi* for a settlement, the situation seems quite similar to the application of two modern autonomous organizations resorting to the court for a settlement. When two bodies are autonomous, a dispute between them cannot be resolved except by the intervention of a third party superior to both of them. Recourse to the court does not in itself either prove total subservience to the state or compromise the guild's independence and autonomy.

One last example affirming this picture of a generally autonomous guild system is the case of the town of Manisa in west Anatolia. Çağatay Uluçay has assembled a large collection of documents relating to that town in the seventeenth century. Many of them are guild related,[32] and several deal with the nomination of guild heads. All, without any exception, specify that it was the guild members who came to court and pointed out the man they wanted for the position; and their wish was always granted.[33] In other documents guild members of many professions declared in court that the nature of their relations was based on old customs and mutual guild agreements. In no case were such relations attributed to governmental regulation of any sort.[34]

We may conclude this topic with a summary of the points of contact that nevertheless existed between the Ottoman state and the guilds:

1. The state backed the customary law; a guild that enjoyed a privilege rooted in custom could secure a state warrant making this right a wish of the sultan.
2. The Ottoman state, especially in times of economic trouble, showed enhanced interest in the affairs of the guilds that were processing gold and silver, which were therefore much less autonomous than other guilds.
3. In times of war the state drafted artisans to its service through a tax imposed on the guilds, and it used the framework of the guilds to extract this service.
4. The Ottoman palace had connections with a substantial number of artisans, who provided it with various products throughout the year and were on the payroll of the palace on a regular basis.
5. In certain places the state used the guilds to levy taxes on the urban population.
6. The government naturally tended to be sensitive to fraud and other illegal activities on the part of artisans dealing with such basic foodstuffs as bread, meat, and the like. It is no wonder that such offenses were even entered into the nineteenth-century codes as penal violations.[35] However, it would be a mistake to view such interference on the part of the government as an interest in regulating the guild system or the urban adult population.

The restrictions the central government sometimes placed on the guilds only peripherally compromised their autonomy. If a particular city had in time of war to send a certain number of artisans to the army, the provision of labor did not thereby become the major function of the guild system. The function of the guilds was determined by what they did on a daily basis, not once in a number of years. And what they did day by day was guard their members against external encroachment on their interests and curtail internal competition as much as possible by fixing production quotas and similar restrictions.

A recent study of the production system of sixteenth-century Jerusalem is relevant in pointing at possible variants of the previous analysis, thus providing us with an all-important comparative perspective.[36] In Jerusalem we find massive involvement of the local government in the affairs of the guilds, designed to ensure an uninterrupted flow of relevant services to the city. For example, bakers and butchers were strictly forbidden to leave town even for a short while; if they wished to do so, they had to apply for permission and often had to provide a replacement.[37] Moreover, millers and bakers were made personally responsible for the uninterrupted supply of good quality bread to the populace.[38] All this was particularly true concerning the butchers' guild, which was "a corporate body formally integrated with the administrative set-up. . . . It was through this channel that the supply of meat became . . . a part of the state establishment."[39] This involvement of the government sometimes found expression in the governor's forceful nomination of the head of the butchers' guild. In 1546, the governor of Jerusalem threatened, beat, and imprisoned a rich local merchant—all in order to force him to accept the post. Such an episode is important and indicative; but no less interesting is the fact that as soon as knowledge of the nomination reached the central government it was rendered null and void, both factually and legally.[40] It must be borne in mind here that this episode relates again to particularly sensitive occupations. We know for a fact that generally the guilds in Ottoman Jerusalem were not much less autonomous than in Bursa, if at all.[41] Even so, such deep involvement of the Ottoman government in guild affairs was not found in, for example, seventeenth-century Bursa—hence, my belief that a real difference between Bursa and Jerusalem did exist. One is led to the conclusion that the distance of Jerusalem from the central government made the difference. If this is so, it neatly affirms the argument of this study that the core area of the empire was more benignly (that is, more bureaucratically) ruled than areas farther afield, mainly because the authority of the central government remained firmer there.

One may ask why the Ottoman government was willing to allow the guilds such a wide measure of autonomy. There are several possible explanations, by no means necessarily mutually exclusive. One factor here may have been a basic indifference on the part of the Ottoman government to what was happening "down below" among the simple folk, as long as no disturbance of the peace, reduction in the tax revenue, or anything of the kind occurred. This is just one part of the wider phenomenon of indifference to the affairs of the civil society, another aspect being the absence of municipalities and the services associated with them. Until well into the nineteenth century the Ottoman Empire did not have budgets for health, education, transportation, charity, or the like. A state that showed such minimal interest in the condition of the urban masses would probably not bother much about laying down detailed production standards for domestic products.

However, it is important to note also that a truly patrimonial state would not neglect such things. Matters about which the Ottoman state was watchful related mainly to state officials; it was also apprehensive about social elements—such as the provincial satraps of important families—that had the potential to develop into a landed aristocracy. The urban common people never constituted a threat to the Ottoman dynasty, so the Ottomans had no real interest in tightly regulating their way of life. A third explanation is purely cultural—the unusually deep belief prevalent in the Ottoman civilization in the absolute sacredness of the old custom. We have seen that, at least ideologically, even the sovereign himself had no right to break a custom and violate its content. The exact source of this deep belief I have not so far been able to pinpoint; but that it was there no one can doubt, nor that it very effectively limited the whimsical, unrestrained will of the ruler. It certainly constituted a major element of this society's belief system, also deeply affecting its legal attitudes in a way similar somewhat to the crucial role of the oath, as analyzed previously.

These observations are true especially for the period up to about the middle of the nineteenth century. For in the latter half of the nineteenth century the guilds suffered a considerable decline, among other reasons because of new state laws especially designed to curb the stultifying economic effect of the old guilds.[42] However, these laws were aimed at promoting economic development and more "rational" social organizations, as they came to be understood; they were definitely not aimed at reducing guild autonomy. I am talking now about a society in which one could find municipalities with budgets for services; a society with a rising bourgeois sector—one expression of which is secular intellectuals such as journalists, novelists, and poets, as well as professional army officers. The old guilds became obsolete in this social framework, and it is only natural that in due course they tended to vanish. But I believe that something deep that characterized them has survived in the society in which they were once a living reality. This was the idea of partially autonomous self-rule enjoyed by a wide range of social organizations. It may or may not be workers' organizations; it may live on also in political parties. But it is my belief that one way or the other the spirit of the guilds goes on living somewhere—otherwise history would lose much of its meaning.

5. PATRIMONIALISM AND BUREAUCRACY IN THE OTTOMAN POLITICAL SYSTEM

IN THIS CHAPTER I try to show the fit between the legal system described previously and the sociopolitical structure of which this law was a part—in other words, the way in which the law was a reflection of the political culture of the core area of the Ottoman Empire. My claim here is that there is a certain resonance between the political and legal setups. I have shown that the law was relatively well structured rather than an area of free bargaining. Here I claim that though the Ottoman Empire was a state based on faceless, bureaucratic rules, it had a clear and limited reach; it was a strong polity, but not as despotic as was usually thought.

In part I draw this conclusion from the structure of the legal system; but in this chapter I put forward some independent evidence to support this argument. My most fundamental argument is that the Ottoman political system was much more bureaucratic—that is, based on objective rules rather than being rapacious, despotic, and whimsical—than is usually thought. The theoretical framework within which I view the Ottoman case and in the context of which I am using the term *bureaucracy* is the Weberian analysis of patrimonial and bureaucratic rulership, supplemented by some modern scholars who follow in Weber's footsteps and who will be called here neo-Weberians. Although I have to qualify severely much of what Weber had to say about the Ottoman Empire, I nevertheless think that he supplied the best available theory within which to analyze this case. The fundamental political principles in the Weberian model that relate to the nature of man in general, or to archaic conditions, should not detain us here. Looking at substantial states in the past, Weber observed in them two basic forms of sociopolitical regime. The modern West was characterized by a form of domination called legal-rational. The other substantial states and empires of the past were characterized by traditional domination based on sacred sources of legitimacy; Weber called their polities patrimonial regimes. The patrimonial regime is a development of the patriarchal regime, in which the ruler is something akin to the head of a family. Patrimonial regime is patriarchal regime writ large—patriarchal regime adapted to rulership over the vast empires of Asia and Africa. But patrimonialism retains the feature of total power of the ruler over the state, akin to the total power of the patriarchal head over his family.[1] What are some of the main features of patrimonial regimes according to Weber? Their most fundamental feature is total power in the hands of the ruler. A closely related trait is complete disregard for the distinction between the official and private spheres. "The political administration, too, is treated as a purely personal affair of the ruler . . . his exercise of power is therefore entirely discretionary."[2] There are hardly rules in a patrimonial regime, just grants of favor:

> All patrimonial service regulations, which would be *reglements* according to our [bureaucratic] notions, are ultimately nothing but purely subjective rights and privileges of individuals deriving from the ruler's grant of favor; in fact, this can be said for the entire system of public norms of the patrimonial state in general. It lacks the objective norms of the bureaucratic state and its "matter-of-factness," which is oriented towards impersonal purposes.[3]

Weber recognizes further nuances within this pattern of rulership. If patrimonialism is a regime of total personal rule, it has a still stronger version, which Weber calls "sultanism" or "Oriental sultanism." It is not clear whether, in fact, the Ottoman Empire served as the model for this type of regime, but it seems certain that in Weber's mind this empire shared these characteristics. What is the difference between patrimonialism and sultanism? Says Weber:

Where authority is primarily oriented to tradition but in its exercise makes the claim of full personal power, it will be called "patrimonial" authority. Where patrimonial authority lays primary stress on the sphere of arbitrary will free of traditional limitations, it will be called "Sultanism."[4]

Weber's modern followers and amplifiers go beyond him by exploiting the empirical data base of modern scholarship unavailable to him, and therefore present us with a paradigm that is considerably more sophisticated. It is true that on the one hand the Weberian view of the Ottoman state as a typical household state is still dominant. To quote Metin Heper, "In line with the metaphor of the polity as a household, the whole country was considered as a single *oikos*; the political realm was identical with a huge Islamic manor."[5] Along with the terms patrimonialism and sultanism, this is of course, an exact Weberian analysis. But in other places the writer has more to say on this regime. He, for example, differentiates between the period up to the late sixteenth century and the later one, that of the seventeenth and eighteenth centuries. The earlier period is characterized as a kind of "enlightened despotism," a benign form of patrimonialism.[6] In more concrete terms, this means that the Ottoman regime in this period was not simply a personal, whimsical, despotic rule; it was rule based on reason, necessity, and *raison d'état*.[7] Then, basing himself on (and citing from) the studies of Halil Inalcik, the foremost Ottoman historian of the present generation, Heper offers an excellent summary of the nature of the Ottoman regime in the sixteenth century:

> During the Classical Age [the period up to the end of the sixteenth century], the Ottoman version of raison d'etat could have led, though did not in fact lead, to arbitrary rule. Instead it showed strong signs of *Rechtsstaat*: the system required all in the bureaucratic center, including the Sultan, to respect absolutely its rules and traditions. "Like pages, the Sultan himself studied with tutors on certain days of the week. He had meticulously to observe ceremony, customary usage determining even the words he had to use on certain occasions".[8]

But this description applies only to the period ending with the sixteenth century. As the Ottoman Empire started to decline, the regime also deteriorated and rapidly became an extreme form of Oriental despotism—that is, an extreme form of personal despotism, with Ottoman officials becoming "plunderers of their own society."[9]

It seems, then, that the basic characteristic of the Ottoman polity as an extreme patrimonial state, according to Weber and the neo-Weberians, is total personal rulership by the sultan, unbound by laws and rules of any kind. Neo-Weberians lay special stress on the lack of such restrictive rules in the relations between the ruler and the periphery—that is, the common people. In this study I intend to focus attention on this latter question, though some analysis is also called for concerning the alleged total lack of laws, rules, "matter-of-fact" types of approach, and the like. These two topics will engage our attention for the rest of this chapter.

In dealing with what actually took place in the Ottoman Empire in the seventeenth and eighteenth centuries, which is the main focus of this work, it is necessary first of all to deal with the issue of the so-called Ottoman decline. There is growing uneasiness today about the very viability of this concept, but I am using the term here in a more limited sense than is usual; I refer to the reduction of the power of the center vis-à-vis other elite groups and the effect of such reduction on the entire state in terms of disorder, chaos, and decline of standards of all sorts. The topic is of some importance here because, as noted, there is a widespread belief that while the Ottoman polity may have been benign, even bureaucratic, in the sixteenth century, it became blindly despotic as part of the process of decline. This, of course, had to have an effect on the legal system, along with other institutions. I have shown that no catastrophic deterioration in standards took place in the legal system; but it is important to show how and why the theory about the decline of the center is exaggerated for the entire polity. Ever since studying at close range the *kadi* court records of seventeenth-century Bursa, I have felt intense uneasiness concerning this thesis, and I want at this point to broaden the discussion of it somewhat, keeping in mind, however, that this is a huge topic and treatment of it must remain tentative.

The study of Ottoman decline started with the so-called *nasihat* literature beginning with Mustafa Ali in the late sixteenth century, a sort of advice to kings on how to run an empire and preserve it from all sorts of predicaments. For long, the *nasihat* literature was perceived as the embodiment of historical reality. Only in recent years have some doubts about it begun to be expressed.[10] Any study of Ottoman decline should, therefore, start with some sort of reexamination of the arguments of the *nasihat* writers, also referred to as memorialists.

The *nasihat* literature invariably speaks about the catastrophic decline in the state of the Ottoman Empire that set in after the Süleymanic era (that is, from the third quarter of the sixteenth century). It maintains that the state could be saved only by reestablishing the institutional format current in Süleyman's time. The memorialists were usually perceived as objective analysts, so it would seem no one ever questioned the accuracy of their statements by trying to verify their facts against other sources. Nor was the internal logic of their arguments ever put to the test. In this section I address myself to some of these questions by way of a sample, not in order to be exhaustive but merely to indicate that the whole decline theory is problematic from the very foundation.

An excellent summary of the main arguments of the memorialists that is perfectly sufficient for our purposes can be found in a study by Bernard Lewis.[11] The first known memorialist was Lutfi Paşa, Grand Vizier to Süleyman the Magnificent, who presented his memorandum as early as 1541. He was the first to observe a decline in bureaucratic standards, and he urged his master to take measures to rectify the situation. The problematic inherent in Lutfi's text starts right away. Take, for example, the role of the Grand Vizier, about which Lutfi has this to say: "The Grand Vizier should be disinterested, without any private aim or spite. Everything he does should be for God and in God and for the sake of God. . . . The Grand Vizier should be frank and honest in his dealing with the Sultan and without fear of dismissal. . . . The Grand Vizier should make appointments and promotions solely on the basis of merit and competence, without favoritism and interest. . . . He should submit to no influence or pressure in making appointments, but follow his own judgment."[12] This is an amazing text, all the more so because it sets the tone for much of the later arguments of the memorialists. According to this recipe, the Grand Vizier should be nothing less than a saint, devoid of any sort of human emotion or passion. What is worse, in this text and similar ones there is no theoretical moral philosophy; the explicit claim is that this (obviously fantastic) description was at a certain historic moment real.

This in a nutshell is the major logical problem with the *nasihat* literature. It depicts the Süleymanic era in impossibly bright colors. If anything was special about the Süleymanic era, it could not have been these incredible social traits. The intellectual and psychological problem raised here probably goes deeper than just that of a small group of thinkers: the decline of the Ottoman Empire after Süleyman was virtually an official ideology. Thus, a late sixteenth-century sultanic order claimed: "In the time of my great ancestor Sultan Suleiman, a law code was composed and distributed. . . . Then no one suffered any injustice...and all the affairs of the empire followed an ideal course."[13] But to come back to Lutfi Paşa, there is an additional problem with his sharp admonitions. Already in the mid-sixteenth century he saw the pitfalls that later came to be considered the most characteristic problems of Ottoman decline—"inflation and speculation, venality and incompetence; the multiplication of a useless and wasteful army and bureaucracy; the vicious circle of financial stringency, fiscal rapacity, and economic strangulations; the decay of integrity and loyalty."[14] The problem here is the tendency to push the golden age ever further back in time. If the Süleymanic age was already corrupt, when was the time of pristine purity? The problem is obvious, the solution much less so—unless we are prepared to change our entire mode of looking at the nasihat literature.

But let us look first at some additional examples. Another famous memorandum is that by Koçu Bey, submitted to the sultan in 1630. The utopian tone is established from the very beginning: "It is a long time since the . . . Sultanate . . . was served by solicitous, well-intentioned, worthy ulema, and by obedient, self-effacing, willing slaves. Today the state of affairs having changed, and evil, upheaval, sedition and dissension having passed all bounds, I have sought occasion to observe the causes and reasons of these changes, and bring them to the Imperial and august ear."[15] Koçu Bey, of course, takes it for granted that the Süleymanic era (1520–66) was a golden age, after which there was only decline. Facts and causes are piled on top of one another without due care for logic. Thus, the first major cause of the decline is the withdrawal of the sultan from the position of effective ruler and administrator of the realm. But the second is connected to the Grand Vizier. In the past this officeholder was nominated only on the basis of "his competence and merit. Once appointed, he enjoyed absolute discretion and power, and was free from any kind of illicit pressure or influence."[16] Just how the Grand Vizier would have been able to possess absolute discretion and power—had the sultan retained his—is not made clear. It is also, of course, factually misleading to claim that the Grand Vizier ever held complete power before the withdrawal of the sultans.

The *nasihat* literature contains, in addition, sections that, while perhaps not based on obvious logical errors, nevertheless do not stand the test of empirical investigation. Speaking about other sections of the Ottoman body politic Koçu Bey notes that they fared no better: "The military fief system, which once provided the backbone of the army and of the countryside, was being undermined and destroyed. The feudal *sipahis* [fiefholders] were being crushed out of existence, and their fiefs given to courtiers and harem women, who sometimes accumulated as many as fifty of them in a single holding. The result was both agrarian and military breakdown."[17]

The *ulema* were another aspect of decline according to Koçu Bey. Again, the utopian terms are highly revealing: in the past, religious officeholders like the *şeyhülislam* "had been chosen as the wisest, best and most pious of the *ulema* and usually held his office for life. Other judges were pious, conscientious and modest, and held office for many years. . . . Now, appointments and promotions among the *ulema* were made without reference to merit, scholarship, or seniority. All went by favor. Tenure of office was brief and insecure, and holders unworthy and grasping. The judges were hated and despised by the people."[18]

Despite their utopian tone, the memorialists were taken for shrewd assessors of Ottoman affairs. The utopian terms, however, are enough to indicate that accurate observers they certainly were not. What they were is much more difficult to establish.[19] In the first place, scholars have noted that the *nasihat* literature is a continuation of the literary genre of advice to kings popular in earlier phases of Middle Eastern history, a genre that tends naturally to take the ruler and his officials to task on various matters.[20] In part, the memorialists no doubt expressed a nostalgia for the pristine conditions of the Ottoman principality by those who had experienced the phenomenal rise of the bureaucratic Ottoman state in the sixteenth century. The early period was characterized by a cozy spirit of togetherness, simplicity, and purity of sacrifice for Islam. Now there was turmoil and probably an increased facelessness.[21] There was unquestionably the group fear of loss of privilege in the face of a rising tide of commoners (*reaya*) swelling the ranks of the administration. Formerly each person knew his or her place in society and realized he had to conform to it. This knowledge, for which the Ottomans used the Islamic-legal concept of *had*, evinced a layered society: everyone knew his position and what his position entailed in terms of behavior. Departure from this pattern was likely to throw the existing social order into anarchy and unrest.[22] This explains much of historian Mustafa Ali's scathing criticism against the Ottoman state. To cite Cornell Fleischer,

> Ali was the child of an age in which the few who were liter-
> ate and learned could hope . . . for a rewarding career as a
> judge, teacher, or member of an expanding bureaucracy that
> needed men of letters. He lived into another age in which the
> government ranks were crowded, when basic literacy was
> more commonly available. . . . Such developments, discerned
> through Ali's eyes and through his life, illuminate the history
> of institutional consolidation as much as they explain the
> emotional and moral distress Ottoman intellectuals experi-
> enced in the face of social and institutional transformation.[23]

Nor is the current image of the Ottoman golden age free of problems. In actuality, very little has been done to demonstrate in what way this age really was "golden." But there is one valuable piece of research—Uriel Heyd's book on patterns of government and administration in sixteenth-century Palestine.[24] This work contains a great deal of information that again bears out the universal phenomenon whereby the golden age tends to recede indefinitely into the past as soon as real facts are drawn into the picture. In other words, the Ottoman administration under Süleyman was already plagued by severe problems. For example, Ottoman weakness in controlling the Syrian provinces, seen by scholars as a typical eighteenth-century problem, was present in just as serious a form in the sixteenth century. Reviewing the Ottoman record with regard to keeping the Bedouins in check, Heyd has this to say: "In this task the Ottomans failed in the period under review despite all their exertions, and many firmans [orders] . . . indicate that the Bedouins succeeded, at least temporarily, in subduing a large part of the country."[25] The Ottomans' main task, says Heyd, was to raise taxes, but this necessitated good and efficient army units. However, "in this period . . . serious corruption and disorganization of these forces set in, and they proved unable to stamp out the almost incessant rebellions and acts of brigandage which devastated the country. At the same time, the efficiency and honesty of the provincial administration began to decline."[26] Furthermore, many see in the later Ottoman custom of co-opting members of local elites into positions of authority in the administration a clear mark of weakness and decline. Few realize that in the "heyday" of the empire the Ottomans had had recourse to this on an even grander scale than in the eighteenth century. To cite Heyd again: "For the sake of administrative convenience and political expediency, some local Arabs, mainly Bedouin chiefs, were in the sixteenth century appointed sanjak-begs [provincial governors]."[27] Many of these "problems" are probably figments of our own biased mode of looking, accustomed as we are to control by modern states that is immensely facilitated by sophisticated communication devices. In other words, many of the signs of supposedly characteristic Ottoman decline are simply pervasive characteristics of many past empires.

As I see it, the whole idea of Ottoman decline is based on an optical illusion of sorts. That the late sixteenth century was a period of economic and social crisis is evident. The question is whether this was the beginning of a long-term development. What is clear beyond this is that people were experiencing a small principality's growth into a vast bureaucratic empire. Now, it is natural that efficiency and honesty are greater in a small principality than in a large and impersonal bureaucracy. But such falling off in efficiency is by no means tantamount to general decline. The limited administrative apparatus of a principality could never fulfill the tasks required of a large bureaucracy. Tax collection on a vast scale cannot be carried out by a bureaucracy in which every official is personally acquainted with all the others. In that sense, corruption and inefficiency are the price paid for growth. It would be absurd to claim that the growth of the empire was a symptom of decline. This paradox, I think, highlights the need to study Ottoman decline with greater care than has hitherto been the case.

Taken together, the opinions voiced by the advice literature and by modern political sociologists contain several statements—some explicit, some implicit—that need to be disentangled for purposes of empirical study. There is first the economic argument, claiming that after the sixteenth century everything in the Ottoman economy, from agriculture to finance and production, deteriorated catastrophically. A second argument is the political-administrative one, which claims that the post-sixteenth-century Ottoman administration became extremely rapacious, oppressive, and predatory, as well as highly chaotic. A third argument is that the end of the sixteenth century saw a drastic and rapid decline in the old form of landholding (the *timar*) and emergence of a new one (the *iltizam*) that was tremendously more rapacious and exploitative. A fourth argument revolves around the drastic decline in the honesty, integrity, and loyalty of the *ulema*, as well as their growing incompetence in carrying out their duties. The root cause of the latter three phenomena seems to be the brevity and insecurity of office and the need to pay for appointments and, hence, to recoup the investment as quickly as possible. The outcome was a general decline in the observance of the old law, both the sixteenth-century *kanun* in the literal sense and the old code of gentlemanly behavior characterizing "the Ottoman way." Thus, the allegedly highly oppressive nature of the Ottoman political system is again seen to be inseparable from the supposed decline of that state. What really went on in Ottoman society after the sixteenth century cannot be learned from the advice literature. To redeem the picture, one needs to look at the primary sources and at the monographs based on such sources, which have become available only in recent years.

As to the first argument concerning Ottoman decline—the economic disintegration of artisanal production, finance, and agriculture—no sign of such disintegration was discernible in my investigation of seventeenth-century Bursa.[28] There were crises, no doubt, but there is nothing to suggest that these were more than cyclical. And disregarding short-term changes, there is an unmistakable increase in the value of estates left by the deceased in Bursa as compared with either the fifteenth century or the beginning of the seventeenth. Certainly more research on other places is called for before we can reach a final conclusion on this issue, but for the time being the decline thesis is called into question.

What about the decline thesis on the political front, or in center-periphery relations? The prevalent version is that the seventeenth and eighteenth centuries witnessed growing despotism of the Ottoman government. But the picture does not tally with what comes out of many primary sources. A relevant case in point is the relation between government and society in a place like seventeenth-century Bursa. To retrieve this side of the picture I have to refer again to the court records of Bursa because I did not deal with this topic in my Bursa monograph. Later I shall draw on additional archival sources to look at the issue in a broader way. The court records of Bursa are useful in shedding light on several of the research questions we have distilled from the discussion of the advice literature. One such topic is the supposedly growing rapacious and despotic nature of the Ottoman government after the sixteenth century. This topic revolves around the relations between Ottoman officials and the city population.

First, it is not entirely easy to locate the government in seventeenth-century Bursa. The city had no governor, whose duty it might have been to carry out the orders of the center. Effectively, the main representative of the government was the *kadi*—and he, after all, was more judge than administrator. The outcome was pretty much a self-regulating community. The city went about its business without any real directing hand. Only a close look reveals the state in the form of officials acting in various technical capacities. These officials, of course, had dealings of all sorts with the local inhabitants, and it is the pattern of these relationships that I propose to investigate here.

Bursa was the main city of a *sancak* (province), the *sancak of* Hüdavendigâr, the governor of which in all probability was usually represented in the city by an acting district governor (*mütesellim*). The *mütesellim*, however, appeared in the *kadi* records only very rarely. One such occasion was the trial of a gang of ten brigands, whom he had apprehended in Bursa's hinterland on suspicion of robbing and killing people. All ten were sentenced to death and handed over to the *mütesellim* to carry out the verdict.[29] In another case a fiefholder sued the *mütesellim* of Hüdavendigâr for attempting to levy a tax of *bedel-i diyet* on "his" peasants, who were legally exempt (*serbest*) from nonfeudal taxes.[30] These are about the only times the district governor was mentioned in the *kadi* record—usually a rather faithful reflection of what was going on in the public life of the city.

The *subaşi* (chief of police) was mentioned much more often, but it is impossible to say anything about this officeholder beyond his role as chief of police. He was never found in any other context or capacity. No complaint against him was ever launched concerning illegal or despotic behavior. We are led, therefore, to exonerate him from any such wrongdoing.

Many other minor officials were, however, mentioned in dealings with the public. Many examples involved managers of sultanic *waqf*s. Citizens sued managers for such allegations as handing village land to outsiders for woodcutting purposes.[31] Because this was obviously against the ancient custom, the *kadi* seems not to have been impressed by the official title of the manager and decided for the plaintiffs. In other cases endowment managers had awarded pieces of arable land to people from outside the village community. In all such cases that came to court, villagers won over *waqf* managers.[32] Villagers often got involved in legal disputes with fiefholders, too; more often than not they won their cases.[33]

A very popular type of dispute in the *kadi* record of seventeenth-century Bursa was between citizens and the official (called *emin beytülmal*) in charge of seizing for the treasury the estates of people who had died in the city without leaving heirs. This official was sometimes overzealous in carrying out his duties, putting his hand on the estates of people staying in Bursa only temporarily who had legal heirs in other places. Such heirs went to court and claimed their rights perforce without any apparent hesitation. In one case we find people from Kastamonu doing this,[34] in another someone from Izmit.[35] Here again the court does not seem to have deferred to authority; in most cases common people won over officials. Sometimes the function of the *beytülmal* was carried out by another official, the *harc hasa emini*, who was the economic agent for the sultan's court in Bursa and in that capacity normally in charge of purchasing various products intended for the court. Because this official represented the sultan rather than, strictly speaking, the state, one might expect on his part a rather lenient attitude to the fine points of law. It is interesting, therefore, to observe that the reality was different. To begin with, this official was sued by common people, just as the *beytülmal emini* was, for wrongfully seizing the estates of deceased citizens.[36] In several other cases we find the *emin* properly performing his duty of purchasing products for the court. No forced purchase was ever discovered or complained about by citizens, and payments seem to have been fair and prompt. In one example the *emin* bought three thousand *kile* of wheat from a sheep owner for the sultan's court and asked the seller to declare that he had received payment in full.[37] In another case an heir of a Bursa merchant took the *emin* to court, claiming that when his father died he was owed 140 thousand akçe from the *emin* for textiles supplied. When this was duly proven, an order was issued to make the payment without any delay.[38]

In many other cases the situation was reversed, and we find officials suing citizens in court. In one case a *sipahi* brought a villager to court and claimed the latter had illegally seized a piece of land in the village. The villager produced a document attesting that he had obtained the land eleven years earlier from the fiefholder at the time, and won the case.[39] Beyond the substantive issue, an interesting aspect of this and several similar cases is that the fiefholder went to court to enforce the law, or what he thought was the law, rather than forced his will on the peasants. The same was true concerning the relations between villagers and sultanic *waqf* managers.[40]

Most legal disputes in the court record of seventeenth-century Bursa show not only that citizens were not easy prey at the hand of state officials, but that in most cases common people won the case. In a typical example the *beytülmal emini* sued a merchant for a sum of money that a man who has now died without an heir had deposited with the merchant; but the merchant now claimed that part of the sum was made up of coins that were deficient in quality. The *emin* insisted that all the coins were of full volume; but because he could not prove this, he lost the case.[41] There is not the slightest hint here that the *emin* was given special treatment because he was the representative of the treasury in Bursa.

In another very telling case we find a representative of the central government coming to Bursa to occupy the properties of a deceased tax farmer to cover a very high sum owed to the treasury by the deceased. Rather than helping himself to the properties of the deceased, the representative proceeded to file a case with the court, which he won; only then did confiscation take place.[42] In another case an agent of the central government was sent to Bursa to collect tax arrears from the guilds. Instead of going ahead with collection, the agent summoned the guild heads to court to settle the issue before the *kadi*.[43] The concern for legality and what might be termed due process are quite impressive. In another document that conveys the same idea even more forcefully, we hear from the two holders of the tax farm of the silver-processing workshop in Bursa. Although an order of the sultan had forbidden anyone to make silver products outside of this establishment, they suspected a non-Muslim, specified by name, of doing this at his house. One might expect them just to have gone ahead and searched the place, but instead they asked the court to authorize their breaking into the house and searching it.[44]

This impression of the government's quite benign treatment of the civil society is corroborated by a study of Suraiya Faroqhi's, who compared the Ottoman and Mamluk approaches to the urban population and said the following:

"Bureaucratic rules and procedures made the actions of the sixteenth-century Ottoman state considerably more predictable than its Mamluk predecessor had been. . . . The expansion of the Ottoman bureaucracy in general, and of the financial bureaucracy in particular, led to an institutionalized system of checks and balances."[45]

Further important evidence on the supposed increasingly despotic nature of the Ottoman ruling class can be culled from studies on the history of the *waqf*, one of the most important Ottoman sociopolitical institutions.[46] A case in point is Bahaeddin Yediyíldíz's important study on Turkish *waqf*s in the eighteenth century.[47] The study is based on a sample of 330 *waqf* documents out of 6,000 said to be contained in the Turkish archive for the entire eighteenth century. The study indicates why historians have to take the institution so seriously. By the late eighteenth century the revenue of the *waqf* was estimated to be one-third of the entire revenue of the Ottoman Empire, and it was more than double the revenue of the entire *timar* system.[48] Among other things this study throws unexpected light on the nature of the Ottoman social and political elite. As noted earlier, the image of that elite, particularly after the sixteenth century, is that of "plunderers of their own society." Moreover, the *waqf* was supposed to be the major device for legalizing this plunder (by endowing ill-gotten property to the family of the founder) because the sacred nature of the institution was supposed to ward off intruders in the form of sultans or treasurers. But the evidence assembled by Yediyíldíz throws very serious doubt on this received wisdom.

To begin with, the information is highly relevant because most of the endowments were established by members of the Ottoman elite. In fact, no less than 65 percent of the institutions were established by *askeri*s (members of the administrative and military elite), 14 percent by *ulema* (religious clerics), and 6 percent by Sufi *şeyh*s. Moreover, 17 percent of the endowments were established by women, of whom almost half were attached in one capacity or other to the Ottoman palace, and most of the rest were probably wives of *askeri*s. All in all, then, about 72 percent of the *waqf*s were established by members of the Ottoman elite.[49] This in itself, of course, says little about the topic at hand. After all, members of the elite may simply have had better reasons than commoners to conceal property by resorting to endowment. We need to look at the purposes for which property was endowed.

Although endowments in Islam are usually either a family type or a public type, this division does not hold in the present case; only 18 percent of the institutions were wholly public, and only 7 percent were wholly private. Fully 75 percent were mixed— meaning that the institution was, in the main, public with some private components, usually expressed by the management's being retained by the family of the endower. An additional private component might be the assigning of surplus revenue to the family of the endower.[50] It is true that such mixed institutions do reserve to the family an important social role within the *waqf*, but it is sometimes forgotten that endowment entails forgoing most of the property for the sake of public purposes. One computation came up with the conclusion that about 10 percent of the revenue of the institutions in question went to management and an additional 15 percent to the family in the form of unilateral gifts—that is, not in return for work performed.[51] The rest, fully 75 percent of the revenue of the entire *waqf* institution, including the private part, went to the upkeep of public institutions. This finding hardly supports the old theory about the nature of the Ottoman ruling elite. Yediyíldíz himself tries to block such an interpretation of the figures he had assembled—for example, by claiming that we should not be deceived by the lavishness of these scions of the elite; they actually saw that most of the money was spent on members of their own class.[52] This is hardly convincing. Mosques, schools for the study of the Quran, public water fountains (the single biggest item), soup kitchens—such institutions are meant for the poor, not for the rich.[53] Obviously, the mixed nature of most of the endowments evinces a mixed motive as far as the founders were concerned: they were seeking to take care of their families, but they might have done so much better by endowing the entire property to their families. So they had something else in mind. For the sake of discussion, let us say that it was merely the wish to immortalize themselves. This in itself is important, for it underlines the fact that these people thought that the way in which common people viewed them was important. It also shows that they were ready to go to extremes to influence this view of the public—not by deceit and greed, but by giving and sharing. However one looks at this mode of behavior, it evinces communal feeling rather than unlimited rapaciousness.

THE CENTRAL GOVERNMENT AND
THE LOCAL ELITE IN THE PROVINCES

A further aspect of Ottoman government and bureaucracy I would like to examine more carefully is the relation between center and periphery in the outer provinces. Major connecting links here are the *ayan* (provincial notables). A number of good studies on the *ayan* of Syria have appeared in recent years, and I shall draw on some of them.

The *ayan* rose to prominence as the central government weakened, so the two elements are often viewed as forming a dichotomy. There is an ongoing discussion in the literature as to whether one of these parties had in mind eliminating the other from the scene. I am particularly interested to find out whether the Ottomans had such a secret dream.

Research on this topic dates back to Albert Hourani and his famous study of the provincial notables who appeared on the political scene in the seventeenth and eighteenth centuries and usurped much of the authority of the central government in the provinces.[54] More recent studies have gone into this topic in considerably greater detail, enabling us to observe more minutely the political dynamics under way. The point I wish to drive home is that reality is a far cry from either the Ottomans' being driven out of the provinces or intending to eliminate other forces from the scene. The generally accepted picture of the growing weakness of the Ottoman government in the provinces is not supported by a careful reading of the evidence. The Ottomans, in fact, quite willingly and intentionally cultivated a local elite to share in government. This is made clear, for example, in a study of eighteenth-century Aleppo.[55]

Aleppin society under the Ottomans was topped by an extremely cohesive social elite, almost a ruling elite, that is highly relevant to this study. Let us look first at the relations between this group and the Ottoman government. Surprisingly, the local elite appears far from being suffocated or oppressed by the faraway imperial power. On the contrary, it constituted a symbiotic part of that government. The Ottoman government itself filled only the two most important posts in the province, those of governor and judge. Scions of the local elite manned a long list of lower, yet crucially important posts, which in Aleppo meant mainly the acting governor (*mütesellim*) and the treasurer and chief tax collector (*muhassil*). In the eighteenth century these two posts were usually the prerogative of one family for many years. Lesser posts—such as those of *mufti, naqib al-ashraf* (head of the descendants of the Prophet), and the acting judges (*nuwwab*) in the smaller courthouses in the city[56]—were also, as a matter of course and routine, filled by the same elite.

On the whole, then, the notables of Aleppo enjoyed a great deal of autonomy and consideration.[57] They seemed at times to occupy a somewhat awkward position between the common people and an oppressive governor. On several occasions they denounced a governor to the sultan and brought about his removal.[58] But on the whole the city's notables had every reason to view themselves as closely tied to the Ottoman wagon. Once a local Aleppin family joined the elite, it tended to remain there safely and securely for centuries.[59] If we keep in mind that these families were both numerous and large, it becomes clear that we are talking here about a substantial segment of the city's population, not just a thin crust. An additional important point to keep in mind is that this upper-crust elite was a genuine local elite that had risen from below, an elite that enjoyed a large measure of legitimacy. All this taken together rules out a picture in which the Ottomans commissioned a small, oppressive social upper layer to rule in their name. In effect, we have here a large measure of co-optation of local elements, with local sensitivities and local commitments. This is not a picture of a central government ruling its provinces with an iron fist.

Late eighteenth- and early nineteenth-century Jerusalem has now also been studied at close range through the *kadi* court records. And here, too, it transpires that the Ottomans were content with controlling the two most sensitive posts—those of acting governor and *kadi*—by sending nominees from the center; lower positions were left to the local elite, making them part of the Ottoman establishment. The claim that this degree of autonomy was forced on the Ottomans by the rise to power of the local families is not convincing. If this were really so, it is difficult to see why the local notables did not lay their hands on the posts of *kadi* and acting governor. What these notables took was exactly what the Ottomans were willing to bestow on them. Here, too, co-optation was the name of the game. Whether it was a forced coming to terms with reality or true liberalism and open-mindedness on the part of the Ottomans makes little difference.[60]

It is a well-known fact that until the late nineteenth century the Ottoman Empire enjoyed among its Muslim population a measure of legitimacy that is almost unmatched in the historic empires—it was never the target of a total revolt, and there was never any known effort to replace the ruling dynasty. This is quite incompatible with the despotic and rapacious nature of that same ruling dynasty. I do not propose here a definitive explanation of this paradox, but I am convinced that part of the explanation can be sought in the aforementioned special structure of the Ottoman polity: on the one hand it co-opted provincial elites into the state councils; on the other hand these upper crusts were not truly ruling elites, but an integral part of the provincial urban society.

NOTES ON THE SOCIOLOGICAL STRUCTURE OF THE OTTOMAN BUREAUCRACY

The internal structure of the Ottoman administration seems a far cry from the Weberian model of a patrimonial bureaucracy in which officials were slaves of the ruler, carrying out his capricious and unreasoned commands. A generation ago such a description was still viable; but as studies of the inner mechanisms of this bureaucracy have begun to appear, the situation has become more complex. Before going into details, let us look at Weber's ideal type of bureaucracy—that is, "real" bureaucracy, which he also sometimes called rational bureaucracy: that of the modern West. Of its ten major characteristics, the following are the most important:

1. Staff members are personally free, fulfilling only the impersonal duties of their offices.
2. Officials are selected and appointed on the basis of their qualifications and merit.
3. There is a clear career structure, and promotion is possible either by seniority or by merit, and according to the judgment of superiors.[61]

There is today an ocean of criticism on the validity of Weber's model as a description of a real-life bureaucracy (emphasizing sociological, or "irrational," factors in the behavior of Western bureaucracies). I shall not discuss this literature because it seems irrelevant to the present study and appears to miss a vital aspect of the Weberian model, the element of comparison. To my mind, Weber was not oblivious to the less than perfectly rational kinds of behavior prevalent in modern Western bureaucracies; he was merely trying to show that they were *substantially* more rational than the historic empires of the past. The fact is that when one compares the modern West to the historic empires of the past, the Weberian model is to a large extent both correct and analytically fruitful. Here I concentrate on trying to show that Ottoman bureaucracy contained important rational elements.

Recent studies on the development of Ottoman bureaucracy in the sixteenth century (by Cornell Fleischer for example) speak of the emergence of two professional paths: finance and chancery. Together these two paths constituted the *kalemiye*, the Ottoman bureaucracy in the narrow sense. Essentially, the institution began to develop only from about the mid-sixteenth century: "By the end of Süleyman's reign [1566] . . . the bureaucracy . . . had grown considerably in size, and chancery and financial specializations had become discrete professional paths and distinct organizational units; official nomenclature and a hierarchical structure of office had been established, and regular procedures of induction, training, and promotion were in operation."[62] Fleischer further speaks of the appearance in this period of "bureaucratic self-consciousness, that emphasized regularity, predictability, hierarchy, and meritocracy in government and social organization."[63] It goes without saying that these developments fit the Weberian definition of bureaucracy.

Predictability, meritocracy, and professionalization are important, and it is highly significant that they did exist in the Ottoman administration. But there were other opposing features in this bureaucracy that should be drawn into the picture as well. The two most important such features—both, unfortunately, greatly underresearched—are the role of *intisab* (personal relations and patronage) in nomination and advancement, and the obviously closely related role of big households in this administration.

The role of the big household has become a subject of serious research only in recent years, and as a result our knowledge here is quite meager. In any event, prosopographic studies have made it clear that although in the fifteenth and sixteenth centuries most high-level personnel ruling the empire tended to come from the household of the ruler via the institution of *devşirme* (Christian boy levy), in the seventeenth and eighteenth centuries there was a rise to prominence of the households of high officials.[64] The same phenomenon was detected through use of the archival nomination books of provincial governors.[65] Metin Kunt has shown that provincial governors who were sons of high officials enjoyed a definite advantage over commoners in terms of admittance into the system and advancement in it once admitted. This established the rising political power of the household of the high official within the Ottoman administration. On a broader sociological scale,

Carter Findley saw the big patrimonial household headed by a high official as one of the main pillars of the pre-nineteenth-century Ottoman political system.[66]

The study of *intisab*—also a new topic of serious empirical research—has recently been given a strong boost by Cornell Fleischer's study on Mustafa Ali, a sixteenth-century bureaucrat and man of letters who wrote enough about himself to enable a reconstruction of his daily problems within the administration. Throughout the book we observe how ascendance was achieved by knowing the right people. Personal knowledge was obviously, therefore, crucial in the Ottoman bureaucracy.

The question is how much all these concepts—households, patronage, and the like—truly dominated the Ottoman bureaucracy. Let us look first at *intisab*. Fleischer's study contains hints that indicate the limits of *intisab*, not just its strength. If ascendance in the bureaucracy was effected to a large extent by personal contacts, the book shows that universalistic values were also very important. Thus, in some chapters about his life Ali admitted that the rapid advancement he achieved was attained at least partially through talent.[67] Admittedly, Ali was by his own standards a failure. He attributed this to the decadence and declining integrity of the Ottoman administration, the rise in importance of *intisab*, and personal relations. Ali felt that *intisab* in his own case had devastating results because all those connected with Lala Mustafa Paşa and his Yemen debacle of the 1560s were marked and pursued by his major opponent throughout their later careers. As a personal feeling this view is perfectly legitimate, but I have a problem when I look at it more objectively. In the first place, Ali's relative failure (for several years after 1578 he was stuck in the office of fief registrar of the province of Aleppo) was at least in part connected with the curious decision he had taken early in his life to quit the path of religious learning and go over to the bureaucracy, in spite of his religious education. That his decision backfired is not entirely surprising. Even more interesting, though, is the evidence that Ali's relative failure was an exception rather than the rule and that he himself realized this. As Fleischer comments, "Ali perceived the Ottoman system to function, ideally, on the basis of impersonal meritocracy and regularity. Given merit, one should be able to plug into the system and receive regular promotions."[68] He decried a situation in which, while this pattern of promotion was the usual case, he was being skipped over for promotion. For most people around him, then, the system of promotion appears to have worked reasonably well and according to the bureaucratic model.

Some years later, when Ali was again looking for a job, he approached a high official of his acquaintance, and this man wrote a letter to the sultan explaining why Ali should be given a post. The main reason was "that Ali's contemporaries in the religious career (*ilmiye*) were already near the peak of their way, at the *mevleviyet* (top judgeship) level, while those at the financial section were also at the near top of that service."[69] Here again, the evidence shows unequivocally that whatever the intricacies of the *intisab* system, there was a strong correlation between seniority and grade even at the end of the sixteenth century. Ali emerges as an exception, not the personification of an ideal gone sour.

Fleischer himself seems at times to agree that the hold of *intisab*, though powerful, had bounds. Observing that Ali received a bureaucratic appointment seemingly without the help of any patron, Fleischer is moved to construe *intisab* as a social pattern in which one initially filled bureaucratic posts under the protection of a patron and then became a free-floating unit in the bureaucracy that took care of itself.[70] This implies that in the higher reaches of the bureaucracy the power of *intisab* was relatively small. Reinforcing this impression is an episode in another study in which the downfall of a vizier did not bring about the fall of his son, also at the time an important official in the bureaucracy.[71]

The extreme looseness of the institution of *intisab* is further evidenced by the following aspects of Ali's story. First, Ali's main patron, Lala Mustafa Paşa, was a full-ranking vizier in the 1570s and 1580s, yet he could not or would not help his client. A second fact that does not say much for the institution of *intisab* is the large number of people that Ali in the course of his life considered his patrons in the Ottoman bureaucracy.[72] All in all, it seems that *intisab* cannot have been the major driving force within the Ottoman administration, particularly as people moved to the higher levels. It was a tough game out there, and a person was on his own. Luck was, of course, extremely important, but so was talent.[73]

As for the big households, the main problem is that we know so little about them. What little we do know about the households creates the impression that we are dealing here with bureaucratic bodies rather than anything resembling extended families, as is implied by the term. As one study shows quite eloquently, the big household appeared in the first place because it had a function to fulfill, that of providing soldiers and low-level personnel to run the empire. So it appears that most household members were not family members. Moreover, despite the importance of families in principle, no lasting dynasties—except for the famous case of the Köprülüs—came into being at the top levels of the Ottoman administration. One student commented on this important phenomenon: "With the exception of some frontier families, there were few examples of members of the same family in prominence for more than two or three generations."[74] The explanation offered is that, besides the effects of the Muslim law of inheritance, the fact that the system was nevertheless a meritocracy and these people had to prove their worth in order to advance.[75]

The bureaucratic nature of the household is also made clear by the fact that most Ottoman officials changed assignments (and places of residence) very frequently—at least once a year. It is extremely unlikely that they would have been accompanied by extended families in their postings around the empire. In fact, there is enough evidence to show that employment in the Ottoman bureaucracy was a classic factor in breaking up families. When the son of Lala Mustafa Paşa (himself a vizier) was made a provincial governor before he was thirty, both he and his father were leading the life of bureaucratic nomads and probably rarely saw each other.[76] When Mustafa Ali chose to pursue the career of an Ottoman bureaucrat, he left his family in Gallipoli, never to rejoin it on a permanent basis. So did his two brothers, who led lives that were only rarely to cross his own.[77]

In one study a potentially enlightening comparison is offered between the Ottoman household and modern anthropological studies of the family in Turkey. Some of the main characteristics of the Ottoman household are not found in this literature, especially the incidence of daughters given in marriage moving into the household of the husband. What we find instead is more often the opposite—absorption of the low-class groom into the orbit of influence of the high-class bride, with a consequent elevation in his status.[78] (Such a man was termed *iç güveyisi* in the Turkish parlance.)

It is more than just symbolic, to my mind, that the premier household in the Ottoman Empire—the sultan's—was, from the sixteenth century on, a far cry from any concept of family current in Ottoman society. It was not based on marriage at all but on concubinage, and an important part of the institution was the bestowal of high status on officials by giving daughters and other female relatives of the sultan to them in marriage (see more about this in the next section). All this seems to point to the fact that the sultanic household had ceased to be a family and had been transformed into a bureaucratic organization.

OTTOMAN BUREAUCRACY AND FAMILY STRUCTURE

It is a major argument of this study that one important characteristic of the society in the core area of the Ottoman Empire, compared to other areas of the Middle East, was smaller families and the commensurately reduced importance of kinship or kinship-simulating institutions. I claim that this phenomenon is connected on the one hand with the structure of the legal system and on the other with the structure of the Ottoman polity as a bureaucratic state. Indeed, it is my argument that the presence of the Ottoman bureaucracy in the core area exerted an influence on the society living there in the development of smaller and more nucleated families. There may well be a logical connection in a culture area like Morocco between the major characteristic of the *kadi* as an arbiter between bargaining individuals and the general tendency of Moroccan society to view individuals in a contextualized manner—contextualized in terms of place of origin, community, clan, and accompanying social customs and customary law. I have, throughout this study, emphasized that none of these traits was discernible in the *kadis'* mode of working in the core area of the Ottoman Empire, and I argue that this was due to the lesser tendency of this society to contextualize individuals in terms of clan, family, village, or any other kinshiplike institutions.

Though study of the historical demography of Islamic societies has hardly started, there seems to be a substantial amount of evidence indicating that, compared to outer-lying areas of the Middle East, the family structure in the core area of the Ottoman Empire tended more to the nuclear (though I am mindful of the vast methodological problems involved in such a claim—for example, the developmental aspect of the life cycles of families). I am by no means talking here about a dichotomy, only about shades made evident by comparison.

Important evidence on the family in the Ottoman Empire outside of the core area under study comes mainly from several studies on the city of Aleppo. One study by Abraham Marcus that bears on the family in eighteenth-century Aleppo[79] makes it clear that ideally and in theory the structure of the family was an extended one, with children living under the same roof as their parents even after marriage: "The extended group of parents and children who remained united in a single residential unit demonstrated a laudable familial closeness and cohesion."[80] Such families tended to split up only after the death of both parents. But the study hastens to emphasize that only the well-to-do could afford such a life-style; the lower classes had to content themselves with living as nuclear families. Of course, the line between the well-to-do and the lower classes was a blurred one, and there is no statistical breakdown of the two models at any given time. Marcus did, however, manage to collect statistics on the size of families. His conclusion is that seven was the average number of members in a family in eighteenth-century Aleppo.[81] When looking beyond this catch-all average, it is important for comparative reasons to note that the author found in Aleppo some domestic groups that numbered several dozen members.[82]

Another study of eighteenth-century Aleppo, this one by Margaret Meriwether, deals more directly with one specific type of family—that of the Aleppin elite.[83] Aleppo had a distinct group of large extended families that constituted the elite of the city. The families in question enjoyed some political power and owned much of the property in the city; but membership in the city's elite was not defined by these two attributes: butchers were wealthy but barred from the elite by their profession; and janissaries also could not hope for elite status, though they possessed most of the political power within the city. Elite status was probably predicated on wealth acquired through a high-status profession such as trade, as well as involvement in Islamic learning. Most important, however, was that elite status in Aleppo was marked by the family name—a phenomenon not at all common in the historic Middle East. Meriwether's study is based on the thousands of allusions to these family names contained in the *kadi* court records of Aleppo and in the biographies of Aleppin luminaries. A comparable scanning of the *kadi* court records of Bursa and a famous biographical dictionary of that town yielded not a single family name. So it seems that this difference between Aleppo and Bursa is impressive and important.

The great majority of Aleppo's elite families were *ulema* (religious scholars).[84] Merchants occupied only second place, although this city drew most of its wealth and fame from international trade. Another important characteristic of these families was that they were by no means newcomers to eighteenth-century Aleppo. A large number actually harked back to the Mamluk period. Also remarkable is that elite status was extremely stable; only very rarely did a family lose its elite status, and indeed many families kept this status for centuries.[85] Of course, all these families were rich—not just the merchants but also the *ulema*. It is enough to look at the religious endowments that some of the scions of these families established to realize that they were indeed wealthy.[86]

These elite families of Aleppo followed the way of life of the extended kin group in a way reminiscent of the kin group in modern Morocco, as described by Hildred Geertz.[87] They tended to concentrate in the central quarters of town and to live together under the same roof, usually in a house traditionally known as the family abode.[88] Marriage patterns were also those prevailing in large-kin-group societies. No less than 18 percent of the matches recorded in this period were between first cousins, with an additional 44 percent of the matches between members of the same kin group.[89]

When one compares Aleppo with the core area of the Ottoman Empire, some interesting conclusions emerge. In another study I described and analyzed the prevailing family pattern in seventeenth-century Bursa,[90] and I found no sign that extended families had ever existed there. Sons possessed separate homes and productive properties while their fathers were still alive and active; it was extremely rare for brothers to share living space or to own property together, and the average number of children per family was found to be no more than 2.5. If juxtaposed with the information from Aleppo, the difference is quite striking.

Also remarkable is the difference between the two areas when we compare patterns of elite family names. In fact, the comparison is particularly revealing. While Aleppo had a very clear social elite composed of tangible families who all bore family names, the information from Bursa shows no sign of the existence of family names. As indicated, neither in the *kadi* court records of Bursa nor in a major biographical dictionary, mostly of religious personages, composed in that city is there mention of family names of individuals.[91] This book is organized around a different concept than are the great Syrian biographical dictionaries of the Ottoman period. Whereas these latter are organized around famous personalities who came to prominence in the city, most of them scions of important local families, the Bursavite dictionary lists personages who happened to die in Bursa during the period surveyed, such as the sons of Şeyhülislam Feyzullah Efendi who were banished to Bursa after the demise of their father in 1703. The difference is symbolic and may be meaningful: the Syrian collections clearly evince more urban, local pride and consciousness, whereas the Bursan collection is clearly more Ottoman in nature. The reason may well be that with the Bursa elite's dispersal of its scions to all parts of the country as bureaucrats, its frame of reference was the entire state, not the locale. In Damascus a rise to prominence was in the context of the city; in Bursa it was in the the context of the empire at large.

Important evidence on the structure of the family can also be had from studying surviving documents on religious endowments (waqf). One type of evidence showing that the extended family was foremost on the minds of scions of the Aleppin elite is the pattern of endowments. Of 463 waqfs recorded in the literature as established in Aleppo between 1770 and 1830, about half were institutions devoted to the family, and a great many of these laid it down specifically that their main purpose was to ensure that the property would be dwelt in by the family in the coming generations.[92] As opposed to this, material from the Turkish culture area of the empire shows much less prominence for family endowments. Here no more than 15 percent of the revenues were destined to go to relatives of the founder.[93] The same point was made in another study of Ottoman social history: "The major portion of the umera [governors] vakífs went to support charitable institutions that they set up; family members, if at all favored, were usually made administrators of the vakíf and sometimes received direct benefits. It was as if it were not worthy of their honor and their high position in society to set up family vakífs, like common people, without establishing charitable works."[94]

Probably the most serious challenge to the thesis on the relative weakness of family ties and relations in the core area of the Ottoman Empire is the case of the Ottoman religious institution in the eighteenth century.[95] When we check the political career paths of high ulema in this period, the importance of the family cannot be denied. For example, no less than twenty-nine of the fifty-eight şeyhülislams who officiated between 1703 and 1839 came from just eleven families. It is thus evident that family connections played a crucial role in entrance and advancement to the very top positions in the religious institution. But again, it must be borne in mind that there is a far cry between this and an extended family form of living. The sons of high *ulema* who received positions necessarily separated from their fathers for the rest of their lives and established their own households. And these households, in turn, were semi-nomadic, having to move every year or so to another place. Moreover, as Madeline Zilfi notes with some surprise, all marriage unions of the 237 topmost Ottoman *ulema* in the eighteenth century were monogamous. And she remarks further: "Contemporaneous observers confirmed—with some surprise—that polygamy was rare among Ottoman officialdom, particularly among the great ulema families."[96] We should also bear in mind that though we currently lack a good explanation for the *ulema* ascendancy in the eighteenth century, the phenomenon was certainly a short-lived one and disappeared within a century as mysteriously as it had arisen. In that sense it was certainly to a large extent exceptional.

We come finally to the nub of the argument in this section, which is not only that families in the core area were less extended and more nucleated than in farther areas of the Middle East, but also that the Ottoman government had a direct, albeit unintended, hand in this. Some evidence along these lines can be culled from Alan Duben's study of late Ottoman Istanbul.[97] Duben reached the "surprising" conclusion that the average structure of the family in the Istanbul area in this period was nuclear and small, and that it differed in this respect from rural Anatolia and other areas of the Middle East. Of the causes that Duben adduces as explanation, one in particular seems to pertain to the late nineteenth century— namely the large-scale immigration of Turks from the rapidly shrinking Ottoman dominions. But I fully concur that other factors in Istanbul's uniqueness were of long standing: "It is hardly surprising that Istanbul, the cosmopolitan capital of the Ottoman Empire and a major port city with dense maritime connections to the whole Mediterranean basin, would differ from the rural, land-locked hinterland of the Anatolian plateau."[98] By the same token, another major factor in explaining Istanbul's uniqueness is more directly connected to the Ottoman bureaucracy. The author found a widespread phenomenon, completely absent in other places, of husbands joining the household of the wife's parents rather than the other way round, as is usual in patriarchal societies.[99] This is clear evidence of the influence exerted by the sultanate on Istanbul society: "The Istanbul custom of residence with the wife's family may have been modeled after the imperial palace tradition where . . .

daughters' husbands, known as *damat*s, traditionally played politically very significant roles in palace and state affairs. . . . The prestigious status of the *damat* was emulated in the microcosm of the elite households of the city, which were linked to the palace both through intricate patron-client ties and a kind of institutional mimesis. The high status of the *damat* in Istanbul was not just something limited to the upper crust of society, but pervaded domestic mores in the city in general."[100] The Ottoman palace's role in influencing the Istanbulite family structure away from patriarchalism is thus lucidly corroborated.

THE *BOOK OF COMPLAINTS* AND CENTER-PERIPHERY RELATIONS IN THE OTTOMAN EMPIRE

Several of these points—patrimonialism versus bureaucratism, the relations between center and periphery, and the question of decline—can be illuminated by an additional documentary source, which to my mind is of exceptional value. This is the record of citizens' complaints to the ruler against wrong done to them by various individuals, chiefly state officials. It was an extremely popular institution in the Ottoman Empire, and complaints were assembled in a series of registers in the central Ottoman archive. Such complaints highlight quite clearly the implied contractual ties that were the basis of sultan citizen relations, and the obligation of the sultan to uphold the concept of *adalet* (social justice)—that is, immunity of the *reaya* (state's subjects) from illegal treatment, especially at the hand of officials. In other words, my claim is that relations between the sultan and his subjects were far from being based on brute force—as seems to be the popular notion. Only recently have scholars become sensitive to these issues. It has been observed, for example, that the preambles to Ottoman laws (*kanuns*) destined for the Arab world were written in Arabic; they were probably intended to be read aloud to elicit a positive feeling toward the Ottoman dynasty—which is, after all, the essence of legitimation.[101] Another scholar has analyzed the relations between the sultan and the janissaries in the seventeenth and eighteenth centuries and has found in them an implied contractual core, the violation of which could easily bring about a soldiers' revolt.[102] I claim here that very much the same thing can be found in the language used by complainants to the sultan in the *Şikayet Defteri* (*Book of Complaints*). The Austrian

Academy has published a facsimile of one such register, which had strayed into the archive of the old Hapsburg Empire. This large volume, containing about 2,800 documents pertaining to nine months in the year 1675, constitutes the basis of the present section. Among other things, this source is an important cultural document because of the clues it contains on how various groups within Ottoman society viewed themselves and the government, which is my main reason for preferring to discuss this document as a unified piece of information.

On perusing the complaints contained in this register, one notes that several conclusions emerge. Some of the complaints involve matters between private individuals and are of little interest in the present study. Others deal with cases brought by one official against another, and many of these are also of little use for the present study. But the major portion of the documents in the register are complaints of citizens against state officials, and they are a highly revealing source regarding the actual relations between these two elements in Ottoman society. In fact, of the 2,800 complaints in the register, about half are truly public complaints.

How can the *Şikayet Defteri* further the study of center periphery relations in the Ottoman Empire? Currently, study of this topic suffers from a predicament: while it is possible to reconstruct some parts of the historical features of elite social groups, such as religious scholars,[103] provincial governors,[104] and even elite individuals,[105] it is very difficult to say anything empirical and concrete about so hazy a social group as "the common people." The value of the complaint register is that it reveals something about Ottoman society in its entirety, including both elite and commoners. Another important aspect of the register is that it lends itself to meaningful statistical analysis. Given the large number of complaints, a statistical breakdown of various types of complaints probably reflects a similar breakdown in real life.

Before I launch into an analysis of the various types of complaints, a word is in order concerning the phenomenon of citizens' complaints against officials in general. Given the prevailing scholarly opinion on center-periphery relations in the Ottoman Empire, it is startling to observe such large numbers of complaints by people in villages and small towns. These were people from the lowest reaches of society, and they were filing strongly worded complaints against state officials, identifying themselves by full name and address. Although the existence of the complaints shows, of course, that wrongs were done, it seems even more telling that common people were fighting back with such enthusiasm and apparent lack of fear. It leads one to suspect possible exaggeration in the degree to which the Ottoman Empire has been considered an extreme form of despotism. The seriousness with which the government viewed these complaints is also indicative.

Two important aspects of the *Book of Complaints* should be noted here. One is the link created between the sovereign and the individual citizen over the head of the official. The other is the courage displayed by ordinary people in putting high Ottoman officials at risk, sometimes grave risk, by exposing them to the possible wrath of the ruler. Regarding the first point, the very fact that citizens complained to the ruler against state officials shows that the assumption did not exist that the ruler would automatically back his officials against his subjects. This evidently harks back to an ancient Middle Eastern pattern of a ruler's suspicious view of his officials and his willingness to seek ways to check bureaucrats' ambitions. Be that as it may, the distinct feature of the *Şikayet Defteri* is the impeccable consideration given by the ruler to every humble complaint. In no document in the register can one discern any sultanic effort to back the usurpation of legal rights by provincial officials or to conceal any act of wrongdoing. While this does not, of course, prove that such usurpation did not take place, it certainly indicates something about the ideological approach of the central government toward the periphery. An example is a complaint by a citizen of Ayntab in southeastern Anatolia. He alleged that a politically powerful man of that town had murdered his son; but as the alleged murderer held strong sway over the local assistant judge (*naib*), there was no chance of his being brought to trial. A sultanic order directed the *kadi* of Maraş (a neighboring town) to have the case transferred to that city.[106]

The large number of citizens' complaints against officials and the unequivocal support given by the sovereign to these complaints should probably caution us against viewing the common people in the Ottoman Empire as too easy a prey at the hands of state officials. But at this point let us go a little deeper and look at some specific topics that appear in the *Şikayet Defteri*.

To my mind the most important are the complaints against *kadi*s, a topic of major importance from the point of view of a study focusing specifically on the Ottoman legal system. Behind citizens' complaints against *kadi*s hides the big topic of alleged judicial corruption and ineptitude, which figures prominently in analyses of Ottoman decline after the end of the sixteenth century. Corruption and bribery by judges were often viewed as the root cause of other major types of decline and disintegration. Because corruption does not usually leave behind archival documents, few topics are as difficult to study empirically as that of judicial corruption. The little research done on this topic is based mainly on various forms of hearsay, extracted for the most part from European travelers in the Ottoman Empire.[107]

Ahmed Mumcu's study of Ottoman corruption tends to differentiate between administrative corruption, such as the sale of offices, and judicial corruption, such as the payment of bribes to judges in return for a biased decision in a court case. In the context of the alleged decline of the Ottoman Empire, the second type is much more important; for it is my feeling that a polity in which the court is thoroughly corrupt can hardly exist for long without undergoing a major change in some form or other. Therefore, I am interested mainly in judicial corruption.

I must, however, begin by saying a few words about administrative corruption, although I hasten to add that the Şikayet Defteri does not, in fact, supply us with evidence on administrative corruption. I suggest viewing with suspicion the prevalent opinion (expressed by Mumcu, among others) that in the so-called period of decline offices were awarded by a kind of auction—with the highest bidder getting the job and, of course, hastening to make good on his investment. While there is no question that all nominations after Süleyman the Magnificent may have involved a payment, this whole point should be approached with caution. I doubt very much whether Mumcu's supposedly characteristic example— someone who paid a big sum of money for a post only to come home and hear that he had been divested of it[108]—is really a fair representation of reality. If it were, it is unclear how officeholders ever managed to take control of their provinces and run them for a year. It seems likely that the level of corruption involved in nominations to Ottoman offices may have been exaggerated.

But let us return to judicial corruption. Mumcu presents a great many details, and we cannot doubt that corruption did exist. But the crucial question is, how widespread was it? After all, corruption, including judicial corruption, is not unheard of today even in Western countries, where it is not supposed to exist. Supposing it was more widespread in Ottoman society, can we assume that it was the dominant factor in the judicial process? This is really the crux of the issue. Since working on the court records of Bursa, I have tended to view with considerable suspicion the allegation that corruption was *the* predominant factor in the post-sixteenth-century Ottoman Empire. The *kadi* records give the impression that the judicial system was, on the whole, fair.[109] Short of colossal forgery, it is difficult to see how and where the modern observer could be deceived by these records on such a grand scale as to come away with a totally false picture. All trial proceedings were attended by witnesses of some sort. Were so many people paid off or deceived? Not very likely, but a nagging question mark remains hanging over this question.

It is fortunate, then, that the *Şikayet Defteri* offers a new kind of approach to the question of judicial corruption in the Ottoman Empire. The many types of complaints found in that register include complaints against *kadi*s. If we are to take the register as representing a real-life breakdown, and if we are to believe that citizens' complaints reflect the truth (an unproven and unprovable assumption, but one that seems plausible), then this source supplies, for the first time, hard evidence on judicial corruption.

I found in the register seventy-one complaints against *kadi*s. This certainly shows that a problem with *kadi*s existed, but I must emphasize that the number of complaints against governors was immeasurably larger. Furthermore, if we carefully check the nature of the complaints against *kadi*s, some features stand out. Almost all were filed against *naib*s (assistant *kadi*s) in small and remote rural areas. There are scarcely any complaints against *kadi*s in large cities. In fact, there is some evidence in the register that *naib*s were morally suspect to start with, in comparison with *kadi*s. A relevant document, sent from a place in the Balkans, claims that although nomination of a *naib* from among the local inhabitants was forbidden, a certain Hamze had managed to get himself nominated to the post, with the result that he has aligned himself with the officials and caused the poor citizens to pay more than the legal rate in taxes. An order was issued to remove that *naib* from his post.[110] One of the few complaints against a city judge was directed against the *kadi* of Bursa, who was accused by *waqf* managers in the city of conducting an inspection tour of the *waqf*s every year, whereas according to the old custom he was supposed to do this every two years.[111] But if anything, such an act on the part of a *kadi* was intended to serve the interests of the populace, not to harm it. The dearth of complaints against *kadi*s in large cities cannot be fortuitous and probably means that with the rise in status came an added measure of social responsibility. This is of some importance in itself, and may indicate that important *kadi*s preserved a modicum of integrity, certainly a valued ideal in this society.

To conclude the general review of complaints against *kadi*s, it may be said that illegal behavior, though extant, was far from being the norm, and every exposed case was treated seriously. Usually, cases against *kadi*s were sent to the administrative area superior to or adjacent to the area of the implicated *kadi*, with orders to investigate and if necessary bring legal action against him. As a consequence, some *kadi*s went into hiding.[112]

If we turn now to a closer look at the complaints against *kadi*s, one of the most distinct feature is the almost total absence of accusations of judicial corruption in the strict sense—that is, allegations of partisan judgment due to bribery. With rare exceptions, all the complaints against *kadi*s involve accusations of exacting illegal taxes—either from the whole community or through illegally high rates for the services supplied by the court. To my mind it is beyond any doubt that taking bribes, if it had become habitual, would not have escaped notice. So we are probably justified in interpreting the dearth of such cases as reflecting reality. And if this is so, then it is certainly a most important conclusion indicating that Ottoman *kadi*s in the so-called period of decline preserved a substantial measure of the integrity for which they had been known in the sixteenth century.

What were some of the actual accusations leveled against *kadi*s? As indicated, most of the cases involved various forms of tax extortion. Thus, inhabitants in the region of Adana complained that their *kadi* did not sit, as is customary, in the *mahkama* (the Islamic court) but preferred rather to roam the villages and deliver judgment there, living all the while at the expense of the villagers and in addition charging them more than the legal rates.[113] In another example the inhabitants of a village in Karaman complained that their *kadi* had pocketed sixty thousand akçe purportedly levied as a tax for the government, and that he charged them more than the legal rate for various documents.[114] In a third example a large body of villagers from the Morea claimed that the *kadi* had exploited a tax collection drive in the area to extort from them various additional taxes, which he then pocketed.[115] This is a very common type of complaint, usually involving quite small sums of money per family or individual.[116] In many cases the complaints were launched by individuals, who claimed that the *kadi*s wronged them in various ways. In one case a Turkman from the region of Manisa claimed that the former *kadi* of that town had charged him the (highly exorbitant) sum of one hundred piasters for issuing a complaint document.[117] In other cases a founder of a *waqf* in Tripoli, Syria, claimed that the *kadi* had illegally appropriated money belonging to the institution,[118] and a Jew from Aleppo claimed that the former *kadi* of that city had imprisoned him unjustly for a month, in addition to extracting sixteen hundred piasters from him.[119] Some complaints depict *kadi*s in very unusual if not bizarre types of behavior. In one example a group of artisans from the area of Gallipoli claimed that their former *kadi* had extorted small sums from them and that when one of them demanded his money back, the *kadi* ordered him beaten, as a consequence of which he eventually died.[120] In another case the inhabitants of a *kaza* in central Anatolia claimed that their *kadi* had extorted from them a large quantity of barley and eighty carts of straw as well as some money. On hearing that the central government had issued a warrant to summon him to the Imperial Council, he ran away to Denizli, and the whole issue was transferred to the inspector of brigands of Anatolia (*Anadolu eşkiya müfetişi*), a high official usually bearing the title of Paşa.[121] People from the area of Güzel Hisar, in the Manisa region, also complained about their *naib,* who was alleged to have behaved in a variety of (unspecified) illegal ways that were severe enough to cause disturbances among the people. This complaint, too, was treated with particular severity by the central government.[122]

Another area of problems with *kadi*s was their handling of estates postmortem. It was the *kadi*'s responsibility to distribute the properties of the deceased to the heirs in accordance with the Islamic laws of inheritance, and he was sometimes accused of illegally appropriating portions of such estates[123] or of unjustly handing over the estate only to some of the heirs—whether for personal gain is not always clear.[124]

Finally, a small number of complaints involved full-scale allegations of bribery to affect the outcome of trials. In one case people from the rural region of Niğde claimed that in a trial involving a land dispute their *kadi* had been bribed to decide against the party who possessed a document of ownership.[125] The *kadi* of Malatya was also expressly accused by a group of citizens of taking bribes that then influenced the outcome of trials.[126] The term *rüşvet*, the modern term for bribery, was apparently much less specific at the time and was encountered only once, in a document in which a *naib* in the region of Silistre was accused by a village of taking a sum from them as *rüşvet* for, among other things, trying to arrange a tax exemption for them.[127] To conclude, if the evidence of the *Şikayet Defteri* is to be believed, then current notions about the total collapse in *kadis'* integrity, competence, and judicial standards has to be viewed as greatly exaggerated. A number of *kadis* were corrupt, no doubt; but our conclusion should be based on the quantitative weight of the evidence, not on the exceptional cases. While the *Şikayet Defteri* lists about seventy complaints against *kadis*, a large proportion of the remaining complaints in the register are filed through the *kadi*—that is, with his help and probably his encouragement—which should be taken as a vote of confidence in him as far as integrity and fairness are concerned. I tend strongly to agree with the general spirit of this finding, because it tallies perfectly with the situation forced upon the reader of the Bursa court records of the seventeenth century.

Another important issue that can be investigated on the basis of the *Şikayet Defteri* pertains to the question of the Ottoman government's oppression and despotism toward the population. As noted earlier, not a single case could be found in the entire register in which the central government itself—the sultan, that is—had acted wildly or unjustly. But what about the officials? I probed the register for cases of despotic behavior—such as arbitrary and illegal executions, large-scale usurpation of property, and the like—on the part of the authorities toward citizens. Admittedly this is a rather fuzzy category; nevertheless, the number of cases of this type is surprisingly small—no more than twelve. In one instance a *voyvoda* (governor of a small rural area) in Zulkadriya province (southeast Anatolia) was alleged by citizens in the area to have extorted sums of money from an individual with no legal justification.[128] In the region of Kanghari it was alleged that the *mufti* and his sons had teamed up with the *ehl-i örf* in order to arrest people and extract money from them, undeterred even by a sultanic order and a *fetva* of the *şeyhülislam* issued against him.[129] In a third example a janissary, citizen of a village in the Bursa region, was accused by the village of robbing them of a whole herd of cattle and sheep.[130]

One might expect to find in a book of complaints a flood of cases involving oppression of non-Muslims by officials. In fact, however, such cases were very few. In one, Christians from the area of Kastamonu complained that officials had obstructed them when they wished to prepare a classroom in their house.[131] Some Jews in Sultaniye filed a complaint against the local *kadi* for extracting money from them, under the excuse of their having committed a certain violation.[132] A final example comes from the region of Malatya, in which the Christians of a village belonging to a *has* fief claimed that fifteen or twenty years earlier they had left the area "because of the severity of oppression" from which they had suffered.[133] Severe cases did occur, then, but they were probably far fewer than formerly believed.

The most common type of complaint in the *Şikayet Defteri* concerns state officials of various types involved in extorting illegal taxes—mostly from communities rather than from individuals. In all I counted 215 such complaints. Because the category is evidently not clear-cut, another tally might come up with a slightly different figure. There is no way of assessing the number scientifically for lack of a comparative referent. However, a total of 215 cases of tax extortions does prove that the Ottoman Empire had a serious problem of order and discipline among its officials in the provinces.

Most of the cases of tax extortion occurred in the context of an armed tour of the province by the governor or, more usually, his acting representative with a varying number of mounted retainers. Such a group would alight on a village, demand hospitality, and in addition extract a sum of money from every household. Most of the complaints in this category of tax extortion related to rural areas. The parallelism that we see here with complaints against *kadi*s and *naib*s is probably not fortuitous; it shows that the central bureaucracy was more effective in keeping Ottoman officials in their proper place in the urban areas. It is interesting to note that the rural areas, those inhabited by semi-nomad Turkmen, were singled out for treatment even worse than that accorded to villages.[134] This point is noteworthy because it indicates that contrary to the situation in, say, North Africa, where the tribes were beyond the control of the state, in Anatolia they seem clearly to have been inferior to the state, if not actually downtrodden. If this finding about the different treatment of urbanites and rural people is valid, it bears out my contention that oppression in the Ottoman Empire was not part of the policy of the state, but its subversion.

To return to the complaints of tax extortion, most of these grievances were filed by village communities or groups of villages. I find it most remarkable that even in the remote corners of this huge empire villagers knew what was legal and what was not, understood the mechanism for lodging a complaint, and were familiar enough with the intricacies of the Ottoman administration to lodge it. But even more surprising is that villagers should cherish the belief that recourse to the sultan might rectify the wrong done to them. Beyond the ideological view of the sultanate that is revealed here, I also read into this tiny piece of evidence that such faith was not misplaced. I rather doubt that a group of sturdy villagers would waste their time and energy on a venture that they felt would have no chance of success. Finally, this whole widespread phenomenon of village complaint has a serious bearing on the gap that is alleged to have existed between village society and the state. Perhaps that old assumption requires rethinking.

The complaints concerning taxation fall into certain discernible patterns. One distinct type of extortion took place when official tax collectors simply charged more than the legal rate. The various types of extraordinary property taxes—such as *avariz, iştira,* and *nuzul*—were especially exploited in this way.[135] The *cizye* was exploited much less—surprisingly little, in fact.[136] In one case a gypsy community in Rumeli complained about the exorbitant *cizye* collected from them. Noteworthy in this complaint is that different rates were mentioned for Muslims and Christians— which shows that Muslim gypsies also paid the *cizye* tax.[137]

Another type of tax extortion was that by *voyvodas,* the local-level administrators of *has* estates (fiefs held by high men of state and ladies of the palace).[138] It was, however, particularly *sancakbeys* (governors of provinces) and even more commonly *mütesellims* (acting governors) who were involved in tax extortion. A sample case is the complaint of "the *ayan* and the poor" of the district of Biga, who claimed that the governor descended on sixteen villages in the area with no less than 130 mounted retainers, extorting six sheep from every village as well as a total of 1,260 piasters from the whole area.[139] Sometimes the charge was made more simply against the officials, *ehl-i örf,* in general.[140] It is interesting and probably noteworthy that the highest level of provincial governors, the *beylerbey* (governor of a province), was very little involved in these illicit operations.[141] In one rare example the people of the *sancak* of Kayseri claimed that three former *beylerbeys* had exacted high sums of money from them in illegal taxation. Following a complaint, the sums were retrieved and placed for safekeeping in the fortress of Kayseri, but they were then stolen by minor officials.[142] In another case a *hakim* (local chief) in the province of Mosul claimed that the *beylerbey* of Mosul had exacted illegal taxes from his people.[143]

Another example concerns the aforementioned inspector of brigands in Anatolia, a high official bearing the title of vizier, who was the subject of a complaint, via the *kadi*, by inhabitants of some twenty villages in the area of Sivas. He was alleged to have levied on each of them private taxes amounting to such minor sums as four to eight piasters.[144] This is a strange sort of extortion and no less a strange complaint, having about it more the air of making a point of principle than being intent on retrieving the money. At the very least the complaint can be plausibly interpreted as meaning that villagers in the remote areas of Anatolia were punctilious and rather stubborn in defending their legal rights even when it came to dealing with the government at the highest level—which tends to support the point made previously.

Despite the substantial number of recorded cases of tax extortions, I am still dubious about the empirical adequacy of the term "plunderers of their own society," as used by Şerif Mardin to describe Ottoman officials after the sixteenth century.[145] In the first place, we should not forget that we are talking about a vast empire, comprising a count of villages probably running into tens of thousands. Seen in this light, 220 cases of overtaxation still leaves the great majority of villages clear of this plight. It should also be recalled that the sum involved per family or individual was often very small, even by the standards of the society in question. Another crucially important point is that tax extortion was probably the main way for officials to cope with inflation, an ever-present phenomenon at this period. As Bernard Lewis has shown, at least part of the dramatic increase in public spending (and hence, probably tax extortion) in the seventeenth and eighteenth centuries was not much more than the updating of former figures of spending and taxation.[146] It may well be that due to inflation, the process of tax collection was, in a way, a kind of bargaining between the officials and the villagers. Only in one or two cases was extortion said to have caused ruin and depopulation. In one such case it was alleged that tax extortion in Aqhisar by a *voyvoda* caused ruination of villages and even the death of Muslims.[147] In another case it was claimed that a *mütesellim* in the *sancak* of Kanghari went on a tour, accompanied by three hundred to four hundred mounted retainers extorting fifty to sixty piasters from each village in the area, a drive said to have ended in the desertion of a number of villages.[148] Such allegations may, however, be exaggerated. On the whole it remains unsubstantiated that there was truly a dramatic rise in ruination caused by officials plundering the countryside, compared to what had occurred in the sixteenth century.

So far I have discussed only tax extortion from villagers. What about urbanites? After all, we often hear that one of the major reasons for the lack of an industrial revolution in the Ottoman Empire was the rapacious nature of the government, expressed in the unpredictable and arbitrary usurpation of productive property and the ruinous overtaxation of commerce. The thesis is that such phenomena created an inauspicious atmosphere for entrepreneurs to come forward and invest in long-term projects. The *Şikayet Defteri* should prove a first-rate source to investigate these old generalizations, which have never, in fact, been documented; but a scan of the register in question fails to substantiate this assumption. There were no cases in the register alleging the capricious, arbitrary usurpation of urban property; the few cases involving merchants had to do with the illegal imposition of excess customs duties.[149]

The *Book of Complaints*, reflecting as it does real administrative and bureaucratic life in the Ottoman Empire in the late seventeenth century, naturally contains a substantial body of information on the decline of the *timar* system (fiefs granted to *sipahi*s in return for military service). While the objection might be raised that this topic is not part of the subject covered by this study, I believe it illustrates my contention that the prevailing view of the structure of the Ottoman polity in the seventeenth and eighteenth centuries is in need of major revision. In the *timar* system we have an excellent window through which to observe the process of the disintegration of old institutions and the rise of new ones—the supposed replacement of the *timar* system by the *iltizam* (tax farming) purported to have brought ruin both to peasants and to the state treasury.

Again, the *Şikayet Defteri* tells an entirely different story, much more similar to what I have detected in my study on the social origins of the modern Middle East.[150] I have found in the *Book of Complaints* about 110 documents dealing with the *timar* system. In all of them the institution, though certainly depicted as being in distress, is nevertheless alive and functioning. As opposed to this, the *iltizam* system, supposed by this time to have eclipsed the *timar*, was mentioned in only about twenty complaints. So there is every reason to believe that in actuality the transformation from one system to the other was only just beginning in this period. The result for the historiography of the Ottoman Empire is that a belief in the supposed ruination and decline brought on by tax farming has to be relaxed considerably. That the *timar* institution was in distress at this time is probably made clear already by the fact that in most of the documents relating to the *timar* it is not the *reaya* (peasants) who complain against fiefholders, but fiefholders who complain against either peasants or other officials.[151]

Several of the phenomena claimed in the literature to have dominated the scene at this time were not encountered at all in the register. One is the claim that while *sipahis* were on campaign, high officials would take over their *timars* and thus amass a number of fiefs.[152] But the *Şikayet Defteri* neither hints at such a process nor provides concrete examples. I interpret this as meaning that the phenomenon was much rarer than we are given to understand mainly by Marxist-oriented social historians of the Balkans.[153] What we do find in the documents are mainly complaints by fiefholders that various administrative bodies or individuals in the vicinity have seized portions of these fiefs or portions of the taxes belonging thereto. The simplest type of case was a quarrel over the supposed borders of the fief.[154] Invariably it was the fiefholder who claimed to have been wronged, never the other way around. Thus, a fiefholder from the province of Segedin complained against the *kadi* and other officials in the area, claiming that they had prevented his representative from collecting the land taxes due to him.[155] Indeed, it was typically other state officials of various sorts who were accused of usurping the revenues of the fief.[156] Again, it was probably not by chance that in the great majority of cases involving fiefholders versus other state officials, the fiefholder was eventually found to be in the right. It is quite evident that the *timar* institution was under threat.

One extreme example, though not entirely atypical, is a complaint filed by the *naib* of Silifke in southern Anatolia. In it he claimed that sometime earlier the *ehl-i örf* of Silifke had proceeded to levy extra taxes on the peasants of a *zeamet* holder in the area, despite their being in possession of an exemption certificate (*serbestname*). Not content with this, the officials gathered a group of some seventy to eighty brigands and sacked the house of the *zeamet* holder himself, and then went on to destroy the building of the *mahkama* (the Islamic court)—a rare but symbolic act.[157]

Statistically, it was more often the provincial governor who put pressure on *timar* and *zeamet* holders, either by demanding higher sums of money for awarding entitlements[158] or by interfering in the affairs of the fief by exacting from the peasants new kinds of taxes (especially *avariz*) that were not registered in the sixteenth-century agrarian *kanun*.[159] But neither did minor officials show much respect for fiefholders' rights; they would seize every opportunity to infringe on them.[160] Even local strongmen who were not part of the Ottoman administration would try to grab their share of the cake.[161] Fiefholders themselves were sometimes subjected to tax extortion, as in the payment of the *tezkre akçesi* to their officers.[162]

A side issue here, even a technicality but one that nevertheless says much on the wider topic, is the way complaints on land questions were handled. An old theory on the decline of the *timar* system asserts that after the sixteenth century, complete anarchy in the record-keeping mechanisms set in, which allowed strongmen of every description to wreck the entire system.[163] The *Şikayet Defteri* tells a different story. All the complaints in the register concerning the *timar* system were resolved by recourse to the old sixteenth-century agrarian surveys—apparently updated in an ad hoc fashion—and additional archival documentation on the *timar* system. This is stated specifically in the documents,[164] and in every case the relevant documents could be traced. Even semiprivate arrangements between fiefholders and those who collected taxes on their behalf somehow found their way into the state archives, information that was on several occasions retrieved and used to resolve disputes between fiefholders (or their heirs) and tax collectors.[165] In fact, from many documents one gets the impression that it was precisely the archive that served as a bulwark against the collapse of the *timar* system. An example is a series of complaints from the province of Varad (modern Rumania) in which people raised sophisticated legal arguments with the intention of taking fiefs from their holders. Recourse to the registers, however, exposed the falseness of these claims.[166]

The complaints in the *Şikayet Defteri* concerning the *timar* institution do reveal some changes as compared with the sixteenth century. One is that in accordance with the claims of critics—for example, the aforementioned memorialists—most of the *timar* holders who figure in the *Şikayet Defteri* were not real warrior *sipahis* but various state officials who drew their pay by way of the fief. This is not to say that real old-style *sipahis* did not appear in it. They did,[167] as did *sipahis* who actually died in battle.[168] Nevertheless, a large number of the fiefholders mentioned in the register were state officials rather than true *sipahis*. But whether such a finding can be interpreted as supporting the decline theory is another matter. To my mind the answer should be emphatically in the negative. These officials had to be supported one way or another.

Another discernible change is that fiefholders now rarely lived within their fief. This found expression in the register in the widespread practice of land taxes being collected by representatives, whether salaried clerks or tax farmers.[169] Yet another apparent innovation was for several people to hold a *timar* or *zeamet* in partnership. Thus, in the region of Ankara three brothers jointly held title to a *zeamet*,[170] and in another case no less than five people together held a *timar* village.[171]

Aside from these changes, the *timar* system seems for the most part to have retained its sixteenth-century characteristics, outstanding among which was the basic right of inheritance enjoyed by sons of deceased fiefholders. This law is supposed to have fallen into abeyance after the sixteenth century, with the state purportedly assigning such fiefs to tax farmers. But no single case of this is hinted at in the register, despite the frequent mention of unoccupied fiefs. In all cases in which a *timar* holder is mentioned as having recently died, his fief passed to his son.[172] In some cases in which the *sipahi* died without leaving a son, the fief was assigned to another *sipahi*.[173] In all cases in which *sipahis* had failed to report for a campaign, the fief was transferred to another *sipahi*.[174]

In sum, changes were taking place in the *timar* system, but we should be cautious in interpreting their meaning or their pace. That changes were taking place is symbolized in the fact that the *timar* was under pressure from the peasants. While some of the old confrontations between fiefholders and peasants still existed, in several cases this classic confrontation was now reversed; fiefholders complained against villagers for trying to avoid tax payment through all sorts of excuses. The very fact that fiefholders now had to resort to the government to secure their basic rights is a telling one.[175]

As noted previously, only some twenty documents in the *Şikayet Defteri* mention the *iltizam*, offering further proof that this institution replaced the *timar* much later than is commonly assumed. In fact, in some of the documents mentioning the term *iltizam*, there is explicit reference to taxes other than agricultural ones, such as *avariz* or *cizye*.[176] It is noteworthy, however, even concerning these types of *iltizam* that the dispute in most cases was not between the public and the tax collector but between various levels within the tax collection mechanism itself, mainly between the tax farmer and the actual tax collector. Where then were the major extortions for which this period is so famous? Keeping in mind our working hypothesis that every serious friction in real life found its way into the register of complaints, the only feasible conclusion is that such friction was not as rife as is usually believed. In any event, in this study I am interested mainly in the agricultural *iltizam*, the institution that replaced the *timar* and that is supposed to have contributed so much to the decline of the Ottoman Empire. Yet very few of the complaints dwell on this topic. Most deal with the leasing by *timar* holders of the office of tax collector, and most are somewhat bizarre in nature. They present us with a kind of *iltizam* institution that is somewhat at variance with the one familiar to us from later periods. For example, in one document we hear that the collector passed on the money collected to the *zeamet* holder without keeping any for himself.[177] In another complaint a quasi-sultanic *waqf* in Istanbul claimed that the lessee in *iltizam* of the *waqf* taxes had not passed them on to the *waqf*.[178] These cases are, of course, strange because the raison d'être of the *iltizam* was to earmark part of the revenue as profit for the collector. Even more lucid in this regard is the complaint of a tax collector who leased (*der uhde ve sipariş*) from a fiefholder the right to collect the taxes of the fief. He claimed that he had collected the tax and passed it on in its entirety, but now the fiefholder claimed they had agreed that six hundred piasters needed to be collected, not the (obviously smaller) sum handed over. Moreover, he claimed he had heard that the sum collected was higher. The tax farmer protested that "I heard" was not an acceptable proof (and in this he was supported by a *fetva* of the şeyhülislam).[179] This cryptic description, necessitated by the coded brevity of the complaints, seems to imply that the tax farmer was supposed to pass on to the fiefholder the entire amount collected. And as noted, this is indeed the bizarre point about all these documents: they do not fit with what we know about the institution of tax farming. In particular, where is the traditional cut for the tax farmer? In all likelihood what we have here is an early stage of the institution in which the collector did his job for a specified salary agreed upon beforehand.

Another irregular case came from a village on the island of Chios. The peasants complained that whereas the taxes on the village were formerly sixty thousand akçe collected by tax farming, some local strongmen had recently offered to raise double that sum. The villagers claimed this was contrary to the law, both *shari'a* and *kanun*, and their argument was supported by the central government.[180] Again, this episode obviously did not involve the regular kind of *iltizam* familiar in later periods. I was able to trace only one regular-looking *iltizam* document; it indicates that a *mukataa* (a tax farming area) was an area taxed by an *emin*, or tax farmer.[181] But even here the internal structure might have been irregular.

Whatever the details concerning the development of the institution of tax farming, it appears that in this entire register there is no single case of complaint by villagers that a tax farmer was imposing on them taxes above the traditional levels. This is obviously a crucial point. If among the hundreds of cases of tax extortion there is no mention of the *iltizam*, this institution must surely have been at a very early stage of development.

A topic of particular interest to the present study is the meddling of officials in legal or quasilegal affairs. One example in the *Şikayet Defteri* of such meddling is the complaint of a villager from the Sivas area that the *mütesellim* sent one of his retainers to the village to capture the plaintiff (no reason is given). Because the man was not at home, his slave was seized and then detained by the *mütesellim* for three months—not on the basis of a trial pending before the *kadi*, but on the basis of *siyaset* (administrative justice). The villager claimed this was illegal, and his reading of the episode was confirmed by the central government.[182] In a similar case, a chief of the Danişmendlu Turkman tribe of central Anatolia claimed that the *mufettiş* Mehmed Paşa seized the plaintiff for supposed highway robbery, locked him up for three months by way of *siyaset*, and then confiscated his horses and sheep. According to the order issued, all this was illegal, and the property confiscated should have been returned forthwith.[183] An interesting point in these two cases is that these high officials were acting to root out crime, so what they did was purportedly within the bounds of their authority. Yet their acts were perceived by the central government as illegal—for the explicit reason that the issue was not referred to the *kadi*'s court for adjudication.

Another topic that appears in the *Şikayet Defteri* and may shed some light on the political system of the Ottoman Empire in the seventeenth century is a substantial body of complaints—about sixty in number—dealing with highway robbery. Most of these complaints were private in nature, consisting of citizens' calls to the government for help against brigands, and in this sense the topic diverges from most others analyzed in this chapter. Nevertheless, these cases are relevant to this study because they raise the question: to what extent was social banditry in evidence?

It was Eric Hobsbawm who coined the term *social banditry* and initiated the issue as a research topic in social history.[184] Hobsbawm had in mind a type of banditry that was specifically directed against authority and the higher classes. Social banditry was social protest no less than banditry in the ordinary sense. As I interpret it, widespread social banditry is a sign of legitimacy crisis, something to be quite expected in the Ottoman Empire in the seventeenth and eighteenth centuries. Seen against this background, it is interesting to investigate the banditry cases in the *Şikayet Defteri* for signs of social banditry.

Of the sixty or so cases of banditry found, in cases in which the social origins of the perpetrator(s) could be identified, all derived from villages. On the other hand the overwhelming majority of the victims were also villagers; in a few cases they were other types of common citizens (for example, traveling merchants). Cases that could be characterized as social banditry were very few in number. If, indeed, the incidence of social banditry can be taken as a rough measure of the degree of legitimacy enjoyed by a regime, there is little evidence that the Ottoman government was viewed with deep resentment in this period.

Let us look at some of the cases. One, contained in a decree sent to the governor and *kadi* of Trabzon and the *kadi* of Of, is about a number of people from villages in the area who formed a band and attacked a house, stole money, and set properties on fire.[185] In another case, inhabitants of a village in Bosnia complained that a group of some eighty robbers descended on the village, consumed their food, and caused them to scatter.[186] Far from being in a state of universal enmity with state officials, brigands sometime cooperated with them against villagers, usually by descending on a village and extracting money and food from the peasants.[187] A particularly severe case is that of a villager from the region of Nigbolu who took over his own village, controlling everything that went on in it socially and economically, all the while beating and cursing the people.[188] This was not an isolated case, though it is difficult to visualize how it was possible in a

Middle Eastern society dominated by tightly woven groups with a very strict code of honor.

A number of cases of banditry have to do with highway robbery in which gangs of robbers, ten or more strong, set upon merchants on the roads. Because these gangs were not particularly selective in choosing their targets,[189] there is little justification to view these incidents as social banditry.

In some cases this brigandage deteriorated into something bordering on civil war. This was found especially in the marginal areas of Anatolia, inhabited mainly by Kurdish and Turkmen tribesmen. In a complaint filed by Turkmen from the Aleppo region, they claimed to have been attacked by Kurdish tribesmen numbering in the hundreds, while en route to their summer camp.[190] Similarly, Turkmen in the region of Kayseri complained of an attack by a group of about forty fellow tribesmen.[191]

Some cases do bear the marks of possible social banditry. An example of this sort was the assault by a group of brigands on the house of an *alim* (religious scholar) for five days in a row—an incident that may have been sparked by social resentment.[192] In another example, on the other side of the empire, such a gang of robbers went further, abducting the family members of an *alim* and threatening to kill them unless the *alim* paid ransom—which he eventually did.[193] In a complaint from the region of Sinop, a *kadi* claimed that a large gang of brigands attacked and sacked his rural estate in that area.[194] There are also several cases of groups of bandits attacking law courts in various places.[195] Additional cases that should probably be classified as social banditry appear in complaints by governors and tax collectors against groups of brigands who had incited people to resist tax collectors[196] or had actually attacked tax collectors and robbed them.[197] While most of these cases were from the marginal areas of Anatolia, some were even from the core area.[198]

Not the least interesting aspect of many of these severe cases of brigandage is the way in which they were handled by the legal apparatus of the Ottoman state. At least in public cases—that is, those involving state officials or state property—one might expect clear and undisputed supremacy of the governor over the *kadi*. After all, even the *kanun* stipulates that public violations of the peace are the domain of the governors, and the *kadi*s should not interfere. Yet almost all cases relating to brigandage were directed to the *kadi* of the region (though often also to the governor) with a specific order to handle the matter through the *shari'a* court. This fact strongly reinforces the conclusion that the supremacy of the *kadi* in the Ottoman legal system in the post-sixteenth-century period was undiminished. It also underscores the view of the Ottoman state itself that it was the *kadi* who held judicial monopoly in the empire. The only exceptions to this rule were the really major disturbances mentioned previously, involving large groups of armed tribesmen in marginal areas. These cases were assigned to the care of governors equipped with proper armies.[199] But aside from cases approaching civil war, the Ottomans were strict in upholding the *kadi's* monopoly. A good example is contained in one of the few cases in the register in which term *siyaset* occurs. In this episode a governor acted as judge and, under the banner of *siyaset*, tried a villager as being an accessory to a brigand and fined him 160 piasters. This procedure was declared illegal and void because the issue had not been dealt with by the *shari`a* court.[200] Beyond its importance in elucidating center periphery relations in the Ottoman Empire, then, the *Şikayet Defteri* provides a significant boost to the argument of *shari`a* supremacy in the seventeenth and eighteenth centuries.

6. SUMMARY AND CONCLUSION

This study has revolved around problems in the relations between state and law in the Ottoman Empire, mainly in the seventeenth and eighteenth centuries. But it has also sought to make a contribution to the wider topic of the relations between state and law in general and the history of Islamic law in the middle period in particular. If we agree that one of the most burning issues in legal anthropology today is the tension among law as theory, imposed law, and law as the interplay of dynamic forces on the ground, then Islamic societies with their sacred traditional code of law, the *shari`a*, should prove important for this entire field of study.

What originally attracted me to undertake this study was my feeling that much was amiss with the current notion of the political system of the Ottoman Empire, and a further feeling that an analysis of its legal system was one possible way to rectify the situation. Since the mid-1970s, when working on my doctoral dissertation on the seventeenth-century city of Bursa, I have had a strong feeling that the picture of extreme despotism that pervades the secondary literature on the Ottoman Empire in this period is highly exaggerated and wide of the mark. The urban society that I saw in my research was very benignly controlled, almost comparable to a medieval European town. I was also fascinated by this question: could there be a connection between what I was discovering in Bursa and the democratic regime of modern Turkey? And that question has remained in the back of my mind, although this study does not answer it. Instead I address another question: was there something in the structure of the Ottoman polity that has eluded the scholars? Certainly, the Ottoman Empire had a very strong center, unlike anything else that has existed in Islam so far. Two scholars have even suggested that modern Turkish democracy is somehow connected with the cohesion of that center.[1] But there is a problem with this kind of thesis. After all, imperial China and Russia also had strong centers, but there the tradition did not lead naturally to democratic outcomes. So the issue is certainly much more complicated than this. My effort to grapple with it has led me to study the relations among law, society, and state in the Ottoman Empire.

The question is, why study law in this context? The first answer is instrumental. As is well known, *kadi* court records are our best source for the social history of the common people in the Middle East before the nineteenth century. In addition, I have always felt that the structure of law in a society reflects the nature of the regime, of the political order. It seems that this link has long been assumed in legal anthropology; hence, I have drawn heavily on what is being done by scholars in this field. Max Weber's frame of reference is also extremely useful here, not least because of the reinforcement it has received from Lawrence Rosen's study on the town of Sefrou, Morocco. But the topic also calls for a macrosociological analysis of the relations between the legal system as a whole and the political regime, a kind of endeavor not usually encountered in legal anthropology. This study, then, has tried to combine historical and anthropological approaches to the study of Ottoman law. On the one hand I have tried to trace change that took place in Islamic law under the Ottomans as reflected in both the work of the law court and the thought of the jurists. On the other hand I have sought to compare the central area of the Ottoman Empire with some of the main models current in the literature of legal anthropology. The main theme in this literature is the tension between imposed law and the more or less free-floating bargaining over issues among litigants themselves and among litigants and judges.

In one such monograph about a present-day Islamic society, Lawrence Rosen has built a general model of Moroccan society, his claim being that the basic features that animate Moroccan society also animate Moroccan-Islamic law. At the base of Moroccan society he finds the individual who bargains his/her position in life vis-à-vis the groups that he/she finds around him—family, clan, tribe, etc.; social context and social obligations are of paramount importance in Moroccan society. On meeting a stranger, a Moroccan inquire first of all about his social origins.

And this is also exactly what a Moroccan *kadi* does at the beginning of a trial. The role of the *kadi* is really no more than to get people back to the negotiating process, for bargaining and negotiation are the key concepts in the Moroccan legal system. This general picture of fluidity, of the predominance of legal process, of social relations, of mediation—over and above the laws and rules imposed from on high (whether by the state or by sacred tradition)—is a major feature of Moroccan law and one that it has in common with a large range of preindustrial societies studied by legal anthropologists all over the world. However, I sensed intuitively that my own area of study was more than a little different, and a search of the anthropological literature indeed revealed that the predominance of process over rule is not necessarily a universal characteristic of all societies and all legal systems. For present purposes I have borrowed a comparative model from Lloyd Fallers that found a measure of correlation between legalism and the institutional structuration of state bureaucracies. I should emphasize that this is not intended to be a universal generalization. (The now defunct Soviet Union, for example, had a highly developed state bureaucracy with a legal system in many ways resembling that of archaic tribal legal systems.) My claim is, however, that within certain parameters and given certain conditions (all of which are problems that have not so far been adequately addressed) the comparison along these lines of some simple societies studied by anthropologists and the Ottoman Empire is feasible and fruitful.

The first topic I dealt with was the process that unfolded in front of the *kadi*. Here I discussed first the theory of Max Weber. Weber's basic idea concerning law was that contrary to Western law, which was rational—that is, individual cases were decided according to a preexisting body of laws that were dispassionately applied to cases in hand—Islamic law was devoid of rationality. In fact, he made *"kadi* justice" a generic term for a legal system lacking objective rules adequate to deal with ever new cases. According to Weber, this basic situation led to the characterization of the legal system in Islam as (1) a system that was totally unpredictable—because there were no rules or enforceable laws, nobody could know what the *kadi* was basing his decisions on; (2) a system that was arbitrary and that denied basic human rights, an outcome of the previous characteristic; and (3) a system with built-in corruption, also an outcome of the first characteristic. For Weber, this state of affairs was mainly the result of the closing gates of *ijtihad*. Rosen has given Weber an interesting twist. He has, in effect, said that Weber was correct: there are no hard-and-fast rules in Islamic law; hence, the discretion at the hand of the *kadi* is boundless. But this is as it should be. Moroccan society is based more on bargaining than on any hard-and-fast rules of conduct, so the Weberian *kadi* fits in perfectly. Instead of being a sternly adjudicating judge, the *kadi* mediates and helps people get back on the bargaining track.

As to the total lack of rules and the resulting total unpredictability and total discretion in the hands of the *kadi*, as far as the central area of the Ottoman Empire is concerned this is entirely off the mark. Most of the legal code in practice was the *shari`a*, with some additions drawn from the *kanun* and from custom. This entire body of law was perfectly known to the litigants; there were no secrets and no surprises. In every case I examined I could identify the law on which the *kadi* was basing himself. Hence I conclude that *kadi* justice in the area of my study was, in fact, very predictable. Moreover, as *kadi*s were in most cases following a clear and evident judicial course, we can conclude that the actual discretion at their disposal was anything but unlimited.

As I looked at the process that unfolded in front of the *kadi*, I also applied several research questions borrowed from legal anthropology and legal historical anthropology. I was struck by the supreme importance in most of these studies of intimate, face-to-face relations that superseded formal rules. I looked, for example, at the role of witnesses, following the lead of Sally Humphreys, who analyzed the role of witnesses in classical Greece. Contrary to Western society, where witnesses are supposed to tell the truth, in ancient Greece witnesses were found to praise the litigant in the most lofty superlatives. This situation arose at a time when Athens was a small community based on personal acquaintance among all its citizens. A similar anthropological interpretation of classical Islamic law suggests the important role there, too, of personal acquaintance: people knew one another and felt close and equal to one another. In this context I have mentioned the ban on usury as the quintessential feature of this world because interest gives the lender an advantage over the borrower. Neither of these societies lived by written documents, and no one could establish legal rights via the use of legal documents. (This is, of course, an exaggerated statement as far as medieval Islam is concerned, but it is at least culturally and ideologically true.) I have applied these and several more such research categories to the Ottoman legal system and have reached conclusions that point to a substantially different mode of social relations.

Let us look first at witnessing. It is true that we have only summaries of cases; we don't know, for example, how witnesses were screened for reliability. But in the summaries, they were simply asked to say what they had seen; and their testimony seems very much like that of objective witnesses in a Western court. It is possible that in real life the *kadi* argued with witnesses about whether or not they really saw what they claim to have seen; but it is important that whatever his decision, the *kadi* molded it according to the accepted legal categories. Moreover, what was applied, according to the summaries, was quite simply the law. There are no signs of groups being involved in the judicial process, and no compromises were struck by the *kadi*. If a person wanted a compromise, he or she had to negotiate it outside of court; the court itself more or less applied the law.

Structural legalism is also more distinct in the area under study when we consider the place of written documents in the law. Despite the continued primacy of witnesses in the judicial process, the Ottoman Empire and its legal system cannot be understood without documents. We all talk about the Ottoman archives as a superb source of information; but it is high time we started thinking about them also as a sociological fact. It is often mentioned that the invention of firearms played a crucial role in the rise of the Ottoman Empire. But it is no less important that paper was invented at about the same time. Documents penetrated deep into the Ottoman legal system, and certainly rights were created by written documents. Anyone who takes a random look at the Ottoman archive will come across thousands of cases of people who established rights according to the various surveys conducted by the government, whether for population or tax purposes. As is well known, what was written in the survey was the law.

But documents also played a crucial role in the *kadi* records themselves. For example, the entire world of credit was based on documents. In seventeenth-century Bursa many thousands of people were enmeshed in credit relations. When they died, the *kadi* had complete lists of these debts, and money was certainly collected on the basis of the documents. In a possibly symbolic way, the

Ottoman Empire also ignored the classical Islamic ban on usury, first by incorporating interest into the *kanun* and then by allowing it openly on a massive scale in the court of the *kadi*—a possible survival of the *kanun*. Can the lifting of the ban on interest be attributed to the development of more bureaucratic relations between individuals in the core area of the Ottoman Empire? I believe this is indeed the case, and Cemal Kafadar has supplied supporting evidence in his study. Following the studies of Natalie Davis, it shows that Ottoman society also witnessed, from the seventeenth century, the decline of group embeddedness and the rise of individuality.[2]

I should emphasize that the elements of bargaining and negotiation did exist in Ottoman law. The law itself was not something that can be said to have been imposed or enacted by a superior authority, though it contained that element too. It was a combination factors, and the particular form of the combination was not imposed. Nevertheless, it is my strong impression that the process of adjudication itself was rather more legalistic than for example in Morocco. At no time in Ottoman law could someone look at a book or even a series of books and find out the law on a specific matter. The law was never enacted in its entirety; it was an amalgamation of various bodies of law—part enacted, part emerging unaided. To know the law in practice one needed to observe the *kadi's* court at work. But to discover a semi-official view of the law, or what it should have been, one had to look at the collections of opinions (*fetvas*) by the Ottoman *şeyhülislam*s, heads of the religious institution of the empire.

Comparing these two sets of social and intellectual activities is one way to investigate the degree to which the work of the *kadi* was based on free-floating bargaining or, alternatively, was anchored in a cohesive body of law that he was trying to apply. Investigation has showed that the law current in the Ottoman Empire in the seventeenth and eighteenth centuries was in an important way an outcome of negotiation and bargaining conducted between such elements as the central government, the religious scholars, and the civil society. The law was an amalgam of *shari'a*, *kanun*, and custom, in proportions decided solely by the interplay of these powers rather than by fiat. On the other hand, investigation has also shown a far-reaching match between the law disclosed by the *fetva* collections and the law as it came to life in the court of the *kadi*. The law of the *kadi* diverged from the *shari'a* in almost exactly the same manner in which the collections, so to speak, admitted into the fold of the *shari`a* new bodies of law such as interest charging. Study of the *fetva* collections has thus enhanced my belief that in relation to Morocco, Ottoman law was quite legalistic—in its mode of execution, if not in its structure.

An important component of Ottoman law was the law of guilds, which mainly had to do with the mode of conduct of the craft corporations. As shown in this study, guild law was in the main an outgrowth from below rather than an enactment on the part of the government. It is noteworthy that Middle Eastern society also had the autonomous guilds so characteristic of the autonomous medieval European commune. Guild law is crucially important to an understanding of the Ottoman legal system mainly in two respects. First, having emerged from below, guild law indicates quite clearly that the Ottoman government was not interested in the total rationalization of Ottoman society through the law. It was content to leave at least some areas of life to be bargained over freely among the citizens. Second, when we look more closely at how guild law was applied in front of the *kadi*, we again find a strong legalistic approach. Trials between guilds were invariably conducted on the testimony of expert witnesses, people not connected with either of the parties. These witnesses were invariably called on to state the law in the matter, which was then acted upon. At least in front of the *kadi* not much bargaining really went on. In essence what I am claiming is that Ottoman law was a combination of centralized imposition and bureaucratization, and a strong element of negotiation as exemplified in the interplay between *kanun* and *shari`a*, and by the acceptance of large chunks of customary law—primarily guild law.

One focus of this study was the application of an anthropological model to compare the Ottoman Empire and some anthropological case studies along a continuum from imposed law to law as process. A second focus was to contribute to the historical anthropology of law through the study of historical change. The realization that the structure of Ottoman law as observed in the eighteenth century was substantially different from that in the fifteenth century brought home to me that transhistoric models about law in general or Islamic law in particular are highly suspect. I have shown that in classical Islam (all of it?) and in fifteenth-century Anatolia, the legal system was diffuse, lacking coherence in codes and enforcement and entailing a multiplicity of authorities and sources of law.

Change appears to have begun in the Ottoman Empire with the enactment of the sixteenth-century penal *kanun*; a minute study the *kanun* shows that basically it was founded on the criminal code of the *shari`a*. Among other things, the *kanun* insisted on the judicial superiority and even monopoly of the *kadi* and his court. Although it is doubtful whether the specifically *kanun* penalties were ever much in actual use, our material indicates quite unequivocally that by the seventeenth century the *kadi* and the *shari`a* court had risen to prominence and seemed to function as a rather coherent and homogeneous system. On the whole we find a process that entailed the rise of the *shari`a* and the *shari`a* court. The important point here is that the *kadi*, in his sources of legitimacy, was not an Ottoman institution. By allowing, and in fact actively supporting, the rise of the *kadi*, the Ottomans in effect agreed to share power. Also, because *kadi* law was a more or less rational and systematic law, and because it replaced a system that lacked any known code or systematic application, its rise meant a higher level of bureaucratization of the law. It has been said of classical Islam that the problem with the *kadi* was his lack of control over the application of his decisions. On the whole I have not observed that in the Ottoman Empire this was a paralyzing problem (though, of course, it is a problem even in modern societies). As far as central government policy was concerned, the line of authority in judicial matters was clear and undisputable— *kadi* decisions had to be heeded by governors and police officials because this was the wish of the sultanate; the policy was clearly anchored in Islamic ethics. The overwhelming weight of the evidence indicates that this was also the social reality.

Part of the explanation for this rise of the *shari`a* court can probably be sought in what Cornell Fleischer has observed as the Ottomans' problem of legitimacy, which led them to insist on their commitment to justice. I believe it is a combination of this factor, the bureaucratic nature of the state, and a compliance to negotiating pressures from below. In terms of the anthropological model used in this study, it is evident that Ottoman law moved along the continuum suggested by Fallers—from a less structured, more negotiated law with less state involvement (characteristic of classical Islam according to both Rosen and Johansen), toward a more legalistically ordered law entailing greater involvement of the centrally imposed element. Thus, in the last part of the study I set out to examine the bureaucratic structure of the Ottoman Empire in the seventeenth century.

The thrust of my argument is that this bureaucracy was based more on rules and procedures and was much less despotic than is usually believed. It was based on power sharing that became more real and tangible the closer it moved toward the seat of power in Istanbul; mainly in the core area around the capital, the word of the government remained relatively effective even in the seventeenth and eighteenth centuries. Within this core area, I have tried to reconstruct the political relations between the city of Bursa and the Ottoman center in the seventeenth century. The gist of my argument is that Bursa lacked any government worthy of the name. It was a self-regulating community, almost like a chartered commune in medieval Europe. In a political sense government, of course, existed, but it was benign and barely felt because on the whole it was highly legitimate. Therefore, this is one major piece of evidence I have used.

Another approach to which I had recourse was a detailed analysis of the *Şikayet Defteri* of 1675. That the Ottoman bureaucracy gave rise to such a vast number of complaints shows that problems did exist, and I am not overlooking them. But there is another side to the coin. It is not the natural tendency of highly despotic polities to encourage, or even to suffer, an institution of complaining against state officials. Also noteworthy is that most of the complaints were filed by low-class individuals, mostly villagers, often against very high officials. All the complaints include exact names and addresses, which evidences a lack of fear that is to my mind remarkable. Another aspect of the complaints that seems to me impressive was the serious and fair treatment accorded to each by the central government. Every complaint was sent to the nearest *kadi* with a strongly worded order to look into it diligently. In no case do we find any effort, direct or veiled, on the part of the sultan to whitewash a case to save a high-placed official. Furthermore, the fact that thousands of villagers sent complaints to the faraway sultan seems to imply that complaining was meaningful in achieving results.

A particularly intriguing chapter in the *Şikayet Defteri* is that one devoted to complaints against *kadi*s, of which there are about seventy. My interest here was to establish once and for all the extent of judicial corruption in the Ottoman Empire, assuming that the common people in the Middle East in the seventeenth century knew best what was really going on. My conclusion is that in this respect, too, the received wisdom on the extent of corruption in the Ottoman bureaucracy is probably exaggerated. Most of the complaints against *kadis* involved charging illegally high rates for the services supplied by the court, with a few cases of participation in tax extortion. I was on the lookout for allegations of bribe taking in order to decide cases, but such complaints were extremely rare. And in my view this must mean that the widespread notion about the disastrous decline in moral standards of the *ilmiye* in the seventeenth and eighteenth centuries is probably very exaggerated.

This study has also sought to make a contribution to the study of the history of Islamic law in the middle Islamic period. We should distinguish here between two topics. One is the application of Islamic law, the *shari`a*, in real life in Islamic countries. The other is the history of the law itself as a body of thought. As to the first issue, studies on the practice of Islamic law in the pre-Ottoman period show that contrary to Rosen's view, the law was not at all a matter of free-floating bargaining but went by the fairly well known codes of the *shari`a* (to the extent that it was applied, of course). Too little is known so far about this pre-Ottoman period to permit the conclusion that the Ottoman and pre-Ottoman sets of law were really the same even in the personal and civil areas. In any event, so far there is no documentary reason to revise Schacht's and Coulson's claims that Islamic law in the pre-Ottoman period had little or nothing to do with the penal law. They were, of course, of the opinion that this applied as well to the Ottoman period, but here they were quite mistaken. If this is so, we are left with a conclusion that the Ottoman period witnessed a historic rise of the *shari`a* and the *kadi*, who now dealt not only with wider *shari`a* jurisdiction but also with such non-*shari`a* matters as agrarian *kanun* and the like. Paradoxically, we may also be mistaken to view the Ottoman period as one of decline, *inhitat*, from a purely Islamic point of view—meaning here from the perspective of the importance of Islamic institutions in the wider society.

As to the second topic, that of Islamic law as a body of thought, this study has sought to contribute some ideas and empirical findings to that issue as well. On the whole I believe the data contained in this book reaffirms the views and findings of a small but growing group of scholars who hold that Islamic law in this period was far from stagnant and motionless. For example, the findings of this study seem to bear out Johansen's view that through the institution of *ifta*, Islamic societies accommodated change within the *shari`a*. I myself found several changes that, although they were initially changes at the practical level of the law court, were also accommodated and accepted at a higher level of self-consciousness, that of the *fetva* collections. There was, for example, an important change in the law of criminal evidence, reflected in the concept of *sai bil' fesad*, and there was a major change in the approach to interest charging. One important social aspect revealed in this latter case is far-reaching pragmatism on the part of Ottoman leaders. It is characteristic, for example, that Ebu Suud and his followers did not justify the cash *waqf* and interest charging through some formal legal device but simply by recourse to the fact that it was an extremely popular institution.

Maybe the foremost protagonist of such an approach in Ottoman society at the time was Katib Çelebi, an autodidact scholar who in his book *The Balance of Truth* set forth his views on politics, society, and law.[3] He had much to say, for example, on the relations between the *shari`a* and various popular beliefs that seem to have run counter to it. To my mind, his view of the crucially important term *bid`a* (illegal innovation) epitomizes his entire mode of thinking. *Bid`a* is an important concept, he says, but it is time we stopped applying it to common customs in the real world—for two reasons. First, we cannot change people's behavior:

> Once an innovation has taken root and become established in a community, it is the height of stupidity and ignorance to invoke the principle of "enjoining right and forbidding wrong" and to hope to constrain the people to abandon it. People will not give up anything to which they have grown accustomed, whether it be Sunna [normative legal precedent] or innovation.[4]

Second, if we look closely, innovation has, in fact, always existed, so that it is impossible to apply the term consistently. The first, commonsensical argument is the general motif of Katib Çelebi's book. It smacks so much of Ebu Suud's views on interest charging as to lead one to think that it really represented a widespread current of opinion among the Ottoman intellectual elite. This is the approach of somebody looking at the world of the *shari`a* from the outside, advising us to take it with a grain of salt, so to speak. The second argument seems ostensibly technical, but on closer look seems to me much more radical because it suggests doing away with the concept of *bid`a* on the strength of arguments that are internal to the *shari`a*:

> In short, there is no point in conducting profound researches into this subject, for if the people of any age after that of the Prophet were to scrutinize their own mode of life and compare it with the Sunna, they would find a wide discrepancy. If everybody were to carry out an honest self-examination, nothing approaching conformity with the Sunna would be found. Scarcely any of the sayings or doings of any age are untainted by innovation.[5]

This view says, in effect, that innovation should be permissible even from the point of view of the strict upholder of the traditional *shari`a*. Katib Çelebi was certainly in favor of innovation, although neither he nor Ebu Suud would probably wish to parade this view in public. I believe, then, that my findings go further than just detecting objective change in Islamic law, and give some support to Hallaq's argument that contrary to prevailing views, the gates of *ijtihad* (individual interpretation) were never really tightly closed in the Islamic middle period.[6]

It might be countered that all the new material that we find in the Ottoman law courts and *fetva* collections are not really innovations or even developments within the *shari`a*, but no more than a compromise with reality—that is, either with customary law or the innovations initiated by the government (and we have seen that several of the new topics in the Ottoman law derived from the *kanun*). Schacht was, for example, of that opinion when he spoke in his classic book about the phenomenon of legal devices:

> Thus a balance established itself in most Islamic countries between legal theory and legal practice; an uneasy truce between the *"ulama"* ("scholars") . . . and the political authorities came into being. The *"ulama"* themselves were conscious of this; they expressed their conviction of the ever-increasing corruption of contemporary conditions . . . and . . . formulated the doctrine that necessity (*darura*) dispensed Muslims from observing the strict rules of the Law. . . . The scholars half sanctioned the regulations which the rulers in fact enacted. . . . As long as the sacred Law received formal

recognition as a religious ideal, it did not insist on being fully applied in practice.[7]

I doubt whether this is a true representation of the Ottoman case. Judging by the structure of Ottoman *fetva* collections, in which new material is treated just like traditional material, there is no sign whatsoever that Ottoman *mufti*s were relating to these new developments as negative in relation to older, supposedly truer legal material. They seemed perfectly comfortable with these newer laws. It is true that they were not calling them innovation and justifying their acceptance as such. But they were certainly closer to that position than to the one suggested by Schacht—that is, that their adoption of these laws was a mere realization of the corruption of the world.

NOTES

1. Carter V. Findley, *Bureaucratic Reform in the Ottoman Empire: The Sublime Porte, 1789–1922* (Princeton, 1980).

2. A good introduction to this whole issue is the four short pieces by David Kertzer, Darrett Rutman, Sydel Silverman, and Andrejs Plakans entitled "History and Anthropology: A Dialogue," *Historical Methods* 19 (1986): 119–28. A more recent introduction to the field, is Shepard Kerch III, "The State of Ethnohistory," *Annual Review of Anthropology* 20 (1991): 345–75, which contains a bibliography of no fewer than 385 items; many are studies just recently published, mostly by anthropologists, and all deal in one way or another with anthropological history. It would hardly be an exaggeration to say that within anthropology, historical anthropology has assumed the proportions of a scientific revolution.

3. A well-known example is Andrejs Plakans. See his *Kinship in the Past: An Anthropology of European Family Life, 1500–1900* (Oxford, 1984).

4. Natalie Davis is no doubt the best known in this genre of studies. See Natalie Z. Davis, "The possibilities of the Past," *Journal of Interdisciplinary Studies* 12 (1981): 227–52.

5. The articles of Rutman and Silverman (n. 2) make this point with particular lucidity.

6. The best study setting out to introduce this approach to social history is Hans Medick, "Missionaries in a Row Boat? Ethnological Ways of Knowing As a Challenge to Social History," *Comparative Studies in Society and History* 29 (1987): 76-98. Nevertheless even under this new paradigm, new anthropological studies seem to relate their findings to

those of former studies. As opposed to this, most historians still write in a way that seeks to distance them from former studies.

7. Clifford Geertz, "Local Knowledge: Fact and Law in Comparative Perspective," in *Local Knowledge* (New York, 1983), 167–234.

8. Lawrence Rosen, *The Anthropology of Justice* (Cambridge, 1989).

9. See book review by Martha Mundy in *History Workshop Journal* 32 (1991): 184–92. In fairness to Rosen it must be acknowledged that his study is nevertheless a convincing looking analysis of a present-day Moroccan court of law.

10. I owe the placement of the present study within this new approach to the study of Islamic law to conversations with Baber Johansen at Washington University, St. Louis, 1991. See his *The Islamic Law on Land Tax and Rent* (London, 1988).

11. Philip Abrams, *Historical Sociology* (London, 1982).

12. Sally Falk Moore, *Law As Process* (London, 1978).

13. Ibid., 1.

14. Ibid., 3.

15. On mediation and similar low-key social processes as legal process, see, e.g., Paul H. Gulliver, "Process and Decision," *Cross-examinations: Essays in Memory of Max Gluckman* ed., Paul H. Gulliver (Leiden, 1978), 29–52; June Starr, "Negotiations: A Pre-Law Stage in Rural Turkish Disputes," in *Cross-Examinations*, 110–32.

16. Moore, *Law As Process*, 2.

17. D. H. Dwyer, "Substance and Process: Reappraising the Premises of the Anthropology of Law," *Dialectical Anthropology* 4 (1979): 309–20.

18. Lloyd A. Fallers, *Law without Precedent* (Chicago, 1969), 326 et seq.

19. Ibid., 326.

20. Ibid., 327.

21. Max Gluckman, *The Judicial Process among the Barotse of Northern Rhodesia* (Manchester, 1955).

22. Sally Falk Moore, "Archaic Law and Modern Times on the Zambezi: Some Thoughts on Max Gluckman's Interpretation of Barotse Law,"

in *Cross-examinations*, 53–77. On the one hand he was trying to prove that the new African nations deserved their independence because their culture—for example, their law—was not inferior to that of the West. On the other hand he was a faithful student of Maine's evolutionism, in the context of which African law represented an ancient and more primitive phase of human evolution in comparison to that of the modern West.

23. Gluckman, *Judicial Process*, 163.

24. Ibid., 164.

25. Ibid., 164.

26. Moore, "Archaic Law," 57.

27. Max Gluckman, *The Ideas in Barotse Jurisprudence* (New Haven, 1965), 16.

28. Ibid., 21.

29. Gluckman, *Judicial Process*, 107.

30. Rosen, *Anthropology of Justice*.

31. Ibid., 11.

32. Ibid., 17.

33. Ibid., 50.

34. It is exactly here that Rosen's conflation cf Sefrou and Islamic law in general is problematic. There are enough studies on the practice of the *kadi* courts in historic Morocco to refute Rosen's assertion that the *kadi*'s mode of thinking and decision making lacked a systematic rational approach. David S. Powers, for one, has published studies that present extensive and protracted law suits—for example, on *waqf* property, from fourteenth- and fifteenth-century Morocco—which show the *kadi* applying the *shari`a* in an extremely careful and rational way, consulting legal experts over fine points of law, and using sharp logic to reach a clear-cut decision. There is no bargaining of any kind, only an uncompromising application of the law. See David S. Powers, "A Court Case from Fourteenth-Century North Africa," *Journal of the American Oriental Society* 110 (1990): 229–54; and his "Conflicting Conceptions of Property in Fifteenth-century Morocco" (Paper presented at the workshop "The Place of Law in Islamic Societies: Historical Perspectives," Washington University, St. Louis, 8–9, May 1992). Cited by permission.

35. See Bernard S. Cohn, "History and Anthropology: The State of Play," *Comparative Studies in Society and History* 22 (1980): 198–221; Silverman, (n. 2); Kertzer (n. 2).

36. See I. M. Lewis, Introduction to *History and Social Anthropology*, ed. I. M. Lewis (London, 1968).

37. See, e.g., Nicholas Thomas, *Out of Time* (Cambridge, 1989), 24–27.

38. See David I. Kerzer, *Family Life in Central Italy, 1880–1910* (New Brunswick, N.J., 1984).

39. The main scholar in this area seems to be Sally Humphreys, an anthropologist who has studied the legal system of classical Athens. See Humphreys, "Social Relations on Stage," *History and Anthropology* 1 (1985): 313–69. The whole issue of this remarkable new journal is devoted to historical legal anthropology.

40. At least this is what is formally claimed by Silverman (n. 2), 125.

41. Moore, "Archaic Law," pp. 9-13. See also now Sally Falk Moore, *Social Facts and Fabrications: "Customary" Law on Kilimanjaro, 1880–1980* (Cambridge, 1986).

42. See, for example, Moore, *Law As Process*, 253, where historical studies are declared to be the wave of the future in legal anthropology.

43. Ibid., 27 and chap. 6.

44. Bernard S. Cohn, "Some Notes on Law and Change in North India," in *Law and Warfare*, ed. P. H. Bohannan, (New York, 1967), 139–59.

45. Maurice Bloch makes the distinction between ritualistic and nonritualistic societies. See Bloch, "The Past and the Present in the Present," *Man*, 12 (1977): 278–92.

46. Discussed in ibid., 283–84.

47. Lawrence Rosen, "Responsibility and Compensatory Justice in Arab Culture and Law," in *Semiotics, Self, and Society*, ed. Benjamin Lee and Greg Urban (New York, 1989), 103.

48. See Bassam Tibi, *Islam and the Cultural Accommodation of Social Change* (Boulder, 1990), 42, 61, 65.

49. See Wael B. Hallaq, "Was the Gate of Ijtihad Closed?" *International Journal of Middle East Studies* 16 (1984): 3–41.

50. The theory is discussed in several places in Ernest Gellner's collected essays, *Muslim Society* (Cambridge, 1984), especially chap. 1 in general and p. 73ff.

51. Gellner later changed his line of argument altogether. In a restatement of his Ibn Khaldun thesis he said: "There are many who hold that the Ottoman Empire makes Ibn Khaldun's account inapplicable to recent centuries. I do not believe this to be so. Under the surface the world of Ibn Khaldun continued to function; it reemerged as the empire declined." See Ernest Gellner, "Tribalism and the State in the Middle East," in Tribes and State Formation in the Middle East, ed. Philip S. Khoury and Joseph Kostiner (Berkeley, 1990), 125. It is obvious that Gellner is speaking here of the place of tribal factors within the social fabric, not of the danger tribes were able to pose to the ruling state, which is, of course, the focus of his former analysis as well as the topic implied by the title of the essay discussed here. In terms of heyday and decline, if tribes ever posed any semblance of a threat to the existence of the Ottoman state, it was in the first period rather than in the second.

52. Max Weber, Economy and Society, (New York, 1968), 1016–17.

53. See, e.g., V. L. Ménage, "Devşirme," Encyclopedia of Islam, 2d ed.

54. See Cornell H. Fleischer, Bureaucrat and Intellectual in the Ottoman Empire (Princeton, 1986), 15, and his extensive bibliography cited.

55. See Albert Hourani, "Conclusion: Tribes and States in Islamic History," in Tribes and State, 303–11. Credit for this idea should probably go to Edmund Burke, "Morocco and the Near East: Reflections on Some Basic Differences," European Journal of Sociology 10 (1969): 70–94.

56. Hans Georg Majer, ed., Das osmanische "Registerbuch der Beschwerden" (Şikayet Defteri) vom Jahre 1675 (Vienna, 1984).

57. In that sense, this source is probably preferable to studying random complaints in the mühimme defterleri as recently demonstrated by Suraiya Faroqhi, although her study, of course, remains very valuable. See Suraiya Faroqhi, "Political Activity among Ottoman Taxpayers and the Problem of Sultanic Legitimation (1570–1650)," Journal of the Economic and Social History of the Orient 35 (1992): 1–39.

58. Mustakim Zade Süleyman Saadeddin, Devhat el-Meşaih (Istanbul, 1978), e.g. 71, 87.

CHAPTER 1

1. One study that does exactly this is Stanislav Andreski, Max Weber's Insights and Errors (London, 1984).

2. I have used documents that are partly court records in the formal sense and partly manuscripts of copies of court records. In the first category I have used the court records of seventeenth-century Bursa. Because I have written about the legal side of these documents before, I have reiterated in this chapter specific citations of Bursa documents. See Haim Gerber, *Economy and Society in an Ottoman City: Bursa, 1600–1700* (Jerusalem, 1988), passim, but especially chap. 9. The main sources used for this chapter are two manuscripts in the Muallim Cevdet Collection, today Ataturk Library, Istanbul, O.18 and K.427, which are respectively court records from eighteenth-century Istanbul and seventeenth-century Edirne. I have also made use of a long series of manuscripts and published books that are, in effect, compilations of court cases that seemingly encompass all areas of life as covered by real court records. These books do not appear to have the intention of presenting to the reader a particular ideology or point of view. They mention murders, prostitution, interest charging, and similar phenomena without much ado. The following are the main collections I have used: Sakk Musazade (Berlin: Staatbibliothek, Preussischer Kulturbesitz, Orientabteilung, or. fol. 4071) (cited as Musazade); Sakk Şanizade Hac Mustafa, same collection, no. or. quart. 1525 (cited as Şanizade); Sakk Mahmud Kara Çelebi, same collection, no. 2393 (cited as Kara Çelebi); Sakk Hízír Efendi, same collection, nor. or. oct. 1999 (cited as Hízír Efendi); Sakk Vehbi (London: British Library, Oriental Books and Manuscripts, OR. 1142); Dabbağzade Numan *Tuhfat al-Sukuk* (Istanbul, A.H. 1248); Çauşzade Mehmed Aziz, *Durr al-sukuk*, 2 vols. (Istanbul, A.H. 1288).

3. Clifford Geertz, "Local Knowledge: Fact and Law in Comparative Perspective," in *Local Knowledge* (New York, 1983), chap. 8.

4. On Weber's theory of law, see *Max Weber on Law in Economy and Society*, ed. Max Rheinstein (Cambridge, Mass., 1969); David Trubek, "Reconstructing Max Weber's Legal Sociology," *Stanford Law Review* 37 (1985): 919–936.

5. Trubek, "Weber," 926.

6. Ibid., 931.

7. True, it was not Weber who invented the term, but the view that he was not referring at all to Islam is certainly not borne out by his writings. Even in the only full-fledged section on *kadi* justice in *Economy and Society* (978)—by no means the only context where the term is mentioned—there is reference to *shari`a* court practices in Tunisia. In the other substantial section on Islamic law in *Economy and Society* (817ff.), obviously emanating from an earlier phase in Weber's intellectual development, the concept of *kadi* justice is not used. But the same fundamental idea seems to permeate the two sections: that Islamic law not only

ceased to develop with the closure of the gates of personal interpretation, but also that an inevitable outcome was that no orderly and systematic law was possible thereafter. Max Weber, *Economy and Society* (New York, 1968).

8. Brian S. Turner, *Weber and Islam* (London, 1974).

9. Ibid., 110.

10. Ibid., 111.

11. Ibid., 116.

12. Lawrence Rosen, *The Anthropology of Justice* (Cambridge, 1989); see also Rosen, "Equity and Discretion in a Modern Islamic Legal System," *Law and Society Review* 15 (1980–81): 217–45.

13. Geertz, *Local Knowledge*, 191.

14. Ibrahim al-Halabi, *Multaqa al-Abhur* (Istanbul, A.H. 1309). The supremacy of this manual in the Ottoman intellectual world was recently documented in a useful study: Şükrü Selim Has "The Use of the Multaqa'l Abhur in the Ottoman Madrasas and in Legal Scholarship," *Osmanlí Araştírmalarí* 7–8 (1988): 393–18.

15. See Donald P. Little, "Two Fourteenth-century Court Records from Jerusalem Concerning the Disposition of Slaves by Minors," *Arabica* 29 (1982): 16–49; Huda Lutfi, "A Study of Six Fourteenth-Century *Iqrars* From Al-Quds Relating to Muslim Women," *Journal of the Economic and Social History of the Orient* 26 (1983): 246–94. These studies are important to the argument of the present study because one cannot claim it was the bureaucratization of the Ottoman Empire that set in motion the application of the *shari`a* in family law, *waqf* law, and civil law. The Ottoman pecularity apparently found expression mainly in the application of the penal law of the *shari`a* and in the augmentation of the role of the *kadi* to cover non- *shari`a* legal matters and many supervisory and even bureaucratic matters.

16. Richard T. Antoun, "The Islamic Court, the Islamic Judge, and the Accommodation of Tradition," *International Journal of Middle East Studies* 12 (1980): 455–67. This is confirmed by experts on Islamic law. Thus, Aharon Layish has observerd that a major differentiating trait between *shari`a* and custom is the destination of the dower. Under custom the dower goes to the woman's guardian; under the *shari`a* it goes to the wife herself. Aharon Layish, *Divorce in the Libyan Family* (New York, 1991), 3–4.

17. Examples: Musazade, ten cases in the first pages of the manuscript; Şanizade, 19b; and Vehbi, 8a–8b.

18. Hízír Efendi, 18b; Dabbağzade Numan, 16–17.

19. Hízír Efendi, 18a.

20. Paul Stirling, *Turkish Village* (London, 1965), 212.

21. Examples: Dabbağzade Numan, 13–14; Vehbi, 12b; O.18, 65–66.

22. Dabbağzade Numan, 11–12.

23. Examples: Vehbi, 10a; Musazade, 14a; Dabbağzade Numan, 20–22; Hízír Efendi, 16a; O.18, 61–62, 26–27.

24. Joseph Schacht, *An Introduction to Islamic Law* (Oxford, 1962), 181.

25. Şanizade, 174b–175a. See also Musazade, 167a–b; Dabbağzade Numan, 306-7, 307-8, 309; Çauşzade Mehmed Aziz, vol. 2, 226; Vehbi, 78b–79a.

26. Dabbağzade Numan, 162, 162–3; Musazade, 166b–67a.

27. O.18, 33–34.

28. Dabbağzade Numan, 311–12.

29. Çauşzade Mehmed Aziz, vol. 2, 239; Dabbağzade Numan, 303–4, 304–5.

30. Vehbi, 81a–82b.

31. Examples: Vehbi, 78a; Çauşzade Mehmed Aziz, vol. 2, 242.

32. Çauşzade Mehmed Aziz, vol. 2., 228-29.

33. Ibid., 239–40.

34. See Sally Falk Moore, *Law As Process*, 226.

35. O.18, 52. See also, Dabbağzade Numan, 166–67, 305–6, O.18, 53.

36. Dabbağzade Numan, 167–68.

37. Ibid, 168–69.

38. Ibid., 295-98, 298-99, Şanizade, 180a.

39. Dabbağzade Numan, 164–65, 165–66; Musazade, 169a.

40. Vehbi, 79b–80a.

41. Musazade, 169b–70a; Dabbağzade Numan, 301, 300–301; O.18, 67–68.

42. Dabbağzade Numan, 290–91.

43. Ibid., 288–89; Hízír Efendi, 37b.

44. Uriel Heyd, *Studies in Old Ottoman Criminal Law* (Oxford, 1973), 111ff.

45. Examples: Dabbağzade Numan, 335; Hízír Efendi, 38b.

46. Dabbağzade Numan, 290; Musazade, 25a.

47. Haim Gerber, "The Islamic Law of Partnerships in Ottoman Court Records," *Studia Islamica* (1981): 110–18.

48. Dabbağzade Numan, 226.

49. Ibid., 225–26.

50. Ibid., 164.

51. Haim Gerber, "*Shari'a, Kanun,* and Custom in the Ottoman Law: The Court Records of seventeenth-century Bursa," *International Journal of Turkish Studies* 2 (1981): 138.

52. Dabbağzade Numan, 346-47.

53. Çauşzade Mehmed Aziz, vol. 1, 114.

54. Ibid., 113–14.

55. Dabbağzade Numan, 336.

56. For examples of *fetva*s in Ottoman records, see chapter 3.

57. The complete lack of intervention in judicial matters on the part of government officials is also forcefully argued by Jennings for seventeenth-century Kayseri. See Ronald C. Jennings, "Limitations on the Judicial Powers of the Kadi in seventeenth century Ottoman Kayseri," *Studia Islamica* 50 (1979): 152ff.

58. Şanizade, 37bff.

59. Musazade, 167b–68a.

60. Çauşzade Mehmed Aziz, vol. 2, 227–28.

61. See, for example, Lawrence Stone, "The Law", in *The Past and the Present Revisited* (London, 1987), 241–51; Douglas Hay, "Property, Authority and the Criminal Law," in *Albion's Fatal Tree*, Douglas Hay et al., (New York, 1975), 17–63.

62. It seems appropriate to mention here Geertz's criticism of Karl Wittfogel for exaggerating the supposed power of some centralized states

in premodern Asia, through a mistake of taking the documentary evidence at face value. Clifford Geertz, "Politics Past, Politics Present: Some Notes on the Uses of Anthropology in Understanding the New States," in *The Interpretation of Cultures* (New York, 1973), 327–41. It seems to me that this essay is overlooked by all those who view Geertz as the prophet of the total supremacy of the individual case over generalizations. Geertz goes out of his way here to show that the unique is useless if it does not at the same time teach us something of the world beyond itself.

63. See Gerber, *Economy and Society.*

64. Dabbağzade Numan, 307–8.

65. Ibid., 299.

66. Ibid., 60–61.

67. Rosen, *Anthropology of Justice,* 20 et seq.

68. William A. Shack, "Collective Oath: Compurgation in Anglo-Saxon England and African States," *Archives europeennes de sociologie* 20 (1979): 1–18.

69. Schacht, *Introduction,* 184.

70. Dabbağzade Numan, 288, 290.

71. Sally Humphreys, "Social Relations on Stage," *History and Anthropology* 1 (1985): 313–69.

72. See Jeanatte Wakin, *The Function of Documents in Islamic Law* (Albany, 1972).

73. Noel J. Coulson, *A History of Islamic Law* (Edinburgh, 1964), chap. 9.

74. Dabbağzade Numan, 306–7. For a similar case, see ibid., 162.

75. Ibid., 290–91.

76. Ibid., 285–86; 286; 310–11.

77. See Rebecca V. Colman, "Reason and Unreason in Early Medieval Law," *Journal of Interdisciplinary History* 4 (1974): 571–91.

78. Roy P. Mottahede, *Loyalty and Leadership in an Early Islamic Society* (Princeton, 1980), 46.

79. Powers, "Conflicting Conceptions of Property."

80. Ibid., 170.

81. See ibid., 172, 318.

82. Lawrence Rosen, "Responsibility and Compensatory Justice in Arab Culture and Law," in *Semiotics, Self, and Society*, ed. Benjamin Lee and Greg Urban (New York, 1989), 101–19.

83. Çeşmizade Mehmed Halis Efendi, ed., *Hulasat el-Ecviba* (Istanbul, A.H. 1289), p. 229, Abdallah, no. 6. This source is a large- format publication consisting of the compilation of several *fetva* collections grouped together according to topic. Every *fetva* within the chapter is numbered, hence the peculiar form of citation.

84. Several cases in ibid.

85. Ibid., Abdallah, no. 8.

86. Ibid., p. 230, Feyzullah, no. 36. Also relevant is no. 28.

87. Example in ibid., *Naticat el-Fetava*, no. 6.

88. Ibid., p. 231, Ali, no. 18, where a robber was killed by a villager while defending the village against an attack by a gang of robbers.

89. Ibid., *Naticat el-Fetava*, no. 24.

90. Dabbağzade Numan, 265.

91. Ibid., 298.

92. Rosen, *Anthropology of Justice*, 40.

93. Ibid.

94. Ibid., 47ff.

95. See Ian Hamnett, Introduction to *Social Anthropology and Law*, ed. Ian Hamnett (London, 1977).

96. See Sally Humphreys, "Law As Discourse," *History and Anthropology* 1 (1985): 241–64.

97. Mary P. Baumgartner, "Law and Social Status in Colonial New Haven, 1639-1665," *Research in Law and Sociology* 1 (1978): 153–74.

98. My grounds for this choice are (a) that although I have seen several thousands of litigation cases in the Bursa court records, I have taken notes on only a small number of them, and this has entailed a selection process that may contain a statistical bias of some sort; and (b) that it is reasonable to expect Dabbağzade compilation to be a random sample— that is, to reflect the real-life population of the relevant universe. By hindsight I can say that the conclusions that I draw from this statistical exercise are entirely commensurate with the impression I have formed from my work on the Bursa court archives.

CHAPTER 2

1. Lawrence Rosen, *The Anthropology of Justice* (Cambridge, 1989), 61.

2. Baber Johansen, "Sacred and Religious Element in Hanafite Law—Function and Limits of the Absolute Character of Government Authority," in *Islam et Politique au Maghreb*, ed. Ernest Gellner et al. (Paris, 1981), 281–303.

3. Ibid., 291.

4. Ibid., 299.

5. Uriel Heyd, *Studies in Old Ottoman Criminal Law* (Oxford, 1973), 1.

6. Noel J. Coulson, *A History of Islamic Law* (Edinburgh, 1964), chap.9

7. Ibid., 125.

8. Ibid., 132.

9. Joseph Schacht, *An Introduction to Islamic Law* (Oxford, 1962), 50, 54–55, 76.

10. Jorgen S. Nielsen, *Secular Justice in an Islamic State: Mazalim under the Bahri Mamluks, 662/1264–789/1387* (Istanbul, 1985).

11. Ibid., 24ff.

12. Ibid., 95.

13. Heyd, *Studies*, 95.

14. Ibid., 95 n.6.

15. Ibid., 105, art. 54.

16. Ibid., 105–6, art.41–42.

17. Ibid., 106, art. 44.

18. Ibid., 106, art. 47; 108, art. 50.

19. Ibid., 112, art. 66.

20. Ibid., 303; Schacht, *Introduction*, 187.

21. Heyd, *Studies*, 130, art. 125.

22. Ibid., 116.

23. Ibid., 122, art.103.

24. Cornell H. Fleischer, *Bureaucrat and Intellectual in the Ottoman Empire* (Princeton, 1986), 8.

25. M. E. Duzdağ, *Şeyhülislam Ebusuud Efendi Fetvalarí* (Istanbul, 1972).

26. Ibid., 138–39, no. 661.

27. Ibid., 139, no. 665.

28. Ibid., 153, no. 745.

29. Ibid., 146, no.705.

30. Ibid., 141, no. 672.

31. Heyd, *Studies*, 150.

32. Ibid., 152.

33. Ibid., 152.

34. Ibid., 154–55.

35. Ibid., 254.

36. Halil Inalcik, *Belgeler* 14 (1980–81).

37. Halit Ongan, *Ankara'nin Iki Numarali Şeriye Sicili* (Ankara, 1974).

38. Galab D. Galabov and Herbert W. Duda, *Die Protokolbücher des kadiamtes Sofia* (Munich, 1960).

39. See ibid., index, under Mord, murder.

40. Ronald Jennings, "The Society and Economy of Macuka in the Ottoman Judicial Registers of Trabzon, 1560–1640," in *Continuity and Change in Late Byzantine and Early Ottoman Society*, ed. Anthony Bryer and Heath Lowry (Birmingham, 1986), 129–54.

41. Ibid., 151.

42. Ibid.

43. Ibid., 152.

44. Ibid.

45. See, for example, Bursa Sicill, *kadi* court records (Bursa: Archaeological Museum), B71/272, 70a, 26 Rebiülevvel 1059; B70/272, 50a, 2 Safer 1059.

46. Ibid., B127/197, 83a, *evail* Safer 1069.

47. Ibid., B42/236, 15a, *evahir* Zilhicce 1031.

48. Ibid., B111/325, 44b, 26 Rebiülahir 1095; B112/326, 12b, 22 Cemaziyelahir 1089.

49. Ibid., B45/239, 83b, *evail* Cemaziyelevvel 1035; B140/355, 59b, 1089.

50. Heyd, *Studies*, 232.

51. See, for example, Bursa Sicill, B92/298, 97b, 1110; B152/368, 99b, Ramazan 1102.

52. Ibid., B45/239, 33a, Safer 1035.

53. It is possible that in Istanbul the *muhtesib* kept more of his former administrative, though certainly not judicial, functions. See Zia Kazici, *Osmanlılarda Ihtisab Müessesesi* (Istanbul, 1987).

54. On *teftiş*, see Heyd, *Studies*, 228–29. The institution is also mentioned several times in the *Şikayet Defteri*. See Hans Georg Majer, ed., *Das Osmanische "Registerbuch der Beschwerden (Şikayet Defteri) vom Jahre 1675* Vienna, 1984.

55. *Şikayet Defteri*, 3b–5, 3b–1.

56. Rosen, *Anthropology of Justice*, 62.

57. Heyd, *Studies*, 242.

58. Bursa Sicill, B285/513, 65b, 1089; B103/316, 1108.

59. Ibid., B42/236, 15a, 1031; B17/197, 18a, 1010.

60. Ibid., B111/325, 44a, 1095.

61. Ménage's note in Heyd, *Studies*, 196.

62. Bursa Sicill, B90/295, 59b, 1081; B112/326, 93a, 1090; B103/316, 38a, 1086.

63. Ibid., B132/347, 12a, 1068.

64. Ibid., B103/316, 36b, 1086.

65. Ibid., B75/276, 61b, 1091. On this kind of punishment see more generally Mehmet Ipşirli, "XVI. Asrin Ikinci Yarisinda Kurek Cezasi Ile Ilgili Hukumler," *Tarih Enstitüsü Dergisi* 12 (1982): 203–48.

66. Haim Gerber, *Economy and Society in an Ottoman City: Bursa, 1600–1700* (Jerusalem, 1988).

67. Ibid., chap. 7.

68. See Dabbağzade Numan, *Tuhfat al-Sukuk* (Istanbul, A.H. 1248), passim.

69. See e.g. Şanizade Hac Mustafa, Staatbibliothek, Berlin, Preussischer Kulturbesitz, Orientabteilung, no. or. quart. 1525, 101b–2b.

70. See, for example, Çauşzade Mehmed Aziz, vol. 2, 32.

71. See e.g. Dabbağzade Numan, 237.

72. See Çauşzade Mehmed Aziz, *Durr al-Sukuk*, vol. 2 (Istanbul, A.H. 1288), 68–69, 69–70.

73. *Şikayet Defteri*, 78b-2.

74. Galal El-Nahal, *Judicial Administration of Ottoman Egypt in the Seventeenth Century* (Minneapolis, 1979).

75. Abraham Marcus, *The Middle East on the Eve of Modernity* (New York, 1989).

76. Ibid., 106.

77. Ibid., 107–8, 114–15, 116–17.

78. Ibid., 119.

79. Rudolph Peters, "Murder on the Nile," *Die Welt des Islam* 30 (1990): 98–116.

80. Ibid, 116.

81. See, for example, Adil Manna`, "The Sancak of Jerusalem between Two Invasions" (Ph.D. diss., Hebrew University of Jerusalem, 1986), 83.

CHAPTER 3

1. Baber Johansen, "Legal Literature and the Problem of Change. The Case of the Land Rent, "in *Islam and Public Law*, ed. Chibli Mallat, (London, in press).

2. Ronald Jennings, "Kadi, Court, and Legal Procedure in seventeenth-century Ottoman Kayseri," *Studia Islamica*, 48 (1978): 133–72.

3. Abdulrahim Efendi, *Fetava*, Istanbul, n.d., 109.

4. Bursa Sicill, *kadi* court records (Bursa: Archaeological Museum), B115/329, 44a, 8 Rebiülevvel 1061.

5. Ibid., B35/229, 26b, *evasit* Şevval 1025.

6. Ibid., 53/247, 3b, 20 Zilkade 1041.

7. Ibid., B116/330, 31a, 3 Ramazan 1082.

8. Ibid., B71/272, 37a, *evahir* Zilhicce 1058.

9. Ibid., B102/315, 68a, 27 Cemaziyelahir 1112.

10. Muallim Cevdet Yazmalari, Atatürk Library, Istanbul, O.18, 58–59.

11. Ibid., 33–34.

12. See Halit Ongan, *Ankara'nin Iki Numarali Şeriye Sicili* (Ankara, 1974), no. 739, 1050, etc.

13. See Jennings, "Kadi, Court," 133ff.

14. Khayr al-Din al Ramli *Al-Fatawi al-Khayriyya* (Istanbul, A.H. 1311).

15. Johansen, "Legal Literature."

16. See Madeline C. Zilfi, *The Politics of Piety: The Ottoman Ulema in the Postclassical Age (1600–1800)* (Minneapolis, 1988), chaps.1 and 2.

17. Al-Ramli, vol. 1, 106.

18. Muhammad Khalili, *Kitab Fatawi al-Khalili* (Cairo, A.H. 1289), vol. 2, 276

19. See Gabriel Baer, *Fellah and Townsman in the Middle East* (London, 1982), 84–85.

20. Al-Ramli, vol. 1, 107

21. Al-Khalili, vol. 1, 162

22. Hans Georg Majer, ed. *Das osmanische "Registerbuch der Beschwerden"(Şikayet Defteri) vom Jahre 1675* Vienna, 1984, 86a–2.

23. Ibid., 85b–6.

24. Ibid., 92b–3.

25. Ibid., 75b–3.

26. There are two editions of this remarkable document. An older one is *Milli Tetebüler Mecmuasi*, vol.2, A.H. 1331, 337-48; a scholarly edi-

tion is Paul Horster, *Zur Anwendung des Islamischen Rechts im 16. Jahrhundert* (Stuttgart, 1935).

27. There are good discussions of the *Maruzat* in Uriel Heyd, *Studies in Old Ottoman Criminal Law* (Oxford, 1973), 183-85; and in Richard Repp, *The Mufti of Istanbul* (Oxford, 1986), 274 et seq.

28. Lawrence Rosen, *The Anthropology of Justice* (Cambridge, 1989), 40ff.

29. Wael B. Hallaq, "Was the Gate of Ijtihad Closed?" *International Journal of Middle East Studies* 16 (1984): 3–41.

30. Repp, *The Mufti*, 279.

31. *Milli Tetebüler Mecmuasí*, vol. 2, 338.

32. Horster, *Zur anwendung*, 25/68 (the first numeral refers to the Turkish original, the second to the German translation).

33. Ibid., 28/70.

34. Ibid., 29/71.

35. Ibid., 58/95–96

36. Ibid., 56/93–94.

37. Rosen, *Anthropology of Justice*, 40ff.

38. Repp, *The Mufti*.

39. See Ibid., passim.

40. Uriel Heyd, "Some Aspects of the Ottoman Fetva," *Bulletin of the School of Oriental and African Studies* 62 (1969): 46–49.

41. Brinkley Messick, "The Mufti, the Text, and the World: Legal Interpretation in Yemen," *Man* n.s., 21 (1986): 102–19.

42. Ibid., 103.

43. Ibid, 107.

44. Ibid., 108.

45. Ibid, 104.

46. The collections used here were Abdulrahim, *Fetava*; Ali al-Murtaza, *Ilaveli Mecmua-i Cedida* (Istanbul, A.H. 1326); Abdallah Efendi, *Behcet el-Fetavi* (Istanbul, A.H. 1266); Ali Efendi, *Fetava*, (Istanbul, n.d.); Feyzullah Efendi, *Fetava-i Feyziye* (Istanbul, A.H. 1266); Minkarizade Efen-

di, *Fetava-i Minkarizade,* Manuscript (London: British Library), Add 7836; M. E. Duzdağ, *Şeyhülislam Ebusuud Efendi Fetvalari* (Istanbul, 1972).

47. Messick, "The Mufti, the Text, and the World."

48. Examples: Minkarizade, 36a ff; Ali Efendi, 133–34, 136–37, 147; Abdallah Efendi, 146–47; Feyzullah Efendi, 140, 145; Abdulrahim Efendi, 103–5.

49. Ali Efendi, 148; Minkarizade, 35b f; Abdulrahim Efendi, 127.

50. Ali Efendi, 133–34; Abdallah Efendi, 145–46; Feyzullah Efendi, 139–40; Abdulrahim Efendi, 99–100.

51. Abdallah Efendi, 578ff; Minkarizade, 139b ff; Ilaveli, different *mufti*s, 559, 560, 562; Abdulrahim Efendi, 326–28.

52. Feyzullah Efendi, 538; On *kasama* cases generally see Feyzullah Efendi, 536–37, 540; Abdallah Efendi, 599–605; Abdulrahim Efendi, 337–38; Minkarizade, 152ff.

53. Abdallah Efendi, 149; Ali Efendi, 142; See also Heyd, *Studies,* 299–301.

54. Abdallah Efendi, 148.

55. See, for example, Feyzullah Efendi, 141–42; Abdallah Efendi, 147.

56. Abdulrahim Efendi, 331. See also Joseph Schacht, *An Introduction to Islamic Law* (Oxford, 1962), 184, where he shows that the *shari`a* had the same kind of law.

57. Minkarizade, 37a.

58. Ali Efendi, 149; Feyzullah Efendi, 146; Abdulrahim Efendi, 128–29.

59. This famous *şeyhülislam* was killed by rebellious soldiers in 1703 for violating the code of behavior expected of a man of his high position. See Rifaat Abou-El-Haj, *The 1703 Rebellion and the Structure of Ottoman Politics* (Leiden, 1984).

60. Feyzullah Efendi, 143.

61. See, for example, Abdallah Efendi, 152.

62. Abdallah Efendi, 153.

63. Ibid.

64. Abdulrahim Efendi, 128.

65. Ibid., 129.

66. Ibid., 101.

67. Baber Johansen, "Claims of Man and Claims of God. The Limits of Government Authority in Hanafite Law," in *Pluriformiteit en verdeling van de macht in het midden-oosten*, ed. C.M. de Moor (Nijmegen, 1980), 60–104, especially 84ff.

68. See Shacht, *Introduction*, 137.

69. See ibid., chap. 11.

70. Udovitch, for example, has written on the concept of *murabaha*, which denoted a sale involving a fixed profit margin for the seller and the seller's obligation to notify the buyer of all his expenses. No loan was involved. See Abraham L. Udovitch, "Islamic Law and the Social Context of Exchange in the Medieval Middle East" *History and Anthropology* 1 (1985): 445–65, particularly 445 and 452ff. Udovitch says it is outwardly difficult to understand how such a complicated transaction could actually exist, bearing in mind that expenses were barely registered in this period. His explanation is that commerce, despite its well-known sophistication in this period, was based on intimate, steady, long-standing relations between seller and buyer within small communities of deep personal aquaintance (see 450). This analysis is doubly interesting for the present study. It is not only noteworthy that the Ottomans completely recycled the classical Islamic legal term; it is also substantively important that this particular institution, the classical *murabaha*, disappeared entirely. Incidentally, it is my argument here that the type of society signified by the term was also transformed.

71. Jon E. Mandeville, "Usurious Piety: The Cash Waqf Controversy in the Ottoman Empire," *International Journal of Middle East Studies* 10 (1979): 289–308.

72. Ibid., 296.

73. Ibid., 297.

74. Ibid., 303

75. Ö. L. Barkan, "Edirne Askeri Kassamína Ait Tereke Defterleri," *Belgeler* 3 (1966): 33, n. 30.

76. Abdallah Efendi, 511; and a similar document in ibid., 512.

77. Ali Efendi, 564, several cases; ibid., 274–75, several cases.

78. Ibid., 564, several cases.

79. Abdulrahim Efendi, 132.

80. Ali Efendi, 226.

81. Ibid., 227.

82. Ibid.

83. Abdallah Efendi, 150. The document was also translated by Neşet Çağatay, " Riba and Interest Concept and Banking in the Ottoman Empire," *Studia Islamica* 32 (1970): 64.

84. Heyd, *Studies*, 122.

85. Minkarizade, 47a.

86. See also the more detailed discussion below and the similar use of the term in Abdallah Efendi, 153, 155.

87. Abraham L. Udovitch, "Reflections on the Institutions of Credits and Banking in the Medieval Islamic Near East," *Studia Islamica* 41 (1975): 5–21.

88. Ibid., 9.

89. Udovitch, "Islamic Law," especially 458f.

90. See Gerber, *Economy and Society in an Ottoman City: Bursa, 1600–1700* (Jerusalem, 1988), chap. 8

91. Ibid., chap. 7.

92. Example in Abdallah Efendi, 266–67.

93. See John R. Barnes, *An Introduction to Religious Foundations in the Ottoman Empire* (Leiden, 1986).

94. See generally Ali Efendi, 245ff.

95. *Ilaveli*, 264, 274

96. See Ali Efendi, 249, 251; Abdallah Efendi, 264, 267.

97. Feyzullah Efendi, 384; *Ilaveli*, 431–43; Ali Efendi, 470ff.

98. Abdulrahim Efendi, 46–47, where there are two occurrences of this usage.

99. Ibid., 92

100. Ibid., 91.

101. Ibid., 327–28.

102. Ibid., 108.

CHAPTER 4

1. See Halil Inalcik, "The Appointment Procedure of a Guild Warden (*Ketkhuda*)," *Wiener Zeitschrift fur die Kunde des Morgenlandes* 76
(1986): 139.

2. The late Gabriel Baer was the pioneer of the study of guilds in
the Ottoman Empire (see his *Fellah and Townsman in the Middle East*
[London, 1982]), but new material, not known to him, imposes on me a
somewhat different line of argument.

3. See Gerber, *Economy and Society in an Ottoman City: Bursa,
1600–1700* (Jerusalem, 1988), chap. 3.

4. Baer, *Fellah and Townsman*, 217–18.

5. Ö. Ergenç,"1600–1615 Yíllarí Arasínda Ankara Tarihine Ait
Araştírmalar," in *Türkiye Iktisad Tarihi Semineri*, ed. O. Okyar (Ankara,
1973), 151.

6. Halit Ongan, *Ankara'nín Bir Numaralí Şeriye Sicili* (Ankara,
1958); *Ankara'nín Iki Numaralí Şeriye Sicili* (Ankara, 1974).

7. Ongan, *Bir Numaralí*, 15

8. Gerber, *Bursa*, 48ff.

9. *Gaziantep Şeri Mahkeme Sicillerinden Örnekler* (Gaziantep,
1970).

10. Ibid. 19.

11. Ibid., 13–14.

12. Ibid., 78–79.

13. Ibid., 32.

14. Ibid., 60–61.

15. Ibid., 7.

16. Ibid., 58.

17. Abd al-Karim Rafeq, "The Law Court Registers of Damascus,
with Special Reference to Craft Corporations During the First Half of the
Eighteenth Century," in *Les Arabes par leurs archives (XVIe–XXe siècles)*,
(Paris, 1976), 141–59.

18. Ibid., 153.

19. Ibid.

20. Ibid., 155.

21. Ibid., 156.

22. Osman Nuri, *Mecelle-i Umur-i Belediye*, vol. 1 (Istanbul, 1922), 404ff.

23. Ibid., 608–9.

24. Ibid., 564.

25. Ibid., 564ff.

26. Ibid., 565.

27. Hans Georg Majer, ed., *Das osmanische "Registerbuch der Beschwerden" (Şikayet Defteri) vom Jahre 1675* (Vienna, 1984) *Şikayet Defteri*, 8b-4. It should be noted that such situations could be met with in other contexts as well. An example is a seventeenth-century Istanbul *waqf* entrusted by an order of the sultan to someone who was not supposed to succeed to the property according to the founding deed of the endowment. The *kadi* was ordered to prefer the founding deed over the decree of the sovereign. See *Şikayet Defteri*, 224a-5.

28. Istanbul Belediye Kütüphanesi (Atatürk Kitaplíğí), Muallim Cevdet Yazmalarí, O.18, 37–38.

29. Nuri, *Mecelle*, 610.

30. Ibid., 646

31. Belediye, O.18, 37–38.

32. Çağatay Uluçay, *XVIIinci Yüzyílda Manisa'da Ziraat, Ticaret ve Esnaf Teşkilatí* (Istanbul, 1942).

33. Ibid., documents 76, 77, 99.

34. Ibid., documents 14, 21.

35. Nuri, *Mecelle*, 640–42.

36. Amnon Cohen, *Economic Life in Ottoman Jerusalem* (Cambridge, 1989).

37. Ibid., 125.

38. Ibid., 102.

39. Ibid., 22.

40. Ibid., 23–25.

41. See Mahmud Ali Atallah, ed., *Wathaiq al-Tawaif al-Hirafiyya fi al-Quds fi al-Qarn al-Sabi Ashr al-Miladi*, vol. 1 (Nablus, 1991). The book contains several hundred documents that bear out this conclusion. It came to my attention too late to be analyzed in detail—as it surely deserves.

42. For antiguild laws see Baer, *Fellah and Townsman*, 184–85; Nuri, *Mecelle*, 662.

CHAPTER 5

1. Max Weber, *Economy and Society*, vol. 2 (New York, 1968), chap. 12

2. Ibid., 1028–29

3. Ibid., 1031

4. Max Weber, *The Theory of Social and Economic Organization* (New York, 1947), 347.

5. Metin Heper, *The State Tradition in Turkey* (Walkington, 1985), 29.

6. Ibid., 28

7. Ibid., 25

8. Ibid., 26

9. Ibid., 31. The cited concept was coined by Şerif Mardin. See his "Center-Periphery Relation: A Key to Turkish Politics?" in *Political Participation in Turkey*, ed. Engin D. Akarli and Gabriel Ben Dor (Istanbul, 1975), 14.

10. See, for example, Rifaat Abou-El-Haj, "The Ottoman Nasihatname as a Discourse over 'Morality,'" in *Melange Robert Mantran*, ed. Abdeljelil Temimi, ed., (Zarouan, Tunis, 1989). See also his, *Formation of the Modern State: The Ottoman Empire, Sixteenth to Eighteenth Centuries* (Albany, 1991).

11. Bernard Lewis, "Ottoman Observers of Ottoman Decline," in *Islam in History* (London, 1973), 199–213.

12. Ibid., 199–200.

13. See Halil Inalcik, "Süleiman the Lawgiver and Ottoman Law," *Archivium Ottomanicum* 1 (1969): 105.

14. Lewis, "Ottoman Observers," 202.

15. Ibid., 203.

16. Ibid., 204.

17. Ibid., 205.

18. Ibid., 205–6.

19. This study does not really deal with this question, which was dealt with extensively by Abou-El-Haj in *Formation*. My aim is merely to show that these memoranda are a far cry from objective social history.

20. See Rhoades Murphy, "The Veliyyudin Telhis: Notes on the Sources and Interrelations between Koçi Bey and Contemporary Writers of Advice to Kings," *Belleten* 43 (1979): 555.

21. Ibid., 556

22. Ibid.

23. Cornell H. Fleischer, *Bureaucrat and Intellectual in the Ottoman Empire* (Princeton, 1986), 9.

24. Uriel Heyd, *Ottoman Documents on Palestine, 1552–1615* (Oxford, 1960).

25. Ibid., 40.

26. Ibid., 43.

27. Ibid., 45.

28. Haim Gerber, *Economy and Society in an Ottoman City: Bursa, 1600-1700* (Jerusalem, 1988).

29. Bursa Sicill, *kadi* court records (Bursa: Archaeological Museum), B17/197, 83a, *evail* Safer 1069.

30. Ibid., B75/276, 56a, 15 Receb 1090.

31. Ibid., A156/207, 136b, 26 Zilkade 1012.

32. Ibid., B17/197, 4b, *evail* Şevval 1010.

33. For example, ibid., B103/316, 16b, 22 Muharrem 1086.

34. Ibid., B71/272, 26a, 20 Zilkade 1058.

35. Ibid., B111/325, 85a, 29 Şevval, 1095.

36. For example, see Başbakanlík Archive [BBA], Maliye Defterleri 9826, 11a, Şaban 1031.

37. Bursa Sicill, B50/244, 22a, 23 Şevval 1038.

38. BBA, Maliye Defterleri 5452, unpaginated, 1 Cemaziyelevvel 1023.

39. Bursa Sicill, B111/325, 129b, 2, Cemaziyelahir 1096.

40. For such cases see ibid., B111/330, 82b, *evahir* Şevval 1082; B59/253, 110a, *evasit* Rebiülevvel 1045.

41. Ibid., B50/244, 102b, *evail* Rebiülevvel 1039.

42. BBA, Maliye Defterleri, 9491, p.126.

43. Ibid., Maliye Defterleri 9878, 96, Muharrem 1108.

44. Bursa Sicill, B115/329, 58a, 5 Ramazan 1061.

45. Suraiya Faroqhi, "Towns, Agriculture and the State in Sixteenth-century Ottoman Anatolia," *Journal of the Economic and Social History of the Orient* 23 (1990): 136.

46. See Gerber, *Bursa*, chap. 8.

47. Bahaeddin Yediyíldíz, *Institution du vaqf au XVIIIe siècle en Turquie—Etude socio-historique* (Ankara, 1985).

48. Ibid., 152–53.

49. Ibid., 163, table 8.

50. Ibid., 13.

51. Ibid., 211, table 12.

52. Ibid., 170.

53. Ibid., 93, table 2.

54. Albert Hourani, "The Fertile Crescent in the Eighteenth Century," in *Vision of History* (Beirut, 1961), chap.2.

55. Margaret L. Meriwether, "The Notable Families of Aleppo, 1770–1830: Networks and Social Structure" (Ph.D. diss., University of Pennsylvania, 1981).

56. Ibid., 219–242.

57. Ibid., 242ff.

58. Ibid., 243–44.

59. Ibid., 100.

60. Adel Manna`, "The Sancak of Jerusalem Between Two Invasions (1798–1831): Administration and Society" (Ph.D. diss., Hebrew University of Jerusalem, 1986).

61. See Martin Albrow, *Bureaucracy* (London, 1970), 44–45, slightly adapted.

62. Cornell H. Fleischer, "Preliminaries in the Study of the Ottoman Bureaucracy," *Journal of Turkish Studies* 10 (1986): 136.

63. Ibid.

64. Rifaat Abou-El-Haj, "The Ottoman Vezir and Paşa Household, 1683–1703: A Preliminary Report," *Journal of the American Oriental Society* 94 (1974): 438–47.

65. Metin I. Kunt, *The Sultan's Servants* (New York, 1982).

66. Carter V. Findley, *Bureaucratic Reform in the Ottoman Empire: The Sublime Porte, 1798–1922* (Princeton, 1980), 30ff.

67. Fleischer, *Bureaucrat and Intellectual*, 64–65.

68. Ibid., 96

69. Ibid., 114.

70. Ibid., 82f.

71. Kunt, *Sultan's Servants*, 50.

72. Fleischer, *Bureaucrat and Intellectual*, passim.

73. An extremely interesting example supporting the same conclusion comes out of the autobiography of an eighteenth-century Ottoman instructor in a religious school, who, though lacking any seeming *intisab* connections, rose almost to the very top of the *ilmiye*, the religious hierarchy, despite being several times passed over in promotion due to the *intisab*. Such episodes enraged the writer to such a degree that it seems quite evident that the regular norm was still seniority and merit. This case again puts things in perspective: *intisab* existed, but the bureaucratic structure functioned even in the eighteenth century. Wherever we scratch the surface, we discover that the thesis of Ottoman decline is highly questionable. See Madeline C. Zilfi,"The Diary of a Muderris: A New Source for Ottoman Biography," *Journal of Turkish Studies* 1 (1977): 157–73.

74. Kunt, *Sultan's Servants*, 55–56.

75. Ibid., 55.

76. Ibid., 48–49.

77. Fleischer, *Bureaucrat and Intellectual*, passim.

78. Findley, *Bureaucratic Reform*, 32–33.

79. Abraham Marcus, *The Middle East on the Eve of Modernity* (New York, 1989), 195–212.

80. Ibid., 197.

81. Ibid., 200.

82. Ibid.

83. Meriwether, "The Notable Families of Aleppo".

84. Ibid., 75.

85. Ibid., 99–100.

86. For an example of such an endowment, see ibid., 78. On the *waqf* institution in eighteenth-century Aleppo, see also Marcus, *The Middle East*, passim.

87. Hildred Geertz, "The Meaning of Family Ties," in *Meaning and Order in Moroccan Society* by C. Geertz, H. Geertz, and L. Rosen (Cambridge, 1979), 315–79.

88. Ibid., 129–30.

89. Ibid., 139.

90. Haim Gerber, "Anthropology and Family History: The Case of the Ottoman and Turkish Families," *Journal of Family History* 14 (1989): 409–21.

91. Ismail Beliğ, *Guldeste-i Riyaz-i Irfan* (Bursa, A.H.. 1302).

92. Meriwether, "Notable Families," 126–27.

93. Yediyíldíz, *Institution du vaqf*, 211.

94. Kunt, *Sultan's Servants*, 55.

95. Madeline C. Zilfi, "Elite Circulation in the Ottoman Empire: Great Mollas of the Eighteenth Century," *Journal of the Economic and Social History of the Orient* 26 (1983): 318–64.

96. Ibid., 331, n. 24.

97. Alan Duben, "Household Formation in Late Ottoman Istanbul," *International Journal of Middle East Studies* 22 (1990): 419–35. This is part of a larger study on the topic by Alan Duben and Cem Behar.

98. Ibid., 425.

99. I have mentioned this information in the previous section as well; I justify dwelling on it again because in Duben and Behar's study it figures as an anthropologically important phenomenon, not just as a semitheoretical custom.

100. Ibid., 427.

101. See Rifaat Abou-El-Haj, "Aspects of the Legitimation of Ottoman Rule As Reflected in the Preambles of Two Early *Liva Kanunnameler*," *Turcica* 21–23 (1991): 371–83.

102. Unpublished paper by Cemal Kafadar, presented to the workshop on Place of Law in Islamic Societies, Washington University, St. Louis, 8–9 May 1992.

103. Madeline Zilfi, *The Politics of Piety: The Ottoman Ulena in the Postclassical Age (1600–1800)* (Minneapolis, 1988).

104. Kunt, *Sultan's Servants.*

105. Fleischer, *Bureaucrat and Intellectual.*

106. Vienna *Şikayet Defteri*, folio 32b, entry 3 (henceforward cited as 32b–3).

107. The main study of corruption in the Ottoman Empire is Ahmed Mumcu, *Osmanlí Devletinde Rüşvet* (Ankara, 1969). Though good in its way, this study is insufficient for my present purpose. Aside from making exessive use of European sources, many of which are to my mind highly dubious, it is basically a collection of facts without any effort to build a general statement.

108. Ibid., 91

109. Marcus reached the same conclusion in his study on eighteenth-century Aleppo. He says, for example, "Residents who went to the shari`a court could usually expect the trial to be fair as well as speedy." Speaking more directly on the issue of judicial corruption in Aleppo Marcus says, "Although venality and abuses tainted the image of the shari`a court, its level of dishonesty was probably within the bounds of ordinary and acceptable judicial practice. In the milieu in which it was set the court performed fairly well and served the cause of justice." See Marcus, *The Middle East,* 111, 113–14.

110. *Şikayet Defteri*, 37a–2.

111. Ibid., 106b–3.

112. For example, ibid., 132a–3; 174b–6.

113. Ibid., 6b–1. There is a similar case from Kayseri in ibid., 67a–3.

114. Ibid., 79a–6.

115. Ibid., 170a–3.

116. Ibid., 56b–5, 7a–2, 26b–2, 199a–6, 197b–2, 139b–3.

117. Ibid., 31a–1.

118. Ibid., 24b–6.

119. Ibid., 220a–3.

120. Ibid., 39b–4.

121. Ibid., 132a–3.

122. Ibid., 92a–7.

123. See examples, ibid., 61b–5; 170b–4.

124. Ibid., 175a–7.

125. Ibid., 116a–7.

126. Ibid., 23b–1.

127. Ibid., 86b–6.

128. Ibid., 132a–5.

129. Ibid., 58b–2.

130. Ibid., 137b–7.

131. Ibid., 212a–5.

132. Ibid., 166b–4.

133. Ibid., 198a–6.

134. Ibid., 21b–6, 2b-4, 2b–5, 120a–1, 179b–2, 213b–5.

135. Ibid., 198b-1, 183a–1, 35a–4, 28a–3, 43a-3.

136. Ibid., 13b–3, 14b–3, 52a–2.

137. Ibid., 180a–3.

138. Ibid., 133a–3, 33b–5, 44b–2, 180b–3, 137b–3, 14a–1.

139. Ibid., 33a–6. For other similar examples, see 50a–4, 50a–5, 164b–6, 28a–7, 182a–3.

140. Ibid., 11a–4.

141. See examples, ibid., 147b–1, 103b–2, 116a–4, 77b–1.

142. Ibid., 34a–4.

143. Ibid., 152b–5.

144. Ibid., 106a–4.

145. Mardin, "Center-Periphery," 14.

146. Lewis, "Ottoman Observers," 212.

147. Şikayet Defteri, 55b-3.

148. Ibid., 38a–3.

149. Ibid., 202b–6, 186b–3, 168a–6, 116b–5.

150. Haim Gerber, *The Social Origins of the Modern Middle East,* (Boulder, 1987), chap.4. It is symbolic of the power of the received version that even scholars espousing the new approach to Ottoman history (such as Rifaat Abou El-Haj in his *Formation,* passim) still reiterate the old *timar-iltizam* model that is not borne out by the documentary evidence.

151. Şikayet Defteri, 27a–2, 32b–5, 208b–4.

152. Bruce McGowan, *Economic Life in Ottoman Europe* (Cambridge, 1984), 56ff.

153. Literature is cited in ibid.

154. Şikayet Defteri, 152a–5, 174a–6, 29a–4, 29a–1, 31a–4.

155. Ibid., 203a–1.

156. See examples, ibid., 145b–4, 180b–4, 212b–3, 213b–6, 219a–1.

157. Ibid., 206b–5.

158. See, for example, a complaint of that sort by the fiefholders in the province of Budin, ibid., 115a–3.

159. Ibid., 115b–3, 131a–2.

160. Ibid., 193b–3, 31b–5, 7a–7, 107b–2, 61b–4.

161. Ibid., 159b–6, 27a–5, 175b–8.

162. Ibid., 33b–4.

163. Ö. L. Barkan, "Timar," in *Islam Ansiklopedisi,* vol.12, 320.

164. See, for example, *Şikayet Defteri*, 189b–4.

165. Ibid., 147a–7.

166. Ibid., 219a–3.

167. See examples, ibid., 29a–1, 42a–6, 82a–4.

168. Ibid., 61b–4, 11b–5, 3a–1, 55b–1.

169. See examples, ibid., 30a–6, 39b–5, 142b–2, 131a–7.

170. Ibid., 97b–4.

171. Ibid., 209b–4.

172. Ibid., 86b–2, 11b–5, 61b–4, 24b–4, 55b–1.

173. Ibid., 3a–1.

174. Ibid., 52a–3.

175. Ibid., 147b–6, 15a–1.

176. Ibid., 193a–3, 163b–5, 92b–3.

177. Ibid., 98b–4.

178. Ibid., 87b–3.

179. Ibid., 75b–3. For other similar cases, see 11a–2, 85b–2, 203a–5, 209a–3.

180. Ibid., 100a–4.

181. Ibid., 44a–3.

182. Ibid., 56b–2.

183. Ibid., 34a–2.

184. See, for example, E. J. Hobsbawm, *Bandits* (New York, 1981).

185. *Şikayet Defteri*, 143a–3. For a similar case from the same region, see 145a–2.

186. Ibid., 22b–2. See similar cases in 14b–6, 15a–4, 43b–6, 193b–1.

187. Ibid., 69a–2.

188. Ibid., 222b–4. See also a similar case from the region of Niğde, 111b–1.

189. See examples, ibid., 10b–4, 116b–3, 83a–5, 163b–6, 48a–2, 65b–3.

190. Ibid., 178a–6.

191. Ibid., 109a–1. For other similar cases, see 47b–3, 44b–3, 45a–5, 193b-2.

192. Ibid., 173b–1.

193. Ibid., 178a–4.

194. Ibid., 57b–5.

195. Ibid., 151b–1.

196. Ibid., 159b–2, from *sancak* Ganghari; 3b–3, from the region of Aydin.

197. Ibid., 212b–1, 142b–4, 137a–2.

198. Ibid., 12a-2, from Inegöl, Bursa.

199. For example, ibid., 178a–6.

200. Ibid., 56b–2.

CHAPTER 6

1. Gabriel Ben-Dor and Engin D. Akarli, "Comparative Perspectives," in *Political Participation in Turkey*, ed. Engin D. Akarli and Gabriel Ben-Dor (Istanbul, 1975), 157–62.

2. Cemal Kafadar, "Self and Others: The Diary of a Dervish in Seventeenth-century Istanbul and First-person Narrative in Ottoman Literature," *Studia Islamica* 79 (1989): 121–50.

3. Katib Çelebi, *The Balance of Truth*, trans. G. L. Lewis (London, 1957).

4. Ibid., 89–90.

5. Ibid., 90.

6. It may be interesting to note that contrary to Schacht's view, D. B. Macdonald, who wrote the article on *ijtihad* in the first edition of the *Encyclopedia of Islam*, was of the opinion that indeed *ijtihad* was never entirely eliminated from the scene. Another study that confirms the existence of *ijtihad* in the Ottoman period (though not necessarily in the Ottoman Empire) is Rudolph Peters, " *Ijtihad* and *Taqlid* in Eighteenth- and Nineteenth-century Islam," *Die Welt des Islam* 20 (1980): 131–45.

7. Joseph Schacht, An *Introduction to Islamic Law* (Oxford, 1962), 84.

SELECTED BIBLIOGRAPHY

MANUSCRIPT MATERIALS

Bursa Sicill. *Kadi* court records. Bursa: Archaeological Museum.

Hízír Efendi, Sakk. Berlin: Staatbibliothek, Preussischer Kulturbesitz, Orientabetilung, no. or. oct. 1999.

Mahmud Kara Çelebi, Sakk. Same collection, no. 2393.

Minkarizade, Fetava-i Minkarizade, London: British Library, Add 7836.

Şanizade Hac Mustafa, Sakk. Berlin, no. or. quart. 1525.

Vehbi, Sakk. London: British Library, or. 1142.

PUBLISHED MATERIALS

Abdallah Efendi. *Behcet el-Fetava.* Istanbul, A.H. 1266.

Abdulrahim Efendi. *Fetava.* Istanbul, n.d.

Abou-El-Haj, Rifaat. "Aspects of the Legitimation of Ottoman Rule as Reflected in the Preambles to Two Early *Liva Kanunnameler.*" *Turcica* 21–23 (1991): 371–83.

—————. *Formation of the Modern State: The Ottoman Empire, Sixteenth to Eighteenth Centuries.* Albany, 1991.

—————. *The 1703 Rebellion and the Structure of Ottoman Politics.* Leiden, 1984.

Abrams, Philip. *Historical Sociology.* London, 1982.

Ali Efendi. *Fetava.* Istanbul, n.d.

Antoun, Richard T. "The Islamic Court, the Islamic Judge, and the Accommodation of Tradition." *International Journal of Middle East Studies* 12 (1980): 455–67.

Baer, Gabriel. *Fellah and Townsman in the Middle East.* London, 1982.

Baumgartner, Mary P. "Law and Social Status in Colonial New Haven," *Research in Law and Sociology,* 1 (1978): 153–74.

Bloch, Maurice. "The Past and the Present in the Present." *Man,* n.s., 12 (1977): 278–92.

Burke, Edmund. "Morocco and the Near East: Reflections on Some Basic Differences." *Archives Europeenne de Sociologie* 10 (1969): 70–94.

Çauşzade Mehmed Aziz. *Durr al-Sukuk.* Istanbul, A.H. 1288.

Çeşmizade Mehmed Halis, ed., *Hulasat el-Ecviba* Istanbul, A.H. 1289.

Cohen, Amnon. *Economic Life in Ottoman Jerusalem.* Cambridge, 1989.

Cohn, Bernard S. "History and Anthropology: The State of Play." *Comparative Studies in Society and History* 22 (1980): 198–221.

———. "Some Notes on Law and Change in North India." In *Law and Warfare.* Edited by P. H. Bohannan. New York, 1967.

Colman, Rebecca V. "Reason and Unreason in Early Medieval Law." *Journal of Interdisciplinary History* 4 (1974): 571–91.

Coulson, Noel J. *A History of Islamic Law.* Edinburgh, 1964.

Dabbağzade Numan. *Tuhfat al-Sukuk.* Istanbul, A.H. 1248.

Davis, Natalie Z. "The Possibilities of the Past." *Journal of Interdisciplinary History* 12 (1981): 227–52.

Duben, Alan. "Household Formation in Late Ottoman Istanbul." *International Journal of Middle East Studies* 22 (1990): 419–35.

Duzdağ, M. E. *Şeyhülislam Ebusuud Efendi Fetvalarí.* Istanbul, 1972.

Eickelman, Dale F. "Is There an Islamic City? The Making of a Quarter in a Moroccan Town." *International Journal of Middle East Studies* 5 (1974): 274–94.

Fallers, Lloyd A. *Law without Precedent.* Chicago, 1969.

Faroqhi, Suraiya. "Civilian Society and Political Power in the Ottoman Empire: A Report on Research in Collective Biography (1480–1830)." *International Journal of Middle East Studies* 17 (1985): 109–17.

————. "Political Activity among Ottoman Taxpayers and the Problem of Sultanic Legitimation (1500–1650)." *Journal of the Economic and Social History of the Orient* 35 (1992): 1–39.

————. "Towns, Agriculture and the State in Sixteenth-century Ottoman Anatolia." *Journal of the Economic and Social History of the Orient* 33 (1990): 125–56.

Feyzullah Efendi. *Fetava-i Feyziye.* Istanbul, A.H. 1266.

Findley, Carter V. *Bureaucratic Reform in the Ottoman Empire: The Sublime Porte, 1789–1922.* Princeton, 1980.

————. "Patrimonial Household Organization and Factional Activity in the Ottoman Ruling Class." In *Turkiye'nin Sosial ve Ekonomik Tarihi (1071–1920).* Edited by Halil Inalcik and Osman Okyar. Ankara, 1980.

Fleischer, Cornell H. *Bureaucrat and Intellectual in the Ottoman Empire.* Princeton, 1986.

————. "Preliminaries in the Study of the Ottoman Bureaucracy." *Journal of Turkish Studies* 10 (1986): 135–41.

Galabov, Galab D., and Herbert W. Duda. *Die Protokolbücher des kadiamtes Sofia.* Munich, 1960.

Geertz, Clifford. *The Interpretation of Cultures.* New York, 1973.

————. "Local Knowledge: Fact and Law in Comparative Perspective." In *Local Knowledge.* New York, 1983.

Geertz, Hildred. "The Meaning of Family Ties." In *Meaning and Order in Moroccan Society* by C. Geertz, H. Geertz and L. Rosen. Cambridge, 1979.

Gellner, Ernest. *Muslim Society.* Cambridge, 1984.

Gerber, Haim. *Economy and Society in an Ottoman City: Bursa, 1600–1700.* Jerusalem, 1988.

Gluckman Max. *The Ideas in Barotse Jurisprudence.* New Haven, 1965.

————. *The Judicial Process among the Barotse of Northern Rhodesia.* Manchester, 1955.

Gulliver, Paul H., ed. *Cross-examinations: Essays in Memory of Max Gluckman.* Leiden, 1978.

Güzelbey, C. C. *Gaziantep Şer'i Mahkeme Sicillerinden Örnekler.* Gaziantep, 1970.

Hallaq, Wael B. "Was the Gate of Ijtihad Closed?" *International Journal of Middle East Studies* 16 (1984): 3–41.

Hay, Douglas. "Property, Authority and the Criminal Law." In *Albion's Fatal Tree*. Edited by Douglas Hay et al. New York, 1975.

Heper, Metin, *The State Tradition in Turkey*. Walkington, 1985.

Heyd, Uriel. *Ottoman Documents on Palestine, 1552–1615*. Oxford, 1960.

————. "Some Aspects of the Ottoman Fetva." *Bulletin of the School of Oriental and African Studies* 62 (1969): 36–56.

————. *Studies in Old Ottoman Criminal Law*. Oxford, 1973.

Horster, Paul. *Zur Anwendung des Islamischen Rechts im 16. Jahrhundert*. Stuttgart, 1935.

Humphreys, Sally. "Law As Discourse." *History and Anthropology* 1 (1985): 241–64.

Inalcik, Halil. "The Appointment Procedure of a Guild Warden (Ketkhuda)." *Wiener Zeitschrift fur die Kunde des Morgenlandes* 76 (1986).

————. "Suleiman the Lawgiver and Ottoman Law." *Archivium Ottomanicum* 1 (1969): 105–38.

————. "Osmanlí İdare, Sosyal ve Ekonomik Tarihiyle Ilgili Belgeler: Bursa Kadí Sicillerinden Seçmeler, *Belgeler*, 14 (1980–81): 1–91.

Jennings, Ronald C. "Kadi, Court, and Legal Procedure in Seventeenth-century Ottoman Kayseri." *Studia Islamica* 48 (1978): 133–72.

————. "Limitations on the Judicial Powers of the Kadi in Seventeenth-century Ottoman Kayseri." *Studia Islamica* 50 (1979): 151–84.

————. "The Society and Economy of Macuka in the Ottoman Judicial Registers of Trabzon, 1560–1640. In *Continuity and Change in Late Byzantine and Early Ottoman Society*. Edited by Anthony Bryer and Heath Lowry. Birmingham, 1986.

Johansen, Baber. *The Islamic Law on Land Tax and Rent*. London, 1988.

————. "Le jugement comme preuve. Preuve juridique et vérité religieuse dans le droit Islamique Hanefite." *Studia Islamica* 72 (1990): 5–17.

————. "Sacred and Religious Element in Hanafite Law—Function and Limits of the Absolute Character of Government Authority. In *Islam et Politique au Maghreb*. Edited by Ernest Gellner et al. Paris, 1981.

Kafadar, Cemal. "Self and Others: The Diary of a Dervish in Seventeenth-century Istanbul and First-person Narrative in Ottoman Literature." *Studia Islamica* 79 (1989): 121–50.

Katib Çelebi. *The Balance of Truth.* Translated by G. L. Lewis. London, 1957.

Kerch, Shepard, III. "The State of Ethnohistory." *Annual Review of Anthropology* 20 (1991): 345–75.

Kertzer, David I. "Anthropology and History." *Historical Methods* 19 (1986): 119–20.

Khayr al-Din Al-Ramli. *Al-Fatawi al-Khayriyya.* Istanbul, A.H. 1311.

Kunt, Metin I. *The Sultan's Servants.* New York, 1982.

Layish, Aharon. *Divorce in the Libyan Family.* New York, 1991.

Lewis, Bernard. "Ottoman Observers of Ottoman Decline." In *Islam in History.* London, 1973.

Little, Donald P. "Two Fourteenth-century Court Records from Jerusalem Concerning the Disposition of Slaves by Minors." *Arabica* 29 (1982): 16–49.

Lufti, Huda. "A Study of Six Fourteenth-century *Iqrars* from al-Quds Relating to Muslim Women." *Journal of the Economic and Social History of the Orient* 26 (1983): 246–94.

Mandeville, Jon E. "Usurious Piety: The Cash Waqf Controversy in the Ottoman Empire." *International Journal of Middle East Studies* 10 (1979): 289–308.

Majer, Hans Georg, ed. *Das osmanische "Registerbuch der Beschwerden" (Şikayet Defteri) vom Jahre 1675.* Vienna, 1984.

Marcus, Abraham. *The Middle East on the Eve of Modernity.* New York, 1989.

McGowan, Bruce. *Economic Life in Ottoman Europe.* Cambridge, 1984.

Medick, Hans. "Missionaries in a Row Boat? Ethnological Ways of Knowing As a Challenge to Social History." *Comparative Studies in Society and History* 29 (1987): 76–98.

Meriwether, Margaret L. "The Notable Families of Aleppo, 1770–1830: Networks and Social Structure." Ph.D. diss., University of Pennsylvania, 1981.

Messick, Brinkley. "The Mufti, the Text, and the World: Legal Interpretation in Yemen." *Man*, n.s. 21 (1986):102–19.

Mintz, Sidney W. "Culture: An Anthropological View." *The Yale Review* 71 (1981–82): 499–512.

Moore, Sally Falk. *Law As Process.* London, 1978.

——. *Social Facts and Fabrications: "Customary" Law on Kilimanjaro, 1880–1980.* Cambridge, 1986.

Muhammad Khalili. *Kitab Fatawi al-Khalili.* Cairo, A.H. 1289.

Mumcu, Ahmed. *Osmanli Devletinde Rüşvet.* Ankara, 1969.

Murphy, Rhoades. "The Veliyyudin Telhis: Notes on the Sources and Interrelations between Koçi Bey and Contemporary Writers of Advice to Kings." *Belleten* 43 (1979).

Nettl, J. P. "The State as a Conceptual Variable." *World Politics* 20 (1968): 559–92.

Ongan, Halit. *Ankara'nín Bir Numaralí Şeriye Sicili.* Ankara, 1958.

——. *Ankara'nín Iki Numaralí Şeriye Sicili.* Ankara, 1974.

Osman Nuri. *Mecelle-i Umur-i Belediye.* Vol. 1. Istanbul, 1922.

Peters, Rudolph. "*Idjtihad* and *Taqlid* in Eighteenth- and Nineteenth-century Islam." *Die Welt des Islam* 20 (1980): 131–45.

——. "Murder on the Nile." *Die Welt des Islam* 30 (1990): 98–116.

Powers, David S. "A Court Case from Fourteenth-century North Africa." *Journal of the American Oriental Society* 110 (1990): 229–54.

Rafeq, Abd al-Karim. "The Law Court Registers of Damascus, with Special Reference to Craft Corporations During the First Half of the Eighteenth Century." In *Les Arabes par leurs archives XVIe-XXe siècles.* Edited by J. Berque and D. Chevalier. Paris, 1976.

Repp, Richard. *The Mufti of Istanbul.* Oxford, 1986.

Rosen, Lawrence. *The Anthropology of Justice.* Cambridge, 1989.

——. "Equity and Discretion in a Modern Islamic Legal System." *Law and Society Review* 15 (1980–81): 217–45.

——. "Responsibility and Compensatory Justice in Arab Culture and Law. In *Semiotics, Self, and Society.* Edited by Benjamin Lee and Greg Urban. New York, 1989.

Rutman, Darett B. "History and Anthropology: Clio's Dalliances." *Historical Methods* 19 (1986): 120–23.

Schacht, Joseph. *An Introduction to Islamic Law.* Oxford, 1962.

Shack, William A. "Collective Oath: Compurgation in Anglo-Saxon England and African States." *Archives Europeennes de sociologie* 20 (1979): 1–18.

Shinder, Joel. "Career Line Formation in the Ottoman Bureaucracy, 1648–1750." *Journal of the Economic and Social History of the Orient* 16 (1973): 217–37.

Silverman, Sydel. "Anthropology and History: Understanding the Boundaries." *Historical Methods* 19 (1986): 123–26.

Skocpol, Theda. "Bringing the State Back In: Strategies of Analysis in Current Research." In *Bringing the State Back In.* Edited by Peter B. Evans, Dietrich Rueschmayer, and Theda Skocpol. New York, 1985.

Starr, June. "Negotiations: A Pre-Law Stage in rural Turkish Disputes." In *Cross-examinations: Essays in Memory of Max Gluckman.* Edited by Paul H. Gulliver. Leiden, 1978.

Stirling, Paul. *Turkish Village.* London, 1965.

Stone, Lawrence. "The Law." In *The Past and the Present Revisited.* London, 1987.

Trubek, David. "Reconstructing Max Weber's Legal Sociology." *Stanford Law Review* 37 (1985): 919–36.

Udovitch, Abraham L. "Islamic Law and the Social Context of Exchange in the Medieval Middle East." *History and Anthropology* 1 (1985): 445–65.

———. "Reflections on the Institutions of Credits and Banking in the Medieval Islamic Near East." *Studia Islamica* 41 (1975): 5–21.

Uluçay, Çağatay. *XVII nci Yüzyílda Manisa'da Ziraat, Ticaret ve Esnaf Teşkilatí.* Istanbul, 1942.

Wakin, Jeanatte H. *The Function of Documents in Islamic Law.* Albany, 1972.

Weber, Max. *Economy and Society.* New York, 1968.

Yediyíldíz, Bahaeddin. *Institution du vaqf au XVIIIe siècle en Turquie— Etude socio-historique.* Ankara, 1985.

Zilfi, Madeline C. "The Diary of a Muderris: A New Source for Ottoman Biography." *Journal of Turkish Studies* 1 (1977): 157–73.

————. "Elite circulation in the Ottoman Empire: Great Mollas of the Eighteenth Century. *Journal of the Economic and Social History of the Orient* 26 (1983): 318–64.

————. *The Politics of Piety: The Ottoman Ulema in the Postclassical Age (1600–1800).* Minneapolis, 1988.

INDEX

A

Abbasides, 60
Abdallah Efendi, Şeyhülislam, 96
Adalet (social justice, on part of state), 154
Adalet (Islamic uprightness, sufficient to give witness), 43
Adjudication, 36; and discretion, 36; state intervention in, 37
Ağa (in eighteenth-century Istanbul—a commoner), 56
Aleppo, 76, 142, 143, 149
Ali Efendi, Şeyhülislam, 82, 96
Ali, Ottoman historian, 63, 134, 146, 147, 148
Amad (intention to kill), 52
Ankara, 67
Anthropology and history, 1–23, passim
Antoun, Richard, 31
Aqhisar, 164
Askeri (official class in Ottoman Empire), 45, 56–57, 65
Avariz (tax on real estate), 163, 169
Ayntab (modern Gaziantep), 114, 116, 117, 118, 156
al-Azhar, 86
ayan (local notables), 141–44, 163

B

The Balance of Truth, 184
Banditry, 171–73; social banditry, 171–73
Barkan, Ömer Lutfi, 103
Bayyina (proof, in Islamic law), 30
Bedel-i diyet (irregular tax), 137
Beytülmal (lit. state treasury, department in charge of seizing estates of people dying without heirs), 45
Beytülmal emini (official in charge of *beytülmal*), 138, 139
Bid`a (illegal innovation), 184, 185
Biga, 163
Blood money. *See under* diyet
Book of Complaints, 22, 154–74, passim; judicial function in, 70–71; *fetva*s in 87–88
Bursa, 29, 30, 33, 38, 40, 47, 56, 57, 66, 67, 68, 72, 74, 76, 83, 114, 115, 116, 118, 151, 136, 137, 138, 139

C

Chios, 170
City (cities) in Ottoman Empire,